Studies in

AFRICAN AMERICAN HISTORY AND CULTURE

edited by

GRAHAM HODGES
COLGATE UNIVERSITY

Afro-Americans in Antebellum Boston

An Analysis of Probate Records

Carol Buchalter Stapp

Routledge
Taylor & Francis Group

LONDON AND NEW YORK

First published 1993 by Garland Publishing, Inc.

2 Park Square, Milton Park, Abingdon, Oxfordshire OX14 4RN
52 Vanderbilt Avenue, New York, NY 10017

Routledge is an imprint of the Taylor & Francis Group, an informa business

First issued in paperback 2018

Copyright © 1993 by Carol Buchalter Stapp

All rights reserved. No part of this book may be reprinted or reproduced or utilised in any form or by any electronic, mechanical, or other means, now known or hereafter invented, including photocopying and recording, or in any information storage or retrieval system, without permission in writing from the publishers.

Notice:
Product or corporate names may be trademarks or registered trademarks, and are used only for identification and explanation without intent to infringe.

Library of Congress Cataloging-in-Publication Data

Stapp, Carol Buchalter, 1946–
    Afro-Americans in antebellum Boston : an analysis of probate records / Carol Buchalter Stapp.
        p. cm. — (Studies in African American history and culture)
  Includes bibliographical references and index.
  ISBN 0-8153-1194-X (alk. paper)
    1. Afro-Americans—Massachusetts—Boston—History—19th century. 2. Boston (Mass.)—Population—History—19th century. 3. Probate records—Massachusetts—Boston.   I. Title II. Series.
F73.9.N4S73   1993
974.4'6100496073—dc20   92-40357
                                                                       CIP

ISBN 13: 978-0-8153-1194-2 (hbk)
ISBN 13: 978-1-138-87817-4 (pbk)

To Marcella Brenner

with admiration, appreciation, and affection

Table of Contents

Table of Contents vii
List of Transcriptions ix
List of Rosters xi
List of Lists xiii
List of Graphs xv
List of Charts xvii
List of Figures xix
Preface xxi
Acknowledgments xxiii

Chapter

   1. Introduction 3

Part I
Review of the Literature

   2. On Black Social History 13
   3. On Probate Inventories 35

Part II
Analysis of the Probate Records

   4. A Multi-Angled Inquiry 69
   5. An In-Depth Investigation 99

Part III.
The Literature Vis-a-Vis the Probate Records

   6. Resonant Reading 127

Appendix
   A. Transcriptions 161
   B. Rosters 211
   C. Lists 231
   D. Graphs 244
   E. Charts and Figures 249
Notes 287
Selected Bibliography 301
Index 308

List of Transcriptions

Transcription   Page

Thomas Cole (35173)

1.1	Will: August 9, 1847	164
1.2	Petition for Execution: August 9, 1847	168
1.3	Order of Notice: August 9, 1847	169
1.4	Executor's Bond: August 9, 1847	170
1.5	Inventory: September 13, 1847	172
1.6	Evidence Perpetuated: September 13, 1847	175
1.7	Order of Notice: April 2, 1849	176
1.8	First Account: April 2, 1849	177

Amy Jackson (32471)

2.1	Will: March 24, 1837	179
2.2	Order of Notice: April 13, 1840	180
2.3	Order of Notice: April 27, 1840	181
2.4	Petition for Administration: July 20, 1840	182
2.5	Petition for Executorship: July 20, 1840	184
2.6	Will: July 20, 1840	185
2.7	Resignation: July 20, 1840	187
2.8	Petition for Administration: August 17, 1840	188
2.9	Order of Notice: August 8, 1840	190
2.10	Administrator's Bond: August 17, 1840	191
2.11	Evidence Perpetuated: October 12, 1840	193
2.12	Inventory: October 19, 1840	194
2.13	Order of Notice: March 1, 1841	196
2.14	First Account: March 1, 1841	198
2.15	List of Claims: March 1, 1841	200
2.16	Request: March 1, 1841	201
2.17	Petition, Sale of Real Estate: March 29, 1841	202
2.18	Bond & Oath, Sale of Real Estate: April 5, 1841	205
2.19	Order of Notice: October 11, 1841	207
2.20	Second Account: October 11, 1841	208
2.21	Third Account: May 9, 1842	210

List of Rosters

Roster		Page
1.	Black Heads of Households in Boston from the Fifth U.S. Census (1840)	212
2.	Prominent Blacks in Antebellum Boston	213
3.	1840s Decedents	215
4.	Literacy Indices of Selected 1840s Decendents (Grouped by Occupation Type)	216
5.	Literacy Indices of 1840s Decedents (Grouped by Occupation Type)	217
6.	Literacy of 1840s Decedents' Peer Group from the Seventh U.S. Census (1850)	219
7.	Signature Literacy among Black Women in Antebellum Boston	220
8.	Literacy Indices of 1840s Decedents' Peer Group	221
9.	Thomas Cole's Personal Network	222
10.	Thomas Cole's Public Network	225
11.	Participation of 1840s Decedents' Peer Group, by Color, in Thomas Cole's Networks	229
12.	Relationship of 1840s Decedents to People Carryng Out Probate Duties	230

List of Lists

Lists		Page

John W. Brown (32656)
- 1.1 Necessities 232
- 1.2 Amenities 232
- 1.3 Luxuries 232

Thomas Cole (35173)
- 2.1 Necessities 233
- 2.2 Amenities 233
- 2.3 Luxuries 233

Primus Hall (33174)
- 3.1 Necessities 234
- 3.2 Amenities 234
- 3.3 Luxuries 234

James H. Howe (34458)
- 4.1 Necessities 235
- 4.2 Amenities 235
- 4.3 Luxuries 235

Amy Jackson (32471)
- 5.1 Necessities 236
- 5.2 Amenities 236
- 5.3 Luxuries 236

| Lists | Page |

William S. Jinnings (32642)
6.1 Necessities ... 237
6.2 Amenities ... 237
6.3 Luxuries ... 237

Edward Lawson (33004)
7.1 Necessities ... 238
7.2 Amenities ... 238
7.3 Luxuries ... 238

Henry Robinson (36092)
8.1 Necessities ... 239
8.2 Amenities ... 239
8.3 Luxuries ... 239

John Robinson (36470)
9.1 Necessities ... 241
9.2 Amenities ... 241
9.3 Luxuries ... 241

John E. Scarlett (33895)
10.1 Necessities ... 242
10.2 Amenities ... 242
10.3 Luxuries ... 242

Peter Williams (35871)
11.1 Necessities ... 243
11.2 Amenities ... 243
11.3 Luxuries ... 243

List of Graphs

Graph		Page
1.	Proportion of crisscrossing decedents' household goods, by necessities, amenities, and luxuries	245
2.	Proportion of crisscrossing decedents' necessities, by generic sets	246
3.	Proportion of crisscrossing decedents' amenities, by generic sets	247
4.	Proportion of crisscrossing decedents' luxuries, by generic sets	248

List of Charts

Chart		Page
1.	Home and Business Locales of Associated Decedents	251
2.	Real Estate Owned by 1840s Decedents	254
3.	Residence by Wards of 1840s Decedents and Network Members in 1830	258
4.	Residence by Wards of 1840s Decedents and Network Members in 1840	261
5.	Home Locales of 1840s Decedents and Network Members in 1830	264
6.	Business Locales of 1840s Decedents and Network Members in 1830	266
7.	Home Locales of 1840s Decedents and Network Members in 1835	270
8.	Business Locales of 1840s Decedents and Network Members in 1835	272
9.	Home Locales of 1840s Decedents and Network Members in 1840	276
10.	Business Locales of 1840s Decedents and Network Members in 1840	278
11.	Home Locales of 1840s Decedents and Network Members in 1845	282
12.	Business Locales of 1840s Decedents and Network Members in 1845	284

List of Figures

Figure		Page
1.	City of Boston (1838), showing home and business locales of associated decedents	253
2.	City of Boston (1838), showing real estate owned by 1840s decedents	257
3.	City of Boston (1835), showing residence by wards of 1840s decedents and network members in 1830	260
4.	City of Boston (1838), showing residence by wards of 1840s decedents and network members in 1840	263
5.	City of Boston (1835), showing home and business locales of 1840s decedents and network members in 1830	269
6.	City of Boston (1835), showing home and business locales of 1840s decedents and network members in 1835	275
7.	City of Boston (1838), showing home and business locales of 1840s decedents and network members in 1840	281
8.	City of Boston (1838), showing home and business locales of 1840s decedents and network members in 1845	286

Preface

The probate records of antebellum black Bostonians offer an ideal opportunity to compare the literature to a primary source, both in terms of content and method. Critical reviews of the scholarship, first, on black social history and, then, on probate inventories as historic sources precede an examination of the probate records themselves and a comparison of the literature to probate records. The study concludes by indicating that the shortcomings of probate records arise from their leaving much mysterious or misunderstood without recourse to other sources while their strengths reside n their intimate and subtle suggestions for understanding a purportedly inarticulate population. Moreover, probate records are extremely compelling primary sources, not only because they prompt the imaginative visualization of artifacts, but also because they are themselves powerful visual artifacts. Their usefulness rests upon this dual dimension as document and artifact; experiencing probate records as artifacts can breathe life into these documents about the dead.

For the sake of brevity, only two packets of transcribed probate records (in visually-inflected simulations of the originals) are reproduced in this edited version, all tables have likewise been eliminated. The complete appendix material is available through UMI. Dissertation Information Service and the Afro-American Communities Project, Smithsonian Institution.

ACKNOWLEDGMENTS

There are many to whom I owe much gratitude: the faculty and administration of The George Washington University; my director of research, James O. Horton (Associate Professor of American History and Civilization at The George Washington University as well as Director of the Afro-American Communities Project at the Smithsonian Institution); and my two readers, Bernard M. Mergen (Professor of American Civilization at The George Washington University) and Dennis A. O'Toole, Vice President and Chief Education Officer of the Colonial Williamsburg Foundation). This study evolved from an opportunity to contribute to the work of the Afro-American Communities Project, housed and supported by the National Museum of American History with funding from the National Endowment for the Humanities and the Ford Foundation; and charged with investigating the lives of Afro-Americans in ten cities before the Civil War.

It is appropriate that I make note of the kindness of Ross W. Beales, Jr., Peter Benes, Beth Ann Bower, Anna L. Hawley, Bernard Herman, Gloria L. Main, Gail F. Mohanty, Barbara Nachtigall, Susan Ostroff, Sally Pierce, Julie Richter, Raymond V. Shephard Jr., Kathryn S. Smith, Laura F. Sprague, Linda Sturtz, Patricia Trautman, and Barbara McLean Ward. The following individuals helped at various stages with the preparation of the manuscript: David Scott Alvarez, Tracey Eberle, Farar Elliott, Dina Rose Friedman, William F. Lynch, Kevin McAnnaly, Philip L. Metzler, Jere A. Trout, Michael Walker, and Andrew J. M. Wheatcroft. Very great appreciation is extended to my friends Susan G. James, Judith Landau, Susan K. Nichols, Barbara F. Weissberger, and Patterson B. Williams. I also wish to thank my family, in particular my mother, Doris W. Buchalter, and my late father, Sam Buchalter, as well as my five siblings--Robert Buchalter, June B. Cohen, Ilene P. Buchalter, Sharon L. Buchalter, and Linda B. Overlie. Finally there are two who merit my warmest regards for caring during some trying times--William F. Stapp and my dear daughter Rosie.

Afro-Americans in Antebellum Boston

CHAPTER 1

INTRODUCTION

The probate records of the black population of Boston before the Civil War constitute the primary source material at the heart of this study. Probate records are official court documents associated with the legal settling of estates. The word "probate" derives from the Latin verb *probare*, "to try, test, approve, or prove," and probate records may best be understood as the bureaucratic paperwork that accumulates during the process of "hearing and determining questions or issues arising in matters concerning the probate of wills or the administration of decedents' estates."[1]

The Process That Probate Records Document

The process of probate in antebellum Boston can be reconstructed in broad terms.[2] It was a practice with a long tradition, transplanted from the European Old World to the colonies, in order to ensure the payment of debts and the assignment of "proper shares" to the decedent's heirs before assets were dissipated. In New England, real estate was included in inventories as a means to establish clear land titles; therefore, the sale of real estate during settlement to meet debts and/or to retire mortgages had to be approved by the court.

Generally, relatively soon after a death, an interested party--a widow, an heir, a creditor--appeared in court, exhibiting the will (if there was one) or testifying to the death of the decedent. Once the will was "proved," the executor/executrix therein named was empowered by the court to execute the will. In the absence of a will, the court appointed an administrator/administratrix. In either case, a bond with the executor or administrator as principal and two others as sureties was posted to guarantee the honest settlement of the estate. Appraisers were also designated to look at the deceased's property and to draw up a list of all "real estate, goods, chattels, rights, and credits," stating current market value. Oftentimes, the executor/executrix or administrator/administratrix compiled lists of debts. If the deceased's personal estate was insufficient for meeting his or her debts, the court was petitioned for a license to sell the decedent's real estate, if any. Commissioners of insolvency might be appointed to review and "allow" claims against the estate. (A widow, however, could exercise certain privileges extended by the protocol of probate to protect her economic rights. By petitioning for an allowance and a dower, she could have the court decree that a portion of her late husband's estate was not subject to his creditors.) A year after the recognition of the executor/ executrix or appointment of an administrator/ administrix, an account was returned to the court with schedules of monies received and disbursed; these accounts were rendered annually until the estate was settled. At every stage in probate--from proving the will to declaring insolvency to returning the accounts--public notice was given through announcements in newspapers.

Probate was a reasonably democratic official procedure, including decedents of all socioeconomic levels, testate and intestate. The argument that this general rule of thumb did not apply to blacks, who would be less sophisticated than whites about legal matters, overlooks evidence that enslaved blacks in the North were familiar with probate procedures. Not only were they classified as property, therefore finding themselves figuring in the settlement of estates, but also they could own and transfer property, therefor finding themselves receiving and bequeathing legacies. If slaves made wills, then surely free blacks were aware of the process of probate.[3] While there may be a number of explanations for the greater presence or absence of probate records for certain categories of decedents, the attempt to avoid estate taxes and the cost of probate itself would not seem to have been factors. There were no estate taxes to avoid in the early nineteenth century. Probate did entail the outlay of cash, however, and, with funeral expenses, comprised the first claims honored in the settlement of an estate.

The most common charges in the Boston probate records were for appraising the estate and serving as executor/ executrix or administrator/ administratrix of an estate; they range from $2.00 to $5.00 per appraiser for inventorying an estate (transcription 1.8) and from $15.00 to $50.00 per executor/ executrix or administrator/ administratrix for settling an estate (transcription 1.8). When the service was provided by a public official, fees sometimes were higher: $18.75 for assisting in the administration of an estate or as much as $120.00 for functioning as the sole administrator (transcriptions 1.8).

Given the limited financial resources of the black community in pre-Civil War Boston, these sums--whether $2.00 on an estate valued at $366 or $120.00 on an estate valued at $800.00--cannot be dismissed lightly. At the same time, as suggested by the two preceding examples, the higher charges generally appear to depend upon variables like the amount of labor involved in settling insolvent rather than solvent estates. The process of probate clearly drained capital from the estate when appraisers and executors or administrators took their fees off the top; however, when widows or heirs acted as the executor/ executrix or administrator/ administratrix, they could be compensated for their

Introduction

service. The overall cost of probate, then, was not generally so exorbitant that it in itself can be regarded as an impediment to the legal settling of estates. Nonetheless, all assets of all estates were by no means officially handled and formally assigned to creditors and heirs through probate.

While the overall procedure follows a recognizable pattern, oddities occur. For example, the settling of estates with no known heirs, carried out by public administrators, had its own rules--the decedent's wealth was held in trust for four years before being turned over to the Treasurer of the Commonwealth. Moreover, the probate records of "typical" black decedents in antebellum Boston have to be approached unprogrammatically, because the documents vary from decedent to decedent, depending upon individual differences in the settlement of each estate.

A Description Of Probate Records As Documents

A decedent's documents are gathered into one file or packet, with a docket number that was assigned chronologically by the court when the process of probate was initiated. The specific content of each packet may consist of a few or numerous items, dating from a single or many years. Each document may have several dates; for instance, the day a petition was submitted to the court as well as the day it was granted. It is the latter date that the register of the court would officially ascribe to the document for record-keeping purposes. Usually there is the inventory that describes and appraises the deceased's real and personal estate; these descriptions can be quite cursory, conceivably because "1 Sofa $1" needed no further explanation to inhabitants of the same social and economic milieu. Often there are the accounts that list sums received from the sale of the deceased's real and/ or personal estate and amounts paid to creditors; along with the notation of mortgages usually included on inventories, the disclosure of debts among the probate records contributes to the determination of a decedent's solvency and net worth, i.e., his or her actual and not apparent wealth. Occasionally there is the will; these can be quite formulaic in distributing assets in catch-all categories to a spouse and children or rather distinctive in itemizing bequests to beneficiaries beyond the immediate family.

Wills are handwritten, but not by the decedents. Those who had the foresight to die testate had their wills drawn up by qualified professionals outside the black community, it can be supposed, to avoid a possible contesting of their decisions about what they bequeathed to whom. As in inventories, the penmanship can sometimes be matched to the hand of one of the signatories--a witness or appraiser. In such cases, the witness or appraiser is invariably a functionary who not only knew how to write but also what to write to ensure the legitimacy of the document. Other instances of handscript documents can also be identified as the work of white professionals who either were administering an estate or were presenting information for a signature. For the most part, these probate records consist of pre-printed forms that were filled out by white public administrators, registers, justices of the peace, and judges of probate or their clerks--Phineas Blair, Samuel E. Sewall, N. C. Cary, Phineas Capen, Oliver W. B. Peabody; but Robert Morris, one of the first blacks admitted to the bar, also performed the legalities of probate once qualified.

Signatures or "x's" from members of the black community are scattered throughout these probate records not only as testators at the bottom of wills, but also as witnesses to wills, as posters of surety, as inventory-takers, and as executors or administrators of estates. An autograph document from a black Bostonian, however, is a rarity among the antebellum probate records; for example, there is an administrative account filed by the brother of a decedent as well as a remarkable letter of complaint from a beneficiary (transcription 2.16). The necessity of observing correct legal formalities limited probate records as a direct expressive medium; they are documents intended for a defined purpose in their own time.

The Research Context And Methodological Rationale

The originals of the probate records under study are stored in the Suffolk County Courthouse, in the middle of downtown Boston today, very near where the decedents lived and worked years ago. The documents were located as part of a larger research effort, the Afro-American Communities Project (A-ACP). Housed at the Smithsonian Institution's National Museum of American History and headed by James O. Horton, the A-ACP is investigating ten different antebellum black communities--Boston, Buffalo, Chicago, Cincinnati, Detroit, New York, Oberlin, Philadelphia, Richmond, and San Francisco.[4] The search for the probate records of Boston's Afro-American community was based on three sources: directory entries for "People of Color," Carter G. Woodson's *Free Negro Heads of Families in the United States in 1830* (roster 1), and a list of racial leaders and activists (roster 2). This highly-controlled strategy produced probate information for 113 black Bostonians who died between 1806 and 1895. An emphasis on antebellum life effectively eliminated the thirty-four decedents whose

Introduction

deaths took place after 1860. Of the pre-Civil War decedents, the occurrence of the most deaths during the 1840s pointed to its selection as the decade upon which to concentrate (roster 3). The very modest number of twenty-three packets of probate records to be studied supported a microcosmic approach, small-scale but multifaceted. The results take on larger significance given their relevance to comparable investigative studies of the probate records of blacks in the nine other cities that comprise the universe of the A-ACP.

Moreover, this intensive focus on 1840s Boston allows careful scrutiny of the efficacy of probate records as sources. Many historians regard the inventories in probate records as valid and democratic transmitters of the material culture and social values of populations for whom few domestic artifacts or personal documents may be extant. While obviously documents themselves, the systematic notation of the tangible in inventories seems to function as a snapshot of the ordinary stuff of everyday life that belonged to people for whom little else may be available for interpretation. Therefore, scholars maintain that probate records are a superior primary source that permits access to populations who have previously been assumed historically inarticulate.

But how credible a source for understanding such populations are probate records? To attempt an answer, it is necessary to proceed by analogy or extrapolation. Abstractly, "a previously assumed historically inarticulate" population for whom both probate records and other sources are available can be selected. Findings based on the probate records can then be compared with conclusions drawn from the other sources. The strengths and shortcomings of probate records as historical conduits for populations for whom information from other sources is limited or lacking can thus be elucidated.

Concretely, Afro-Americans were chosen since they represent par excellence a hitherto alleged inarticulate constituency whose historic voice has been emerging emphatically through recent scholarship. Focusing on antebellum Boston in particular permitted reference to the advanced state of the literature pertaining to its black population. This model study of a small sample of the probate records of a formerly presumed mute--but now well-heard--historic constituency can therefore argue that probate records offer a subtly shaded interpretation of that constituency, sometimes complementing and sometimes contradicting conclusions based on other sources.

The Historic Context And Socioeconomic Factors

The Afro-American community in antebellum Boston enjoyed a

heritage of racial pride while suffering the hardships of racist discrimination. Both pride and discrimination helped to bind black Bostonians together and motivated the community to strive for mutual betterment and abolition of slavery. The collective memory must have recalled with a mixture of appreciation and frustration the valor of Crispus Attucks, provocateur and hero of the Boston Massacre in 1770, as well as the achievements of the "Bucks of America," a black unit from Boston commanded by a black during the Revolutionary War.[5]

Black Bostonians must also have remembered their forebears' shrewdness and persistence in securing their own emancipation. The nature of northern slavery, with its rapid social acculturation, created an arena for action, and the rights accorded slaves in colonial New England--to petition, to receive trials, to sue in court--opened the way for the slaves' activism on their own behalf. The enslaved clearly recognized these windows of opportunity and vigorously exploited them.[6] Massachusetts blacks, in particular, brought their facility with English and familiarity with legal processes to bear in their determined demands for freedom. In the 1770s, a sophisticated grasp of the rhetoric of egalitarianism informed petitions seeking release from bondage submitted to the governor and the general court by a committee representing Massachusetts slaves; in 1778 and 1780, a calculated reference to the principle of no taxation without representation was cited to justify two free blacks' refusal to pay land taxes on the grounds that blacks were barred from voting in Massachusetts; in 1783, a deliberate invocation of the words "all men are created free and equal" from the 1780 state constitution converted one slave's suit against his master for failing to honor a promise of manumission into a judicial declaration of liberty for all Massachusetts slaves.[7]

Black Bostonians before the Civil War knew, therefore, about the forceful use of violent confrontation and the adroit exercise of limited power as means to pursue equality. This proud race legacy was offset, however, by mainstream racism that attempted to keep blacks less than equal. Job and housing discrimination in antebellum Boston indicates that Afro-Americans, despite their small numbers, were perceived as a threat to white prosperity and proprieties.[8] Increasing only slightly from 1,875 in 1830 to 1,999 in 1850, they decreased from 3.1 percent to 1.5 percent of Boston's total population over the same period of time because of the influx of the Irish. These two thousand blacks lived for the most part in residentially-distinct sections of town, especially on the lower slope of Beacon Hill.

At mid-century, the majority were no more than thirty-five years old, but a high infant mortality rate kept the proportion of blacks under ten years of age small compared to that of whites. Women only slightly outnumbered men until after age fifty, when a higher male death rate increased the imbalance. Almost two-thirds of black Bostonians were northern-born, with about 45 percent hailing from Massachusetts. Southern- and foreign-born blacks constituted approximately 17 percent and precisely 9 percent of the population, respectively. Mulattoes accounted for 21 percent of Boston's "people of color" in 1850, and, although they were only 18 percent of the black work force, they held a quarter of the most skilled occupations.[9]

Every black Bostonian sought employment and shelter in the face of an extremely restricted opportunity structure. A commercial city that expended the majority of its capital resources to develop a system of outlying mill towns, Boston had little other than its port to offer in employment for the blue collar worker.[10] The majority of black men therefore found work as mariners and dock laborers, both low-paying and irregular occupations, since prejudice barred them from almost all skilled jobs. A handful of enterprising businessmen succeeded as hairdressers, caterers, or clothiers, while a few professionals pursued careers as doctors, lawyers, ministers, or teachers. Women contributed substantially to the economic survival of black households and the community at large, despite racist and sexist constraints placed on their occupational aspirations and earning power. Confined for the most part to domestic labor, Boston's Afro-American women generated a small but steady income that often made them the financial mainstay of the family.[11]

Boston's blacks can thus be described as both integral and peripheral to their city's economy. Shut out from competition with white Yankees, squeezed even more by the influx of Irish in the mid-1840s, blacks provided a pool of labor that could be hired or fired at will when commerce fluctuated. Racism relegated blacks to the most menial and least stable jobs, which inflated the egos of working-class whites while it enhanced the power of upper-class whites.[12] But mainstream society's attempts to marginalize Afro-Americans economically and socially were strenuously resisted by race leaders and ordinary folks alike. Enormous reservoirs of hope, charity, energy, and faith fueled black Bostonians in their collective efforts for socioeconomic advancement; the dual factors of heritage and hardship united the community to improve its own lot and to take action against slavery.

The particulars of the suffering and fortitude of the Afro-American community in antebellum Boston are now to be viewed against the panorama of black social history. And once this wide-angle backdrop is in place, the uses of probate inventories are to be canvassed. Antebellum black Bostonians will next again come under scrutiny--via their probate records. And, last, findings from the probate records will be contrasted with the literature, to induce a more resonant reading of both.

Part I

Review of the Literature

CHAPTER 2

ON BLACK SOCIAL HISTORY

Scholarship that pursues an understanding of the daily lives of plain people in the past inherently reverberates with compelling urgency. Although a logjam of statistical tables and charts frequently halts the discourse, social history can almost be defined as historical research informed by social conscience. At its very best, the intellectual and the emotional dimension are equally activated and engaged.

Black social history is infused in particular with pride and anger. Scholarly arguments are no less cogent by necessity for being impassioned; but in its tenor, the literature of black social history reads as if it is finding a voice of its own analogous to that of the people it studies. The issue of overcoming conscious and unconscious barriers to learning about the lives of common Afro-Americans from *their* viewpoint threads throughout the literature. The story is by no means irretrievable, but it can primarily be told only via unexpected or unconventional paths.

Black social historians therefore seek documentary and/or material evidence that in some way captures the thoughts and beliefs of people who have been written out of history. Probate records, which bridge the documentary and the material, bear historical testimony to the tangible world of the Afro-American community in the past. Subject to both rigorous analysis and subtle coaxing, probate records with inventories listing personal possessions offer a down-to-earth perspective on a number of themes found in black social history. Its verbal contentions, moreover, can be weighed against mental recreations of the movable property and the communal interactions of antebellum black Bostonians, an undertaking all the more poignant for its sense of retrieving what so easily can be believed to be lost.

The Social Historian As Activist

The unacknowledged truism that the writing of history reflects a scholar's own time as much as the period discussed finds confirmation in the work of current social and urban historians. The link between their historical cold data and contemporaneous hot issues is anything but tenuous. The questions these scholars ask of the past, the sources to which they turn, the analytic methods they employ, and the interpretations they advance (even champion) arise from their acute awareness of the very real impact of ahistorical perceptions of the past on the formulation of public policy.[1]

The Philadelphia Social History Project (PSHP) can serve as an excellent case in point. Its central scholarly concern may have originally been with "how the processes of urbanization and industrialization shaped both the development of the nineteenth-century metropolis and the experience of its diverse population groups," but its driving force sprang from a question of critical importance in the last third of the twentieth century--"whether the burdens and disabilities faced by black Americans were peculiar to their historical experience or simply obstacles which every immigrant group entering society had to overcome." As Theodore Hershberg states boldly, the results of investigating this question have "clear implications for public policy." He pointedly addresses the inadequacy of popular solutions to the socioeconomic plight of urban blacks, and then explicitly embraces as a new goal for PSHP research "the purposeful study of history to shed light on issues of contemporary social policy" since "contemporary social science literature, which provides the intellectual and scientific context for policy making, suffers from a terribly distorting ahistorical focus."[2]

Similarly, James Horton wishes to combat ill-informed assumptions about the past that underpin erroneous assessments of current social difficulties. In addressing the National Urban League Conference on Black Families, Horton argued that Daniel Patrick Moynihan's 1965 report, *The Negro Family: The Case for National Action*, rested on shaky historical evidence when it contended that the black community was irrevocably weakened by the destructive repercussions of slavery and urban poverty on family relationships. Like Hershberg, Horton does not shy away from drawing attention to the implications for setting public policy of a more accurate understanding of the past.

> Social history is bringing to light much information which is of central importance to social policymakers. Soon, we may be able to provide the historical background which will aid in our understanding of the pressing problems of contemporary society.[3]

This deliberate probing of the past in full consciousness of history's contemporary relevance has generated intense inquiry into the roots of current social ills and injustices. Furthermore, cognizance of marked socioeconomic inequities in a nation that declares equal opportunity for all fuels a search for the origin of the incongruity between the ideal and the real. A cadre of scholars has therefore turned its attention in particular to measuring the historic reality of the American ideology of egalitarianism. In their quest, they habitually and overtly wrestle with method, going to great lengths to develop unimpeachable, empirical sources.[4] Two sequential studies of Boston exemplify these strategies, investigating social and economic stratification through analyses of tax lists and town offices in the periods 1607 to 1771 and 1771 to 1790. Each study documents increasing inequality, culminating by 1790 in a rapidly advancing concentration of wealth and political power among the "merchant princes," accompanied by a burgeoning of the numbers of propertyless "proletarians"--during the very time of profuse egalitarian rhetoric. These ideologically-charged conclusions assertively deflate the cherished American myth of equal opportunity, revealing its disjuncture with reality quite early on in American history.[5] These powerful findings are not to be gainsaid, yet an exclusive focusing on wealth and political power as the key indices of achievement has tended to deflect historians' attention from what may actually have constituted success and satisfaction in the everyday lives of ordinary people in the past.

Social History's Moral Dimension

A deeper examination of the imperatives of social history scholarship makes abundantly clear that it requires a balanced perspective. Social historians' findings not only may become the basis for public policy, but their interpretations also carry the responsibility for doing justice to the values of the men, women, and children who lived in the midst of broad socioeconomic conditions that only hindsight clarifies. In short, social historians' conclusions and judgments are freighted with both political and human meaning and ultimately possess, therefore, a profound moral dimension.

What might have seemed of purely academic interest thus transcends ivory tower rumination when scrutinized for its actual import for those who experienced it. Take the issues of geographic and property mobility, both of which--on first glance-- would seem fairly clearcut indices of success and satisfaction. Substantial geographic mobility in the past appears undisputed, but its significance is open to debate. What is a scholar to understand when he discovers that "only 5 to 8 percent of the Afro-American men [in Boston] listed in the 1850 census could be traced to the 1860 census"?[6] Conventionally, lack of persistence--transience--has been regarded as negative; it has been said that populations in the nineteenth century moved on when they had established neither an economic nor a social foothold.[7] Yet, geographically-mobile populations can be regarded positively, by virtue of their choosing "a strategy to maximize opportunity."[8] Horton has carefully delineated the affirmative character of the multiple, short-distance moves over several decades that brought Southern black migrants *to* Boston by 1850. They were drawn to Boston--kin and friends had already established an active community amidst moderate racial tolerance--for good reasons.[9] On the other hand, geographic stability may signal reluctance to forsake familial and kin loyalties.[10] Staying or leaving is a decision individuals and families make within a context of cultural and structural variables;[11] therefore, transience, in and of itself, is not open to a single interpretation. Transients may represent society's winners as well as its losers.[12]

Property mobility also resists simplistic interpretation. The two sequential studies of Boston that assertively deflated the cherished American myth of equal opportunity nonetheless conceded that there was a degree of genuine property mobility: in the period 1687 to 1771, "commercial prosperity had raised the purchasing power of every social group" and from 1771 to 1790, there was the "possibility of moderate economic success."[13] But the discrepancy in Revolutionary Boston between the rhetoric of egalitarianism and the reality of economic and social stratification perceived and decried by today's historians may blind them to the significance of property mobility ("the possibility of moderate economic success") for those achieving it. Given the ideology of American culture, this preoccupation with determining the authenticity of the openness of American society and testing the validity of the American success ethic is understandable. Dismay over misdirected anger (poor whites harassing blacks instead of joining with blacks to take common action against the wealthy) and impatience with a quiescent social order (middle-class deference to the elite) may be justified,[14] but overlooking the complexities of property holding distorts the values of a large proportion of people in the past.

Michael Katz at first appears to propose a strict constructionist stance on the advantages of those with capital (the business class), who are in a position "to appropriate a disproportionate share of scarce and desirable resources," and, by implication, to accumulate even greater wealth and power. This entrepreneurial drive is understood to dominate other considerations in social relations.[15] But when he, along with Michael J. Doucet and Mark J. Stern, examines the issue of home ownership among certain ethnic groups and non-whites, they discern a different attitude from that held by the business class, an attitude that had little to do with property as a marketable commodity or its "exchange value."

[A] home for a working man meant not only a modest source of capital accumulation but even more the only realistic protection he could acquire against the common and expected difficulties inherent in working class life.[16]

This attitude of "use value" toward home ownership may have made owning a home inconsequential for social mobility when strictly construed (*i.e.*, if only joining the class controlling capital were to be regarded as constituting genuine mobility for a member of the working class, homeowner or not). "However," they clarify, "if social mobility is defined as an individual's perceived improvement in his life situation, then home ownership was indeed consequential."[17] This "perceived improvement" deserves acknowledgement, since achievement needs to be weighed on more than economic and political scales. The attainment of security or respectability rather than higher social status--if culturally valued--comprised success.[18] Thus, even if home ownership by the working class may ultimately have served the interests of the business class (through handsome profits from investing in mortgages and through limiting the working class's recourse to geographic mobility as a strategy for betterment),[19] it would be a mistake to dismiss this sign of property mobility as minor or as a form of capitalistic chicanery. Starting with virtually nothing by way of property and getting off the bottom can represent a reasonably lofty objective for the poor--white and black--at any time.[20]

Scholars today detect the reality of historical inequality and seek the ideological basis for the quiescence of populations who apparently learned "they should be losers--or that they are not entitled to the highest rewards and greatest pleasures offered in their time"--i.e., those who did not try to alter the social order.[21] Yet interpreting the significance of staying or leaving and the meaning of owning a home demands considerable sensitivity to what represented losing or winning in the lives of people in the past. Persistence may signal either choice or necessity; real property may represent a marketable commodity or a homestead; the unbridled pursuit of enhanced social and economic status could eventuate in the sacrifice of life's "highest rewards and greatest pleasures."

Contradictions In Black Social History

Students of black history, in particular, find themselves confronted by a curious paradox: condemning the American system historically for its endemic racial discrimination and structural economic dislocation, yet celebrating the vital social cohesion of the black community engendered by that discrimination and dislocation. In the eighteenth century, both race and class functioned as societal dividers, but in the first quarter of the nineteenth century race became the more prominent social distinction. The demise of the potential for political or economic alliances between blacks and whites--when race became in the public rhetoric the "strongest determinant of equality among men"--was a lamentable block to the integration of Afro-Americans into the wider society.[22]

A pervasive prejudice against blacks prevailed, as is persuasively documented in many of the studies emanating from the PSHP. In evaluations of the nature of work for Philadelphians in the mid-nineteenth century, an overall analysis proved infeasible because:

> The most severe handicaps were faced by blacks. They were so excluded from the broad range of opportunities generated by industrialization that figures on black employment were not included in the essay's data tables.[23]

When examining the uses of urban space, the discovery of the critical importance of industrial affiliation--rather than ethnicity--in determining residence must be tempered because:

> The other major finding concerns the one ethnic group that was an exception to the ecological generalization: black Americans. The ecological "rules" that governed access to job opportunities were "suspended" for blacks.[24]

In investigations of the family, its economy, and the organization of the life course, colorblind analyses are impossible because:

> even when the internal characteristics of their families were similar to those of whites, black families appeared to be following a different set of rules. This suggests a very different world view. The opportunities generated by industrialization were not equally available to all Philadelphians. When black families observed the city and the narrow range of options available to them, they apparently behaved differently, creating short- and long-run family strategies very much unlike those of whites.[25]

And, finally, when looking at the experiences of subgroups within the larger population, dependence on typical categories must be abandoned because:

> Afro-Americans have always been less able than whites to differentiate their community along the usual stratification axes of occupation and wealth . . . . blacks used factors unique to their experience such as free or slave-birth, the attainment of freedom before or after the Civil War, and intra-group color differences.[26]

Yet conditions that would seem unavoidably to precipitate total social disarray gave rise instead to a community with a sense of identity, a belief in mutual welfare, and a commitment to civic activism. Never fully surrendering self-definition, Afro-Americans mobilized survival strategies that developed organically from their Old World heritage interacting with their New World milieu. Even in slavery, black folk thought conferred expressive autonomy,[27] while festivals and celebrations preserved elements of African culture.[28] Choosing group loyalty over individual advancement, distinctive domestic and kin arrangements evolved in the face of slavery and formed the touchstones of black communalism. Insecurity about the duration of blood and marital ties prompted blacks to enlarge familial and kin obligation into social obligation.[29] Thus the individual was bound to the community and vice versa--the hostility of the larger society made "individualism an unaffordable luxury" for black Americans in the nineteenth century,[30] encouraging instead a climate of cooperation, the development of community leaders, and an agenda of common concerns.[31] Since blacks were uniformly denied access to the American mainstream, they found intraracial solidarity both a prudent and effective instrument for improving their lot economically and politically.[32]

Such ethnic cohesiveness may have been characteristic of many groups of people who relied on a "defensive mode" of adaptation to cope with the accelerated uncertainty of the nineteenth century,[33] but the disproportionate hardships meted out to blacks by American society no doubt intensified their turning inward. The mechanisms adopted by the black community--whether institutional like the church or informal like kinship networks--blended pragmatism with creativity; the communal order and values that ensued met the practical and cultural needs of the community's members.[34] To be sure, there was diversity within the black community--even dissension over issues like integrated or separate schooling. But both the relatively small sizes of the various Afro-American communities in the antebellum urban North and the readiness of whites to stigmatize all blacks equally bred economic and social interdependence.[35] Internal and external forces thus both nourished and necessitated the building of the black community, that--like the black historical experience overall--can be seen as unique.[36]

Analyzing The Black Community

This element of distinction has prompted today's social historian to undertake particularly careful testing and application of the "usual and customary" categories of sociological analysis--occupation, wealth, education, gender, etc. When data about the black community neither fit the pattern nor lend themselves readily to the typical explication, scholars have inquired more deeply, seeking to mesh the qualitative with the quantitative.[37]

Stratification within the historic black community is a good case in point. Superficially, the black communities in antebellum Boston and Philadelphia could be assessed as largely undifferentiated--and thus unstratified--if one depended upon the classic axes of occupation and wealth. Scholars have indeed documented that there was little occupational diversity. In antebellum Boston, two-thirds of black males were semi-skilled or unskilled workers (domestics, seamen, and laborers) and fewer than one-third were skilled workers or small shopkeepers (hairdressers and barbers, blacksmiths, and clothing dealers), with 1 to 2 percent of blacks at the top of the occupational scale as doctors, ministers, teachers, and lawyers. Likewise, in antebellum Philadelphia, 80 percent of the black male workforce was unskilled (all but 10 percent in the same five occupations--laborer, porter, waiter, seaman or carter), 16 percent was skilled (one-half of whom were barbers and shoemakers), and 4 percent was white collar (vending cart proprietors). For black women, occupational diversity was similarly constricted. In antebellum Philadelphia, 80 percent of the black female workforce did daywork, 14 percent were seamstresses, and 5 percent were vending cart proprietors. Black women in antebellum Boston made up 90 percent of the occupational category of domestics, the category accounting for 20 percent of the entire black workforce. In the skilled and entrepreneurial group, black women took in sewing and boarders.[38] In short, the vast preponderance of black workers carried out unskilled or semiskilled jobs, with very little differentiation in occupation.

The black population, systematically barred from occupational opportunities regardless of aptitude or skill, fell back on the menial labor or service jobs deemed permissible by the wider society.[39] Therefore positions that among whites would be considered lower middle class were considerably more prestigious and relatively lucrative within the black community.[40] Barbers, for instance, could accrue status within the black community through their shop's functioning as a community center or could gain wealth through the patronage of white customers.[41]

When wealth as a potential stratifier is examined, the key point that emerges is that "it was extremely scarce and anyone at any occupational level who held any property was rare."[42] In 1860, only 6 percent of the Boston black community held real property and just 15 percent held personal property. Among the antebellum Philadelphia black community, three out of five households had $60 or less total wealth. But what little wealth there was to be found in the black community was distributed unevenly. In Boston, skilled and entrepreneurial workers (less than one-third of the workforce) held 60 percent of the property, while professionals more often than not held no property. In Philadelphia, the richest 10 percent owned 70 percent of the wealth.[43]

Although careful scrutiny detects a not inconsequential --even if limited--social hierarchy whose principles of stratification reflected the realities of the black experience, simple economic class analysis to determine the internal differentiation and social structure of the historic black community will not suffice. The vast majority of antebellum blacks were uniformly ensnared by lowly labor and grim poverty. Consequently, intra-community distinctions arose along noneconomic lines in accord with the black community's historic development and unique characteristics. Factors that differentiated antebellum Afro-Americans included free or slave birth, working as a live-in servant, subtenanting, color differences and church affiliation.[44] Investigating such sociocultural nuances with full appreciation for their meaning within the historic black community demonstrates understanding of a population hitherto "*rendered* historically inarticulate," whether through lack of scholarly tools or interest.[45]

Empathetic Perplexity

A central concept cited by social historians as verification of their having accurately located the voice of ordinary blacks in the past seems to be "choice." Detecting patterns of decision-making grants to Afro-Americans in the past a species of autonomy that coincides with today's ideas about self-determination. Moreover, evidence of exercising choice effectively contests characterizations of blacks as compliant accessories to their own subjugation. Social history scholarship finds that, no matter how hard pressed, Afro-Americans were active in shaping their own lives and the world around them. As slaves, blacks were "able to structure in positive ways many of the circumstances surrounding them"--their relationship with their owner, their kin arrangements, their cultural expressions.[46] Slavery limited choice but did not totally "take over" the enslaved; through decision-making independent of slaveowners' beliefs and practices, Afro-Americans shaped their own history.[47] Afro-American traditions, worldview, and lifestyle developed dynamically in answer to experience and needs;[48] this adaptability and resilience countered the brutality of slavery and racism with alternative modes of affirmation and autonomy.

Empathy for these alternative modes "turns up the volume" on the heretofore muted voices of Afro-Americans, allowing recent scholars to identify previous scholarly misjudgments, ranging from blindness to the internal order of the black community to incomprehension of room usage in a black tenant house, installed backwards in a museum exhibit.[49] Once perceived and explicated, the unnoticed or misunderstood gains an aura of the self-evident. But getting it "backwards" arises from ever-present reservoirs of point-of-view that--if not overtly examined--can compromise the interpretation of historical evidence.[50] Even conscientious scholars cannot entirely escape value judgments reflecting their own time, class, and taste; historiography suggests that scholarship, always influenced by contemporaneous forces beyond the pure search for knowledge, can take on a pressing immediacy through confronting problematic ideological and moral issues, ostensibly in the past. When approaching black social history, therefore, the task of balancing empathy with analysis becomes particularly perplexing. Certain topics require deep and sensitive inquiry--internalized racism,[51] black sexism.[52] Moreover, celebrating the adaptability and resilience of black culture to counteract negative assessments of Afro-Americans as accessories to their own victimization endangers hearing the full voice of the historic black community.[53]

Certainly, child-naming practices and leadership in community organizations connote instances of self-determination from which scholars can infer the values of black culture.[54] Entries in slave birth registers and "broadsides" describing black organizational activities[55]--while not conscious articulations of individual choice (as might be found in diaries and letters)--do leave a trail of behaviors that not only conveys aggregate data about the mass of everyday Afro-

Americans in the past but also reveals personal information about particular Afro-Americans long ago. A specific slave couple--Huldah, Jr., and Little Bob--named their five children--Jenny, Edward, Elijah, Adeline and Sylvia--for a maternal grandmother, two maternal uncles, and two paternal aunts.[56] Literally and figuratively, this family is no longer nameless; by bringing to light both the content and significance of a slave birth registry (compiled for the use of the master and conceivably a symbol par excellence of ownership), the free will of these enslaved parents to define for their children a kin network that referred to their own particular familial ties is clarified. Similarly, a certain barber, John J. Smith, can be identified as one of the typically married, upwardly-mobile men in their mid-forties (increasingly Southern-born and mulatto) who engaged in reform and protest activities in antebellum Boston--in his case, specifically in the underground railroad, assisting fugitive slaves. By attending to the particular as well as the general characteristics of an activist (derived from censuses and city directories, etc., themselves compiled for purposes indifferent to individual personalities),[57] the choice of a certain small businessman to act in accord with his own principles is underscored.

This curious reversal of emphasis from the anonymous mass to the nameable individual shifts the scale in black social history.[58] The most vivid example of this inversion can be found in Horton's "Life and Times of Edward Ambush: An Illustration of Social History Methodology."[59] After describing recent scholars' rejection of traditional themes in American history (which concentrated on white male power) as the nation's full story, Horton stresses the importance of studying the community to understand the poor and the oppressed:

> The lives of the exceptional few cannot alone bring a full understanding and appreciation of the richness of the black American experience. . . . An understanding of the communal roots of exceptional blacks will bring greater appreciation of their individual achievements and, more important, it will focus attention on the real strength of Afro-American society, its community.[60]

Individualism thus takes a back seat to the collectivity. But to illustrate social history method, Horton uses documents in the public domain to trace the life of an individual, Edward Ambush of Washington, DC, who--although "a person of no greater or lesser significance to history than any one of his neighbors"--virtually personifies the American success ethic. In seven documents--from an agreement with his master to "hire out" on commission (1841) through a manumission agreement (also 1841) to a DC directory listing (1845) to the federal census (1850) to a tax record (1855) to his will and inventory (1864)--Edward Ambush's life is partially reconstructed. His age, birthplace, marital status, spouse's name, number and names of children, wealth, property holding, and literacy are all teased out through the careful accumulation and cross-checking of all pertinent "scraps of evidence." Edward Ambush gradually takes on a recognizable, individual identity the more he can be linked to a certain life history, a specific wife, a particular home address. And finally, the biographical data gain a fully human dimension when the door of Edward Ambush's dwelling figuratively swings open upon his death, and the inventory of his personal property provides a tour of his home. During his twenty-three years as a free man, Ambush--along with his wife Elizabeth--acquired the basic domestic accouterments for sleeping, eating, storing, and cleaning. While remarkably austere by twentieth century standards (and even in comparison to the lifestyle of the wealthy in the eighteenth century), a "Safe & Contents" (valued at $6.00), a "Refrigerator" (valued at $5.00) and a "Large Family Bible" (valued at $20.00) do represent acquisitions beyond essential, unspecialized furnishings. As Horton points out, Edward Ambush's legacy was not negligible; aside from a foundation of property holding, he was able "to pass along the opportunities of freedom to future generations."[61] Moreover, the investment in a family Bible, "which no doubt, had recorded in it birth, marriage and other important family information,"[62] can be recognized as an act consciously laying claim to what was once only noted by third parties (in slave birth registries, censuses, etc.). The last item of the final public document giving access to Edward Ambush's life therefore implies the establishment of a private, self-generated record.

Perhaps the Ambush family Bible, emblematic of choice and continuity, is somewhere extant, but for the most part social historians rely on "indirect records" to decipher "revealed preferences." These indirect records--documents most frequently produced by government functionaries--list "material" aspects of life that disclose selection, however constrained by attitudes or circumstances: where people lived, what jobs they held, what familial settings they created.[63] Inventories present an intriguing twist upon this concept of the indirect record that documents the material aspects of life; as a document, it permits indirect access to actual material culture. Probate inventories may have been officially generated, but they allow for a species of secondhand intimacy with the personal possessions of the long-deceased (within the context of a routine enumeration of household goods) that is extremely powerful. Edward Ambush's "Large Family Bible," even if physically lost to posterity, manages to project a strong presence that eloquently reveals preferences.

It is this caliber of understanding that motivates the careful scrutiny of a select pool of probate records rather than the wholesale study of numerous probate inventories. Collected systematically in large quantities and analyzed statistically, inventories can deliberately be wrung of their association with specific individuals in order to determine the common experience of large segments of society. At the other end of the spectrum, a sole example often is guarded protectively and minutely examined expressly because of its association with a single, usually "significant," person. For students of black social history, avoiding either extreme to the exclusion of the other is paramount; knowing what inventories can convey about the historic black community as a whole, as well as about particular Afro-Americans in the past, has relevance.

Probate Records As Passport

Selected probate records from the black community in Boston before the Civil War can thus serve as a passport into the homes of people whose household possessions have largely not survived as artifacts to be cherished by descendants or to be displayed in museums for what they say about the everyday material realities and cultural values of Afro-Americans in the past. Therefore a sensitive reading of the characteristics and contents of these particular probate records in light of appropriate themes and issues found in black social history studies raises two interesting prospects: the interpretation of the personal and communal meaning of now-vanished physical goods and the investigation of specified scholarly contentions with probate records as evidence.

Undermining The Monolithic Myth

Scholars have argued persuasively that the historic black community was not monolithic. This adamant affirmation of diversity springs in large part from the need to disabuse white Americans of their racist tendency to view all blacks as the same.[64] At the same time, the distinctive context of the Afro-American historic experience masks the ready detection of heterogeneity and precludes the customary analysis of internal diversity.

Scholarship has identified pertinent socioeconomic differences--occupation, geographic origin, skin color--within antebellum Boston's black community that correlate with differences in residence, job skills, and association. Moreover, scholars have overturned conventional expectations about the positive relationship between typically more elevated occupations and greater wealth, as well as the very assignation of social status to a particular occupation.[65] Will the contents and value of probate inventories mirror such distinctive features of differentiation and stratification in the black community? For instance, one wonders if a hairdresser's possessions at death will reflect his occupation in terms not only of the tools of his trade but also of his relative affluence and high status.

Also, what clues do probate records offer for sustaining findings that skin color had socioeconomic consequences in the black community? Scholars have tread lightly when discussing this particular dimension of differentiation. Although they agree upon the decline of color over time as a determinant of status in the black community, the acknowledgement of the earlier importance of color can provoke uneasiness and controversy. No matter that the explanation for the disproportionate wealth and power of the mulatto lies in environmental advantages from which mulattoes benefited (greater access to opportunities than blacks during slavery, more likely manumission, more rapid urbanization), the valuing of lighter over darker skin--substituting for the inapplicable mainstream system of stratification using occupation and wealth--bespeaks the internalization of racism within the black community.[66]

The most telling evidence leading to this disturbing finding concerns marriage patterns. Even in Boston in 1860, where mulattoes "were over represented [in wealth holding] by less than six percentage points, with less than 45 percent of the city's black wealth" and lived intermixed with darker blacks on "Nigger Hill," mulattoes married mulattoes: 72 percent of the mulatto men married mulatto women. And when mulattoes did marry darker spouses, a pattern emerges that indicates a greater prizing of lighter rather than darker skin color among antebellum Afro-Americans. A dark man who was "well situated financially and/ or occupationally" was more likely than a black laborer to win the hand of a mulatto woman; conversely, a dark woman was more likely to wed a light-skinned laborer than a mulatto who was "well situated financially and/ or occupationally."[67]

Moreover, real property ownership can be correlated with color-coded marriages. An analysis of the four possible kinds of unions among Afro-Americans--mulatto men/ black women, black men/ black women, black men/ mulatto women, and mulatto men/ mulatto women--discloses an upward progression of real property ownership in antebellum Philadelphia:

> only 3.4 percent of the marriages between mulatto men and black women reported real property ownership, while black men with black wives reported twice that proportion; black men with mulatto wives three times the proportion; and mulatto men with mulatto wives approach four times the proportion.[68]

Thus, although possessing real property was rare, mulatto women--whether married to mulatto or black men--were more likely than their darker sisters to share a degree of economic security. The economic worth of fair color--for women, in particular--is spelled out rather dramatically in these marital patterns. Will probate records substantiate observations of intraracial differences in the black community? For example, one wonders if the community members who appear in each other's probate records will reflect intraracial exclusivity or diversity?

Looking At The Black Family And The Black Woman

Recent scholarship has effectively combatted characterizations of the black family and community--historic and current--as disorganized; rather they were and are organized both in accord with Afro-American values and in reaction to pressures from the wider society. During slavery, kin networks complemented settled two-parent families as a highly rational response to the ever present threat of the separation of blood relatives.[69] But the legacy of enslavement did not in itself produce the preponderance of matrifocal families nor the dominance of kinship networks among today's poor blacks: the grueling experience of life in the nineteenth century urban North did. Research shows conclusively that "settled slave marriage 'models' and domestic arrangements existed in all types of slave settings" and "the typical ex-slave family was composed of a poor husband, his wife, and their children." In fact, "in all settings," despite changing its shape between 1880 and 1930, "the typical black household (always a lower-class household) had in it two parents."[70] Similarly, in Boston, "the vast majority of black children in 1860, over sixty-five percent lived in two-parent households," while "only sixteen percent of black Boston households headed by women contained children."[71]

An emphasis on "the typical" and "the vast majority," however, perhaps casts a too-positive glow on these findings. The power of scholarly language to stress one interpretation over another based on exactly the same statistical findings plays a role in sorting out the data on family composition in Philadelphia from 1850 to 1880, eventuating in a clearer understanding of the origins of the black matrifocal household. When compared to German immigrants, Irish immigrants, and native American whites, blacks had the lowest proportion of couple-headed households with children, thus already manifesting a noticeable prevalence of matrifocal families in the mid-nineteenth century. Two diametrically opposed phrasings of this finding are then offered:

> We could say that blacks are more than twice as likely as foreign and native-born white Americans to live in households headed by a female. Such a statement emphasizes the differential. Alternately, we could point out that the great majority of all ethnic groups live in couple-headed households. Even among blacks, only one fourth of the households were headed by a female. Moreover, among the various ethnic groups there is a difference of only 17 percentage points between the group with the lowest proportion of female-headed households--the German Americans--and that with the highest, black Americans. Obviously, this characterization tends to minimize the differences by underscoring the similarities.[72]

Such scholarly wordplay convincingly demonstrates that the significance of the pattern lies less in focusing on the magnitude of the observed differences than on its source. "Urban economic and demographic factors" are held accountable for black male absence:

1. Since female-headedness varies inversely with wealth, the job discrimination faced by Afro-American men--limited primarily to unskilled labor--ruled against a black father's producing adequate income to provide for his family.

2. Given high mortality rates among Afro-American males, three-quarters of all black female household heads were widows; at least a quarter of the married Afro-American women with children were widowed by age 40.

3. Black female single-parents could manage to keep their children while holding down steady jobs as domestics,

seamstresses or taking in boarders, whereas black male single parents--with irregular income--may have found it preferable to send their children to live with friends or relatives.

With no evidence to the contrary, poverty and death thus loom as the agents responsible for denying stability and continuity to Afro-American households. Slavery undeniably strained black families; but the impact of the urban experience--with its economic discrimination, privation, and disease--resulted in the matrifocal Afro-American family. "To the extent that the female-headed family appeared during [1850-1880], it emerged, not as a legacy of slavery, but as a result of the destructive conditions of Northern urban life."[73] Thus, matrifocality would seem to have a material dimension. Does the settlement of estates of black decedents in antebellum Boston contribute to understanding the rise of the matrifocal family? For example, one wonders if the narration of personal possessions in inventories tells of security and comfort or of uncertainty and subsistence.

The ardor of the debate about the origin of black matrifocality with its attendant kin network reciprocity--bonding through swapping--suggests unresolved tension between admiration for the resilience of Afro-Americans placed in abhorrent circumstances and aversion for the outcome of that resilience. What can be praised as pragmatic can also be judged as tragic. Today's poor black family is "embedded in cooperative domestic exchange, prov[ing] to be an organized, tenacious, active lifelong network." But these "patterns of co-residence, kinship-based exchange networks linking multiple domestic units, elastic household boundaries, [and] lifelong bonds to three-generation households" also produce "social controls against the formation of marriage that could endanger the network of kin, [thereby emphasizing] the domestic authority of women . . .[while limiting] the role of the husband or male friend within a woman's kin network."[74]

This negative corollary to the adaptive social order that prevails in today's poor black community--a social order evolved to accommodate the barriers to assimilation and acculturation erected by white society--should not elude scholarly acknowledgement. But in the nineteenth century, before the influx of the Great Migration of Southern blacks in the twentieth century overtaxed Northern black communities,[75] mutual aid seems to have supplemented rather than supplanted dependence on the two-parent family. Do probate records offer clues about this intermeshing of the familial with the communal? One wonders, for instance, if those who took the inventory or served as administrators represent either eligible candidates among family, kin, and friends or primarily leaders of the black community carrying out customary responsibilities for their fellow Afro-Americans.

Cooperative behavior and matrifocal households were realities in the historic black community that indicate the struggle to adjust to economic hardship. But appreciation for resourcefulness of Afro-Americans ought not to obscure the painful lot of the preponderance of black women entrapped in a racist and sexist society. It is now recognized that the ordinary Afro-American woman has borne a double burden. Being female *and* black, she has been required not only to live out gender ideals of deference to men but also to carry out economic and social roles--to raise her family and elevate her race--without questioning patriarchy or seeking autonomy. The strictures of this Herculean task have led to misperceptions of black women as either "inadequate" or "superwomen." Regardless of which bias, black women have been regarded as problems and deviant,[76] virtually as perpetrators of the very system that has oppressed them.

"Ironic" insufficiently describes the average black woman's situation as breadwinner within her family, the black community, and the wider society. Readily accepted by both whites and blacks as domestic laborers in the antebellum North, Afro-American women could live-in, do day work or wash, sew, and/ or take in boarders at home. Although for the most part unskilled and with little opportunity for advancement, these occupations had the great advantage of bringing in a relatively steady income. Black women were for the most part relegated to labor that was deemed appropriate for their race and sex; racism and sexism therefore together forced them to work at menial jobs that produced little cash and conferred minimal power.

> Racism helped create economic conditions that made it impossible for black men to support their families without the supplementary incomes of their wives and contributed to the number of black women, without men, called upon to support families on their own. . . . Sexism was also a handicap because it further curtailed black women's earning power beyond that already limited by racism. This made total independence for black women all but impossible even as limited economic opportunities for black men made wifely dependence unpractical.[77]

So most black women worked, even if their true numbers escaped the attention of government functionaries. The 1860, 1870, and 1880 censuses in the urban Ohio Valley may show that "only fifty-one percent of [black] female heads of family listed an occupation . . . , the majority of whom (almost ninety percent) were listed as 'domestics' and 'washes and irons,'" but the full extent of female employment clearly went unrecorded when some wards in Cincinnati show every black woman employed while others reported no black women with occupations.[78] Similarly, in Providence the 1850 census listed only eight women (2 percent of the workforce) with occupations, leaving uncounted the "significant numbers of housewives who supplemented family income by taking in other people's laundry, caring for other families' children, or occasionally cooking meals for other families." Although the 1860 census showed women as 37 percent of Providence's black workforce (listing 204 females with occupations),[79] even these higher figures are unlikely to reflect fully the prevalence of black women working for pay.

Taking in wash, for instance is known from newspapers, letters, tax lists, and other records to have been a major source of income for black women in antebellum Boston. Yet the 1850 census lists not a single black washerwomen. The Boston city directory indicates that there were at least twenty-five black women who took in laundry; but surely that figure--no more than the 1860 census listing of thirty black washerwomen--barely hints at the number of Afro-American females in pre-Civil War Boston who toiled over other peoples' laundry long before the days of automatic washing machines, tumble dryers, and steam irons, even before the advent of hot running water.[80] Will the contents and value of personal property correlate with the working role of black women? For instance, one wonders if the enumeration of household goods and remuneration in administrative accounts will document work-for-pay within the domestic setting.

Verifying Black Cultural Values

Although the historic black community was impoverished, scholars concur that Afro-American property-holders were to be found in antebellum American. The 1860 census shows that, although "nearly eighty-eight percent of black households were without appreciable amounts of property," "fifty-three blacks owned significant amounts of property in [Providence] that year." The amount of property-holding ranged from personal property valued at $30 to both real and personal property valued at $5500, with a median of approximately $900.[81] In Philadelphia, the total wealth (real and personal property combined) for three out of five households in 1838 and 1847 amounted to $60 or less;

but the wealthiest 30 percent held from $200 to $300 worth of property in 1838 and from $400 to $600 worth in 1847.[82] In the 1850 census, Philadelphia blacks held real property with a mean value of $103.[83] The 1860 census records that 4.5 percent of black Bostonians held real property, up from 1.5 percent in 1850 (but this increase is probably simply a reflection of better reporting rather than an actual gain); when all the property held by that 4.5 percent of Boston's black population in 1860 is distributed evenly, it only amounted to $91 per capita.[84]

By any measure, then, Afro-Americans were not in general amassing substantial amounts of wealth in the form of personal and/or real property. Systematically denied--either by law or custom--equal access to economic opportunities that would have yielded a comfortable income, or even an adequate one, blacks were not in a position to accumulate much in the way of personal and real property. At the same time, the privilege of holding property seems to have been one of the few prerogatives accorded to blacks: in the South, the "only right to escap[e] unscathed was [the free Negro's] ability to hold property";[85] while protecting his life and property but going no further was the stance taken by Lincoln and the Republican party.[86] In Massachusetts, along with the right to receive trials and to sue in the courts, even slaves had had the right to own property.[87]

This allegiance to the sanctity of private property put a premium on competition and acquisition within the wider society, associating property ownership with individual endeavor and volition. Within the black community, however, individualism was for the most part set aside in favor of the collectivity. The expansion of familial and kin obligations to social obligations, the everyday realities of common hardship, and the unanimous opposition to slavery fostered a spirit of mutuality that would seem to conflict with notions of individual gain and the pursuit of material possessions for personal gratification or dynastic aggrandizement. Afro-Americans may well have had mixed attitudes about the accumulation of property.[88] Did blacks in antebellum Boston limit their individual prosperity for the sake of communal advancement? One wonders, for instance, if the inventoried household goods of black decedents of increasing wealth will deviate from the ladder of necessities to amenities to luxuries typical of preceding populations who gradually became beneficiaries of the eighteenth century "consumer revolution."

One aspect of property-holding among blacks that has drawn scholarly remark was their propensity to invest in real--as opposed to personal--property. In Providence, this "marked preference for real over personal property" is documented by the tax lists for 1829 to 1840, which show that never less than 92.5--as much as 96.5--percent of the value of the property held by blacks was comprised of real property.[89] The actual amount or value may often have been quite scant: "in 1850 urban free blacks were roughly one-half as likely as American urbanites in general to own real estate" and "many of the urban black landholdings were . . . of slight value";[90] but, given the barriers blacks had to surmount to acquire sufficient capital for purchasing real estate or land in the days before thirty-year mortgages, these figures indicate an aspiring after and a sacrificing for an objective that seems to transcend predominantly practical concerns.[91] The sense of continuity that infuses black cultural thought, despite the disruptions of slavery and poverty, perhaps was finding tangible expression in terms that could be understood by the wider society. Are there items enumerated in these inventories that bespeak a consciousness of legacy? For example, one wonders if the movable property of a black homeowner will show any greater degree of family heritage than that of a non-homeowner.

The probate records from twenty-three pre-Civil War black Bostonians thus promise to lend further insight into questions about diversity in the community, about the family and women, and about cultural values. Looking at the lists of household goods--and thereby recreating mentally the physical domestic world of Afro-Americans of some 150 years ago[92]--offers a window through which to come to understand a population that has been studied from other viewpoints. Just as tracing Afro-American folk thought contributes to a recognition of blacks as "actors in their own right,"[93] studying probate records leads to an appreciation of long-deceased blacks as individual human beings in their own right. It is for that microcosmic glimpse into the everyday lives of Afro-Americans in antebellum Boston--within a framework of black social history themes and issues--that these particular documents are best suited.

CHAPTER 3

ON PROBATE INVENTORIES

Scholarship that avails itself of the evidence embedded in probate inventories ranges from a passing reference to intensive manipulation, from a localized focus to trans-Atlantic comparison, and/or from a small sample to total coverage. Yet all have in common four decisive factors that structure each study: when--the specific date(s) to which the documents are confined, where--the exact locale(s) from which the documents are gathered, who--the particular population(s) to whom the documents are related, and how many--the precise number(s) into which the documents are clustered. A refreshing degree of scholarly flexibility and initiative appears to have been exercised in determining these key parameters; it seems scholars have elected to explore not only the historical information preserved in inventories but also its effective mining.

From Passing Reference To Total Coverage

Upon occasion, probate records associated with the historic Afro-American population receive short shrift because they simply "confirm that the wealthiest members of the black community spent relatively little on personal luxuries"; they are adjudged "not that revealing since community leaders and property holders are already covered in the narrative sources" while no records exist for total unknowns.[1] Such cursory usage contrasts sharply with examples of energetic usage. Probate records, when intelligently meshed with archaeological findings, have been shown to explicate the life of a totally unknown Afro-American, Black Lucy.[2] Clearly, the limited degree of access to the presumed inarticulate--and, in particular, to problematic population constituents like women, blacks, and Native Americans--demands both delicate and forceful tactics in extracting clues from probate records.

It is striking that the geographic and numerical dimensions in scholarly studies of inventories cover the spectrum of possibilities, from one site to whole towns, counties, regions, or colonies--either treated individually, in the aggregate, or comparatively. A single will, in association with a substantial inventory, of a laborer who possessed seven acres in Skunk Hollow on the New York/ New Jersey state line may be cited; or, conversely, "approximately 4,000 probate inventories from three areas--York County, Virginia, and Anne Arundel and Somerset Counties, Maryland" can be examined.[3] Careful attention may be lavished on attaining an unbiased sample that is defensible,[4] whereas equally thoughtful campaigns have been mounted to gather every extant household list in the designated time/ space frame.[5] It is dramatically apparent from the scholarship that great numbers of inventories can be amassed for appraisal by full sweeps of nearby sites over substantial time periods. Some historians have chosen, however, to control the numbers, for both practical and conceptual reasons, by unbiased sampling.[6] This scholarly buoyancy in the face of an *embarras de richesse* finds further expression in the chronological scope exhibited by research using probate records--at the extremes, encompassing groupings of inventories from one year to approximately three hundred years as the basis for analysis or contrast.

For instance, one study concentrates upon a single year, analyzing and contrasting randomly selected distant sites; Alice Hanson Jones's carefully chosen sample counties of the American colonies in 1774 are given individual, regional, and overall attention.[7] Another study encompasses sixty-three years, accruing material from deliberately chosen nearby sites; Gloria L. Main's appropriately clumps six counties of one American colony from 1656 to 1719 for individual and collective consideration.[8] A third study spans three centuries, playing with the findings from deliberately selected far-distant sites; Carole Shammas holds sixteenth and seventeenth century English shires up to an American colony in 1774 for contrapuntal analysis.[9]

Thus the common decisive factors of when, where, who, and how many are manipulated with ingenuity. Even the strategy of "amassing impressive numbers of inventories by full sweeps of nearby sites over substantial time periods" can be refined in keeping with a scholar's delicacy of tactics. Main, to illustrate, sensibly chooses upon occasion to rely on calculations based on inventories of young fathers, thereby reducing the number of documents she is considering from 3533 to 604.[10] Different objectives reasonably lead to different configurations for study and analysis, confirming that scholarship explicating and exploring probate inventories is in a healthy state of becoming.

Scholarly Caution

At the same time, the literature pertaining to probate inventories--whether advising on their use or mining them as historical repositories--regularly counsels and acknowledges the exercise of scholarly caution. There is considerable thought dedicated to assessing the advantages and disadvantages of inventories as primary sources, as well as great care devoted to assuring their legitimacy as accurate sources.

Inventories As Primary Sources: Advantages

The claim of inventories on the attention of scholars surpasses even that of Mount Everest on mountaineers. Although they are *there* on a scale comparable to that of the Himalayan peak, it is not principally sheer magnitude that establishes their importance. Probate inventories, knowledgeable scholars aver, can provide access to hitherto inaccessible populations, with immediacy and particularity.

These historical records encompass all classes in person-by-person coverage, according to Alice Hanson Jones, with "many cases where possessions are very scanty, others of middling wealth, and still others of the rich."[11] They are distinctly "free of the influence" of prominent individuals, Gloria L. Main similarly affirms, permitting the "sole objective guide" to the lives and values of a cross section of the populace.[12] Both scholars repeatedly celebrate the bounteous depth of detail in these records,[13] in which the decedent's possessions are assiduously tallied and priced. Indeed, the assigned valuations enjoy a strong claim on veracity by virtue of the contemporaneous legal constraint of sworn appraisal, both undistorted by undervaluation for the sake of estate tax evasion as well as confirmed by the sales returns on those occasions when the possessions were auctioned.[14] Inventories therefore deserve respect as democratic, detailed, and dependable sources.

But sheer numerical abundance ought not to be belittled, particularly since probate inventories lend themselves readily to quantification.[15] This plenitude of historic material moreover represents a "systematic recording of economic and social data" that Main finds admirable.[16] Persuasively and eloquently, she catalogues the attractions of inventories, ranging from the practical--"the only guide to the deceased's means of earning his living, his family status, and the style in which he lived"--to the reflective--insight into "the cultural assumptions that guided [the purchase of household items]"--to the imaginative--"the effect is to call up in the mind's eye of the modern reader" the domestic environment.[17] Lois Green Carr and Lorena S. Walsh further elucidate the contributions of probate inventories to the scholar's understanding of a range of issues in economic and social history:

> if the records are sufficiently complete, the historian can aggregate the value of inventoried property in various ways that allow him to estimate per capita wealth. He can then chart over time and place economic growth or decline and the ways

in which it contributed to or eroded the welfare of various social groups. When linked to biographical information about the decedents, inventories also permit studies of the relationships of wealth and the process of its acquisition to systems of social stratification.[18]

As Peter H. Lindert declares: "There they are, those *enticing* probate inventories, awaiting us."[19]

Inventories As Primary Sources: Disadvantages

Yet these historical resources do not provide for historians an unqualified entree into the lives and values of the totality of the populace. Inventoried individuals are distinctive; probate records can be eccentric; sheer magnitude has its drawbacks. Scholarly enthusiasm requires tempering in the face of such serious hindrances.

"The set of persons whose estates yield surviving probate inventories is a biased slice of society," the eager but astute Lindert warns.[20] Since wealth is the most critical factor in being inventoried--and occupation is the most significant determinant of wealth--a disproportionate number of estates of more lucratively employed decedents will be inventoried.[21] Indeed, neither the dying nor the living population finds full coverage in extant records. Main acknowledges the unrepresentativeness of the documents by raising the crucial question, "How typical are these men and their property?" Her reference to coverage's "leveling off to 40 percent [of male decedents] in Massachusetts. . . . during the nineteenth century" certainly lifts her question out of the rhetorical.[22] Jones, speculating on this lack of probate, proposes two probable explanations:

1. No wealth or so little no need to bother (drifters, ne'er-do-wells; the possessionless young, the generous old).

2. Unofficial and undisputed distributions of assets among heirs.[23]

Simply put, not everyone who died had his estate inventoried, for whatever reason. And no matter how numerous, "probate records do not tell us the wealth of non-probates."[24] Since they undisputedly fail to encompass all the *dying*, even 100 percent of the inventories from a designated time and place will fall short in yielding irrefutable access to the *living* population.[25] Over and over again scholars name the two principal sources of bias that set owners of probated estates apart from everyone alive at the time--age and socioeconomic class.[26] That the dead are apt to be older and wealthier than the living is carefully and continually argued by Main:

> Decedents, of course, tend to be older on the average than living adults, and because older men have had longer earning lives than younger men, their accumulated assets tend to be greater, as well . . . . the mean wealth of probated estates tends to be higher than the mean for the living population of free adult property holders subject to probate.[27]

But Main also hastens to warn against precipitously assuming that "all those missing constitute a homogeneous class of downtrodden propertyless proletarians."[28] Moreover, to Jones, the actual wealth of probated decedents hinges on more than the appraisal of their inventoried estate--"'debtor' and 'poor' were not synonymous, nor 'creditor' and 'rich.'" Since assets provide the collateral for the extension of credit "high debt was very apt to go hand in hand with high assets," without indicating "borrowing for consumption needs or survival."[29]

Probate inventories can be demonstrably incomplete in coverage--and inconsistent in valuation--of assets. Despite the impressive detail of many inventories, the decedents' assets and liabilities may not have been well covered. Real estate (except in New England) is not included, while the personal estate and debts are often inadequately spelled out. Lindert suggests that clothing may have been "hidden in nondescript categories such as 'other things unseen' or it was omitted altogether as unsalable" while cash may have been "allocated informally among survivors even before probate took place."[30]

Carr and Walsh carefully consider the "things that inventories do not include, some of them unexpected": items of no market value, like fresh fruit; items overlooked by careless appraisers or concealed by heirs, like clothing; items omitted as a reflection of local custom like the basic bed and pot vouchsafed the impoverished widow or legacies mentioned in wills; items affected by the seasons, like crops; or debts receivable unidentified at the time of appraisal.[31]

Three major types of absence are proposed by Anna L. Hawley. First, there are objects "not really missing" but rather accidentally or deliberately unreported. Accidental non-reporting includes failing to list specific goods because they were overlooked or had no market value or were lumped together under catch-all designations like "a parcel of lumber." Deliberate non-reporting includes not listing items because they constituted the widow's dower or will-specified legacies or, conceivably, criminally-concealed possessions. Second, there are objects "truly lacking," because of the decedent's stage in the life-cycle or because of poverty. The inactive or dependent elderly frequently distributed assets before their death, whereas the poor never acquired certain desirable possessions like feather bedding. Third, there are objects "culturally-perceived as lacking." Contemporary standards may raise anachronistic expectations about household possessions and domestic practices. Decedents would not notice the absence of forks or soap, given historic standards of civility and cleanliness.[32] Main, for her part, tries to mediate between accepting and dismissing inventories as absolute records of household goods. She weighs the negative evidence with sensitivity, questioning the significance of missing items like spoons and beds, conceding that they may have been either absent from the estate or withheld from the inventory. Perhaps the appraisers took pity on the impoverished widow and deliberately overlooked the bedding to guard it against avaricious creditors. Readily available substitutes for spoons--like shells--may have served the household. Certain classes of objects, she contends did not get inventoried because they were homemade or free, perishable, protected by custom from the auction block (clothing worn by children, wives, and servants), formally bestowed upon the widow before her husband's death, or recognized as the widow's reserve.[33]

Jones, too, accompanies her opinion that inventories are likely to be under--rather than over--statements of the deceased's wealth by a non-judgmental supposition of "occasional omissions, oversights, etc., on the part of the appraisers or those who assembled the objects for their inspection."[34] Thus even the possessions of the dead who were subjected to inventorying were not totally catalogued and evaluated, so care must be taken when determinations about the deceased's role as head of household are based on the presence or absence of bedding furniture and kitchen utensils in the inventory.[35] Indeed, the presence--as well as the absence--of certain possessions that purport to indicate literacy cannot necessarily be interpreted with complete confidence. Books and desks may figure in a decedent's probate inventory, but like looms, they are not guarantees of that decedent's command of the skills requisite for proficiency.[36]

Scholars are furthermore wise to proceed with caution on two other accounts. Although both the subsequent auction sale prices verify the valuations assigned to the assets and the lack of federal taxation mitigated against undervaluation, attention must be paid to making values comparable over time.[37] And probate inventories, like all historical records, are not preserved in orderly perfection, nor are those that are preserved replete with all the desirable data.[38] Indeed, the very advantages of inventories can be discerned as disadvantages. Their prized numbers are genuinely "formidable,"[39] whereas their extolled detail are legitimately "alarming."[40] Scholars must concede with Main that "all we know is what a man owned when he died, not how or when or in what order he obtained his goods"; she maintains that the contents of probate inventories "are not readily interpretable."[41] It is consequently imperative to be sensitive to the fact that, in Jones's words, "Records made for purposes quite different from our present interest do not fully answer our questions at some crucial points."[42]

Inventories As Accurate Sources: Sampling

Probate records lend themselves to a multiplicity of scholarly objectives and methods, all dependent upon the strictures of depth and breadth inherent in these historical sources. How they are chosen, grouped, and manipulated directly affects scholarly conclusions based upon this promising but problematic window on the past.

At the risk of oversimplification, two models for sampling from the vast universe of probate records can be discerned in the literature. On the one hand, there is propounded the value of "a small, rigorously selected, statistical sample"--geographically spread but time restricted.[43] On the other, there is the recommendation to take "the full population of probate documents for a single place instead of sampling several similar places more lightly"--geographically restricted but time spread.[44]

Jones, who advocates sampling, insists that if unbiased, its results are generalizable to the universe from which the sample is drawn. With great attention to avoiding measurement error and to proper weighting procedures, she establishes "a reasonably close approximation" of the wealth of decedents in her targeted time and place, which in turn--with further weighting from data outside the probate records--yields trustworthy information about the wealth of the living.[45]

But Lindert, sensitive to the costs of team efforts required by aggregate conclusions, speaks briskly to the typically lone scholar, advising him strongly "to squeeze all the science and beauty he can from exceptionally good local data sources."[46] He mentions as an ideal a geographically limited but time protracted study par excellence in which an unimpeachable death record for one locale over some fifty-five years is compared to extant probate records, yielding the following conclusion:

> In general probate records are a much better source for the analysis of change over time within a small area than for the study of differences between regions and classes.[47]

Main, however, manages to integrate a degree of geographic extent with the passage of time--albeit each in moderation-- to render a credible account of "a particular geographical region . . . in the context of a particular cultural and political system at a particular stage in its evolution."[48] Coverage of the total assemblage of every probate record associated with a major population constituent for the selected time period validates her findings.

But a special population constituent rarely enjoys such extensive and reliable coverage over a predetermined time. Indeed, problematic population constituents--women, blacks, Native Americans--are regularly eliminated from or limited in purportedly inclusive studies.[49] Rather than clarifying unbiased sampling techniques or carrying out elaborate computations, the scholar attending to the presumed inarticulate struggles mightily to accrue, in adequate number, undisputable historical evidence for a defensible time period. Even then, the elite of the non-elite can dominate as shown in Kathryn S. Smith's study of black Washingtonians in the early mid-nineteenth century:

> The 41 inventories in my sample must be an elite group. There were about 6,000 free blacks in the District in 1830. By 1850 there were about 11,000. Those who were visible enough in the city to be identified by occupation in directories before 1835 or wealthy enough to own land before 1845 are by definition a select group numbering only 410 names, or about 4% of the total 1850 free black population.[50]

Inventories As Accurate Sources: Validating And Correcting

Main proclaims authoritatively:

> The historian wishing to use probate records must tailor his use of them according to the kinds of available evidence on the population of potential wealthholders such as vital records, militia lists, tax rolls, land warrants, civil and criminal court

proceedings, town meeting minutes, and other documents which identify inhabitants by name.[51]

She proceeds to use tax valuations as an independent source to construct analogous figures to compare with the wealth distribution evident in probate records.[52] And, although Jones asserts that tax lists are extremely questionable sources for whatever use since she "found a very poor correlation between taxed wealth and probate wealth for identical persons, with differences going erratically in both directions," she subsequently does acknowledge the utility of tax lists along with other parallel and complementary evidence to identify age at death or occupation (particularly information from genealogical research, wills, deeds, and land grants).[53]

The scholarly challenge, however, does not lie so much with the inadequacy of inventories as complete accounts of all the wealth of those inventoried, challenging as that may be.[54] Rather, inventories neither record nor reflect the entire population's assets. They are both age- and class-biased, requiring more-or-less elaborate correction depending upon their degree of skew and the variety of corrective action necessitated by the objectives of the study.[55] Scholars are advised to design the sampling so that it can be tested against another source,[56] yet they are warned to beware of comparing records that have essentially the same biases--like church vital records and probate records.[57]

Nonetheless, cross-checking sources can prove to be immensely revealing for a population that is underrepresented in probate records. Carried to its apogee by Suzanne Lebsock in *The Free Women of Petersburg: Status and Culture in a Southern Town, 1784-1860*, testing for accuracy by comparing outcomes based on different sources unveils what has previously been regarded as hopelessly shadowy. When discussing women's work, Lebsock turns first to the 1860 census, where she discovers that free black women were more likely to be employed than white women, which is congruent with arguments that black women worked out of the necessity of supplementing the low incomes earned by black men and/ or in continuation of their slave experience of labor regardless of marriage and childbearing. But, Lebsock declares, cross-checking with other sources reveals that white women appear to have worked to a far greater degree than recorded in the census. "Alternative sources" give the lie to Petersburg's 1860 census. Only three women in medical occupations? "A search of all the other available records reveals the names of twelve medical women, all of whom were practicing in 1860." Nine women teachers? "Other sources show that there were at least forty women teaching in Petersburg in 1860." Nine women boardinghouse keepers? "The business section of the city directory for the same year listed eighteen female boardinghouse keepers, and in the personal section of the same directory, ninety women were named as having taken in boarders."

> It is not clear whether the census taker was not asking or whether the people were not telling, but the result was serious undercounting . . . . Alternative sources suggest that married women were far more active than the census admits; eighteenth-century patterns of female enterprise survived well into the nineteenth century.

This profuse but diffuse documentation presents a serious challenge to scholarship as well in its resistance to profitable subjection to systematic analysis. Lebsock, torn between being "impressed with the evidence that does exist" and "mourn[ing] what can never be recovered," advocates a tentative tone as appropriate to generalizations.[58] Multiple sources carefully gathered and interpreted thus open up for the scholar's understanding--through large quantities of information often in bits and pieces--previously hidden populations.[59]

Scholars may cast about for approaches that respect the aforementioned caveats pertaining to the accuracy of inventories as sources,[60] but the study of special population constituents like women, blacks, or Native Americans imposes restraints that foreclose both the opportunity for, and necessity of, elaborate correction.[61] The same distortions of age and class may obtain, but they occur amid so small a total pool that every instance merits attention. The matter of scale--meager now rather than grand--thus comes full circle in significance for the study of probate inventories. The literature recommends that the prudent scholar move cautiously, cognizant of the advantages and disadvantages intrinsic to this variety of historical evidence, while exercising the controls of sampling, verifying, and correcting--when requisite--to ensure that these alluring primary sources prove to be securely accurate sources.

Model Methods And Pertinent Findings

While predominantly convergent in principle, scholarly analyses of bodies of probate inventories diverge in practice. Almost unanimously the scholars seek revelation of specific qualitative variations (for instance, frequency of possession of a certain class of items among the specific population groupings) beyond simple quantitative differences (like the calculation of overall wealth). But the scholars proceed in their conceptually-equivalent undertakings quite idiosyncratically.

Review Of Analyses: Quantitative

Two strictly quantitative analyses, in fact, set two different objectives and employ different variables. In the first instance, Carole Shammas investigates some 538 inventories over the relatively short time of seventeen years (1660-77), from three distinct locales (Worcestershire, England; East London; and Tidewater Virginia) to identify the rank order of four determinants of wealth (region, occupational status, education, age). Multiple Classification Analysis, with Total Personal Wealth derived from estate inventories as the dependent variable, makes clear that occupational status was the most significant determinant of wealth, followed by age and education, with region the least critical factor. Subtleties in interpretation, however, can arise even in such straightforward calculations; education, while overall of third importance, increased the mean wealth for every occupational status group, but considerably more for the privileged orders of gentlemen, professionals, and merchants than for farmers and laborers.[62]

In the second instance, shifting wealth patterns revealed through the analysis of inventories as indicators of wealth are also placed in their socio-historical context. Russell R. Menard, P.M.G. Harris, and Lois Green Carr concentrate on seeking wealth distribution at three different points in time over the relatively lengthy span of forty-seven years via 1,735 estate inventories from four adjacent locales (Calvert, Charles, Prince George's, and St. Mary's Counties in Maryland). Essentially the quest concerns identifying changes over time in equality of wealth distribution--shifts in the proportion of decedents whose estates fall into lower, middle, and upper wealth categories during 1632-1642, 1658-1665, and 1683-1687. Their findings reveal the greatest degree of equity was enjoyed by colonists of Maryland's lower Western shore during the middle two decades of the seventeenth century, connected to--but not solely dependent upon--income from tobacco. Moreover, the estate inventories' rich detail is acknowledged to exceed in potential for insight into the past mere exploitation for a "statistical description of the distribution of wealth." Menard, Harris and Carr deliberately disengage from advocating the grouping of inventories into "rigid categories based on total estate value" which would be "artificial, lumping together some dissimilar estates while separating others which show a similar use of assets, source of income, and style of life." These scholars clearly wish to promote attention to the qualitative as well as the quantitative dimension of probate inventories.[63]

Review Of Analyses: Quantitative Plus Qualitative

The most thoroughgoing combination of qualitative and quantitative analyses is accomplished by Alice H. Jones and Gloria L. Main in their respective major studies of the colonies in 1774 and of six Maryland counties from 1656-1719. Their commonality in purpose and resolve nevertheless yields distinctive--even individualistic--analytic strategies. For example, both scholars group the decedents into three wealth classes, but they affix different labels to these groupings: for Jones in *Wealth of a Nation to Be*, "high," "middle," and "low," while for Main in *Tobacco Colony*, "rich," "middling," and "poor." Equally individualistically, Jones classifies wealthholders into three age groupings (twenty-one to twenty-five; twenty-six to forty-four; forty-five and older), whereas Main groups decedents into four life cycle stages (single, married with young children, married with one child of age and other(s) under age, married with adult children).[64]

More substantive, however, is the distinctive categorization of nonfinancial assets. Jones proposes seven different methods to analyze "kinds of physical assets"; Main, on the other hand, employs just two categories of nonfinancial assets. Nonetheless, upon a closer look, Jones's third analytic method--"By purpose (producers' goods; consumers' goods)"--appears to be virtually identical to Main's two categories of nonfinancial assets--"Consumption Goods" and "Capital." With the exceptions of slaves and servants (whom Main includes in Capital and Jones omits form both producers' and consumers' goods) and spinning wheels (whose assignment to Consumption Goods by Main contradicts their designation as "equipment within the house for use in production" by Jones), conceptually there is broad agreement.[65]

Main's relatively simple two-tier system is considerably less complex than Jones's multifaceted treatment of the same species of historical data. Jones's variations of groupings essentially offer a variety of perspectives on the same body of information. Whether simple or complex, therefore, the shared objectives of both qualitative and quantitative analyses unite the two historians. Jones computes aggregate and per capita wealth and its distribution in the thirteen colonies in 1774 in practically every telling configuration, alongside investigations of the particularities of possessions disclosed in the probate inventories. Ultimately she concludes that the standard of living for the typical free American in 1774 was substantial, even for the "poor" colonist.[66]

Although less elaborately, Main also attends to the overall wealth achieved by decedents in the selected counties of Maryland from 1650 to 1720, in association with calculations dependent upon the actual contents of their probate inventories. She concludes that the level of living for both rich and poor settlers remained rudimentary during those seventy years.[67] Thus, Jones and Main elucidate statistical data by analyzing the data's original material expression in inventoried goods.

Review Of Analyses: Qualitative

Four chiefly qualitative studies exhibit a range of scholarly attention to the quantitative domain--from foil for consumption to fleeting calculation to no mention. Regardless of the degree of textual and tabular consideration of overall wealth, however, the scholars' preoccupation is clearly on life styles. Thus the specifics of possessions predominate in the analysis of probate inventories.

Lois Green Carr and Lorena S. Walsh, in "Inventories and the Analysis of Wealth and Consumption Patterns in St. Mary's County, Maryland, 1658-1777," document the interplay between overall wealth (in nine strata) and consumption behavior (in association with the possession of nine items). They measure changes in life style discernible among the white inhabitants of St. Mary's County, Maryland, over 119 years (1658-1777), scoring 2,613 inventories for the presence of "items that stand for varying levels of comfort or luxury" as well as scrutinizing them for the occurrence of "assemblages of goods that various consuming groups possessed." Carr and Walsh draw conclusions that correlate noticeable modifications in the regard for and manipulation of personal possessions with distinctive differentiation over time among social groups at different wealth levels. They disclose that, from the mid-seventeenth to the mid-eighteenth century, the material conditions of the poor became less austere, the middling more comfortable, and the elite quite elegant as each wealth-level acquired consumer goods to its full economic capacity.[68]

Kathryn S. Smith briefly notes overall wealth before concentrating on the components of that wealth in "Household Inventories as Sources for the Study of Nineteenth-Century Non-Elites." Her "several different ways of interpreting the information" recorded in forty-one inventories of black Washingtonians over a forty-five year span (1831-76) leap swiftly from the aforementioned look at the total value of the inventories by occupations to five analyses that focus on the actual contents of the inventories. Smith's conclusions entail evaluations of the quality of life discernible in the inventoried goods associated with different occupational categories. She shows that a conventionally lowly occupation like waiter or hackman could be materially rewarding for Afro-Americans in a service economy like the new federal district.[69]

Lorena Walsh, however, discusses solely the composition of household goods revealed in probate inventories in "Urban Amenities and Rural Sufficiency: Living Standards and Consumer Behavior in the Colonial Chesapeake, 1643-1777." Her search for "ordinary amenities" beyond "commonplace decencies" and on to "touches of elegance" explores four thousand probate inventories from three relatively nearby locales (York County, Virginia; Anne Arundel County, Maryland; and Somerset County, Maryland) over about 135 years (1640s-1777). Walsh's conclusions identify a chronological change and a geographic difference in styles of living, as revealed in the listings of the material goods of three broad strata of folk. She determines that the urban elite acquired the possessions and practiced the rituals of social refinement, the middling regarded comforts as essentials, and the poor sought out hitherto unavailable conveniences, while the rural population maintained more traditional spending patterns.[70]

Carole Shammas's "Domestic Environment in Early Modern England and America" corresponds predominantly in spirit and substance with this latter study. Her review of the "tools of domesticity" tabulates 823 inventories from three distant sites (Oxfordshire, England; Worcestershire, England; and Massachusetts) over three centuries (1550-91, 1669-70, and 1774). Shammas's conclusions distinguish a two-stage change in acquisition of commodities associated with sociability in the home among four personal wealth categories. She indicates that, in the sixteenth century and then more emphatically in the mid-eighteenth century, the house became a more comfortable environment, with poor, average, above average, and affluent families all enjoying to some extent the transformation of the domestic setting through a shift from home to market produced goods.[71]

These four qualitative studies concentrate principally on the itemized goods, without the apologetic acknowledgments commonly expressed in the quantitative studies for neglecting the opposite domain. Interested more in the social meaning of particular possessions than in the economic issue of overall wealth, Carr and Walsh, K. S. Smith, Walsh, and Shammas study probate records primarily to ascertain the status and values of various population groups. The specifics of the distribution of personal property are analyzed for insight into historical life style choices.

Learning From Analyses Of Inventories: About Stratification

A more sustained look at the conclusions drawn in the major, balanced studies by Jones and Main permits instructive learning from both the quantitative and qualitative analyses, i.e., about both stratification and possessions. A quick look first, however, at the findings in two of these scholars' smaller-scale studies focused principally on stratification reveals the characteristic individualism.

Jones in "Wealth Estimates for the New England Colonies about 1770" states that her data indicate a

> wide spread from low to highest wealth . . . . Physical wealth ranged from essentially nothing but the clothes on their backs for the relatively small servant and slave fraction of the population and about $93 for the poorest probated wealthholder . . . a widow [of unknown age] . . . to about $108,000 . . . for the richest probate . . . [a] merchant . . . who died aged 72.

When comparing the wealth of the probate-type living (the sample decedents adjusted to reflect the range of ages of everyone alive at the time) by occupation, Jones finds a clear wealth hierarchy: 40 percent of the physical wealth was held by the upper 10 percent, while the poorest 20 percent held only 1 percent of the wealth.[72]

Main in "Inequality in Early America: The Evidence from Probate Records of Massachusetts and Maryland" says

> The distributions of wealth in colonial New England seems to have remained stable under conditions of rapidly growing population and with little gain in productivity per capita attributable to technological improvements. Expanding markets for their manufactures and shipping services permitted economic growth to raise the standard of living without also enhancing inequality . . . . Close examination of the probate evidence for New England simply will not support the thesis that some irresistible force levered open a widening gap between rich and poor.

This "picture of stability" in the distribution of wealth in New England was not "cracked" until after the (political) Revolution--but before the

Industrial Revolution. Main attributes this change to the "growth of wealth at the top rather than the expansion of the propertyless."[73]

Such seemingly disparate conclusions about stratification in virtually the same locale at virtually the same time, however, is not truly contradictory. Jones discloses the existence of an emphatic inequity in wealth in 1774 in New England; Main discovers continuity in the unequal distribution of wealth in colonial Massachusetts. Economic inequality is documented; in both small studies, probate records reveal pronounced stratification, even if in answer to different scholarly inquiries about wealth patterns.

This slight tilt in the angles of approach figures in the findings of the major studies. Jones in *Wealth of a Nation to Be* states that "wealth was distributed quite unequally among the free wealthholders" and that

> New England was poor with unequal wealth distribution, the South was rich with unequal wealth distribution, and the middle colonies were much closer to poor New England than to the rich South in average amount of wealth, but those assets were much more evenly distributed. . . . the nearest approximation to a size distribution of wealth for the entire population of the colonies in 1774, free and nonfree . . . shows that over half of all the physical wealth (including nonfree human wealth) was held by the top 10 percent. Only 3 percent was held by the entire poorer half of the universe, including all free wealthholders and the nonfree males who might conceptually have been possible wealthholders. This was surely not egalitarianism.[74]

She then carefully investigates whether total wealthholding and its makeup are linked to "interesting socioeconomic characteristics" like age, sex, occupation, and residence. Very systematically, in some thirty-three tables, Jones sets forth the figures related to wealthholders in five socioeconomic groupings and their associated kinds of wealth. For instance, the possession of land (real estate), first, in all thirteen colonies and, then, New England, the middle colonies, and the South is shown in three different configurations:

1. The percentage of wealthholders who had any land.
2. The average monetary value of the land.
3. The percentage of total physical wealth the land represented.

On Probate Inventories 51

In each table, Jones tabulates the land of *all* wealthholders and then of the five socioeconomic groupings.[75] Her findings about the significance of age, gender, locale, and occupation are clear:

> a pattern of rising wealth, starting from a low point under age 25, up to a peak around age 60 [with] some dropping off in average wealth in later years to successively lower levels.
>
> Men probate-type wealthholders were much more strongly represented than women in the two upper-wealth groups, and they had higher average wealth in each region. The women fell most heavily in the low-wealth interval in all regions, most strikingly in New England.
>
> In the most urban region, New England, there was no relative predominance of urban cases over the rural in the high- or middle-wealth groupings; indeed most urban were in the low-wealth group. . . . New England's urban wealth inequality was only slightly greater than its rural inequality.
>
> The strikingly richest occupation classes were "esquires, gentlemen, and officials" in all regions and merchants in the two northern regions. . . . At the other extreme were most mariners (excluding captains) and laborers. . . . In between, in the northern regions, were the professionals, farmers, "shopkeepers and artisans," who were widespread more nearly equally among the three wealth intervals.[76]

Jones thus refines her pronouncement of economic inequality on the eve of the Revolution with meticulous attention to the particulars of stratification. She further proposes an overview of wealth distribution, looking both backward and forward from the pivotal point in time of the eve of the Revolution. She hypothesizes:

1. Wealth inequality rose, but not dramatically, up to 1774. New England and the South had high levels of inequality, with the Middle Colonies more moderate.

2. Wealth inequality increased some to 1860-70, possibly continuing and peaking around 1890 or 1929 or 1940, with a mild downdrift to the 1950s, with little change since.

In summary, the distribution of wealth in the thirteen colonies on the eve of the Revolution was "on a par" with today's inequalities, while a higher degree of inequality obtained in 1860 and 1870.[77]

Main in *Tobacco Colony* clarifies her determination of the continually rising value of all estates over the seventy years of study by documenting the asymmetry of this overall increase. Sorting estates into three separate strata of poor, middling, and rich, she finds

> The richest 10 percent registered increases on all fronts the entire span of time. The bottom 90 percent of estates was perhaps a little better off, in terms of material goods, at the close of the period than they had been earlier, but the rich were far richer, no matter [by] which measure.

When Main seeks an explanation for this mounting inequity she turns to the "provenance" of a "small but enterprising class of men." Their ascendancy can be linked to early arrival in Maryland with sufficient funds or good connections; even the initial status of freeman conferred an advantage for accruing wealth for passing on to descendants, who then compounded the imbalance in the distribution of wealth during the following generations. Main documents a connection between this constancy of stratification and the acquisition of specific assets--land and slaves. In the case of the latter, she delineates three strata of white planters after 1700:

> a large class at the bottom who owned neither servants nor slaves, a narrowing middle class who owned a few bound laborers of either type, and a small but growing class at the top who owned six to twenty servants or slaves.[78]

In an examination of "the *course* of inequality over time" (her emphasis), Main tries to determine if the structure of wealth-holding has been historically consistent--that is, consistently unequal. In "Inequality in Early America: The Evidence form Probate Records of Massachusetts and Maryland," she develops the following geography and chronology of the distribution of wealth:

- Early South (seventeenth century)
    - Unequal wealth distribution
    - Small class of well-to-do and large class of poor
- Preindustrial Northeast (from colonial times to the Civil War)

- Varied wealth distribution
- Rural communities relatively egalitarian while cities inequitable
- Maryland in the eighteenth century
  - Increased inequality in wealth distribution
  - Handful of very rich planters (through trade and money-lending)
- Massachusetts by 1830
  - Unequal wealth distribution
  - Considerable inequality in agricultural areas (through immigration and industrial development) while even greater inequity in cities (through the growth of the very rich, whose taking advantage of opportunity and credit contrasted with the concentration of the mobile poor)

In both locales, although at different times, Main concludes that the sizable and sudden bound upward in inequality arose from the increase of wealth at the top rather than the expansion of the propertyless, thereby excusing the Industrial Revolution and the great growth of the cities as the culprits in "what now appears an irreversible leap forward in the degree of . . . concentration" in the distribution of wealth.[79]

Both Jones and Main, then, turn to the comparison of particular assets--land or slaves--to help clarify large-scale economic stratification. The two scholars agree that, aside from some pockets of time and place, the distribution of wealth has been typically unequal in America. For the most part, a small number of decedents usually have controlled a large percentage of the total assets of any place at any time.

Learning From Analyses Of Inventories: About Possessions

Jones in *Wealth of a Nation to Be* speaks of "peering, as it were, into . . . households . . . by way of the probate inventories." The decedents' belongings tell about "modes of production, implying the character of economic development," but they also reveal "consumption goods, implying life styles made possible by the economic development." Land, when owned (and real estate--land and buildings--was owned by three-quarters of the wealthholders in Jones's sample), represented "a major and highly significant asset." The most universal possessions, however, fall into her categories of consumers' and producers' goods:

Virtually everyone had some consumers' goods, usually at least some pots and pans and a few articles of clothing or bedding. Likewise virtually everyone . . . had some form of producers' goods--an axe or tool, equipment items such as wool cards or harness, a bushel or quart container, if not crops and livestock.

The extent and kind of consumers' and producers' goods can be associated with three wealth levels, each level constituting about one-third of all free wealthholders. The low stratum--unlikely to own land or slaves and frequently without livestock--possessed rudimentary tools and equipment, along with a few sturdy garments. The middle stratum occasionally owned real estate, usually possessed basic farm and household producers' implements along with some livestock, as well as a modest assortment of functional consumers' durable goods. The high stratum owned land--and, in the South, slaves--and possessed extensive producers' goods and livestock along with some impressive items of consumers' durable goods.

Telling evidence in probate inventories about the diversity of household appointments and differences in apparel contributes to an understanding of the disparity in daily lives in 1774. Looking at bedding (almost always present, though ranging from straw pallets to fine bedsteads with feather mattresses) or tableware (from earthenware to silver) or apparel (from the decedent's immediate clothing to fancy specialized garments), Jones develops a rank-ordering of the colonists in "degree of affluence of consumer living." In the eleven subgroups, (1)slaves and (2)indentured servants are at the bottom, followed by (3)low-wealth widows and (4)laborers and mariners. Next, (5)middle- to low-wealth artisans and shopkeepers and (6)farmers rank just below (7)middle- to high-wealth lawyers, doctors, and ministers, who are surpassed by both (8)high-wealth widows and (9)Middle-Colony and New England farmers and artisans. Finally, (10)major city merchants, esquires, and captains come right below the (11)top-ranked Southern wealthy planters and farmers. Leaving aside the slaves and indentured servants about whose life style the probate records provide only indirect evidence, Jones concludes that "the level of living attained on the eve of the American Revolution by typical free colonists, even the 'poor' ones, was substantial."[80]

Main in *Tobacco Colony* concludes from "an examination of the unspoken system of priorities" among the three strata of planters (inferred from "the selection of household goods found at successively higher wealth levels") that "rich and poor placed investment ahead of consumption and lived at a level that proved spare, crude, and unselfconscious." Over the span of seventy years, the day-to-day living and material conditions of ordinary folk barely altered. Moreover, "in a society still rude and only recently emerged from raw wilderness, many of Maryland's economic leaders had not yet acquired the wealth, the style, or the distinctive habiliments of a class apart." Yet the majority of slaves lived below the norm, even if a rough-and-rude norm, as borne out by the lack of adequate bedding, the sine qua non of human possessions in early eighteenth-century Maryland. (Clothing for slaves, servants, and poor planters was across the board insufficient.)

As for housing, three types can be surmised from 111 room-by-room inventories (from all six counties under study, 1656-1719); each associated with approximately one-third of planters' families. The poor had one or two rooms; middling households had three rooms, usually two on the ground floor with a loft above, and an auxiliary structure; the rich had five or six rooms with additional buildings. Within these domestic spaces, the room-by-room inventories reveal a "helter-skelter quality of objects and functions"; the full range of inventories discloses that there were pronounced consistencies among the life styles of all three strata. An analysis of the consumption goods of young fathers at every level of wealth over the entire time, however, reveals some degree of choice-making, reflecting differing perceptions of the need for comfort, convenience, or civility. A multitude of chairs in an estate predicts a decedent of the very richest class, while the quality of bedding--rather than the number of beds--took priority for all classes. Overall, there was a gradual ascent of increasing abundance rather than sharp distinctions among the strata.[81] Main, like Jones, therefore utilizes the ownership of specific possessions or constellations of various goods to decipher consumption patterns.

From Artifactual Pre-literacy To The Consumer Revolution

But what of the nature of the possessions? Jones in "Wealth Estimates for the New England Colonies about 1770" finds "that the wealth of 1774 was, in general outlines, surprisingly like that for the United States in 1966." Producer and consumer durables together, it seems, constituted around 11 to 12 percent of physical wealth for both New England colonists in 1774 and United States citizens in 1966. More specifically, colonial holdings in consumer durables like "an occasional riding chaise or carriage, often books, especially a 'large Bible,' occasionally a painting" when joined with clothing and furniture and cookware and dining utensils added up to a similar percentage of wealth represented by the same category of goods in 1966, even counting the value of possessions rather inaccessible to people in 1774 like automobiles, refrigerators, and televisions. Thus, "the great change over the years in the nature of individual items which make up the several major wealth categories" must not be obscured by "the similarity in general profile of wealth in 1774 and in 1966."[82]

Main, however, in *Tobacco Colony* maintains that "from 1650-1720 Marylanders led the plain life from choice and not of necessity" in pursuit of "a life style that appears to have valued a strong back, a good bed, and a full stomach more than cleanliness or 'niceness.'" These preferences, regardless of wealth level, reflected persisting and consistent cultural values that placed priority on building capital rather than on "comfort, convenience, and civility." For instance, almost everybody appears to have devoted similar percentages of overall wealth to clothing. The value of the apparel of the rich may have been two times greater than that of the middling class and four times greater than that of the poor, but expenditures on clothing for everyone amounted to a similarly small consumption asset overall.

Nonetheless, Main does argue for a degree of correspondence between different wealth levels and particular consumption patterns. In order to discern choices she focuses on young fathers at ten levels of wealth over the entire time of seventy years (1650-1720), comparing holdings in beds, iron cooking utensils, pewter, arms, brass, chairs, hand mills, books, silver, warming pans, pictures and curtains, chamber pots, and personal ornaments. "A strong positive correlation between [increasing] personal wealth and [increasing] diversity in consumption goods" emerges. Also, clear preferences among all wealthholders for beds, iron cooking utensils, and pewter is contrasted with the class-related priority placed upon possessing matched chairs.[83]

Walsh concurs with Main's findings and then carries the analysis forward in time in "Urban Amenities and Rural Sufficiency: Living Standards and Consumer Behavior in the Colonial Chesapeake, 1643-1777." In the first phase (1643-c.1715), commonality rather than differentiation in domestic props prevailed among all economic levels. The ordinary householder possessed the basics of "a good bed, a few cooking pots, something to eat food off of, a chest or two for storing goods, and a gun for hunting"; the middling added "chairs, tables, bedsteads, sheets, chamber pots, and interior lighting"; the elite amplified these "basic needs with an overlay of modest amenities," choosing individual chairs, a dining table, candles, pewter, beds with linens, varied cooking equipment, even pictures or mirrors.

It was in the second phase (c.1715-1777), Walsh explicates, that all three levels entered into expanded consumption, even though to different degrees in chronological sequence. By 1715, the elite acquired fine possessions; by the 1730s, the middling, comfortable furnishings with touches of elegance; by the 1750s, the poor, ordinary amenities previously foregone. At the same time, town dwellers manifested an appreciably greater level of conspicuous consumption than their rural counterparts; moveover, country dwellers managed to improve their domestic situation without increasing the proportion of wealth expended on household goods related to sleeping, cooking, dining, seating, storage, etc. Specifically, the rural improved traditionally established prerequisites--first, "the good feather bed" and, second, cooking and eating implements--becoming more comfortable without vastly shifting their spending patterns towards consumerism. Yet all wealth levels of white Chesapeake colonists "dramatically changed their styles of living," Walsh concludes, participating to varied degrees in the "increasingly sophisticated material culture" unfurling in the first half of the eighteenth century.[84]

Thus, a significant and dramatic shift in the nature of possessions evident in probate inventories gains the spotlight. Unlike the constancy over time in the inequity in the distribution of wealth, the use of wealth changed in the early eighteenth century for all wealthholders. Main in *Tobacco Colony* describes uniformity in life styles across the economic spectrum from 1650 to 1720, with consistently little attention to consumer goods; Jones in "Wealth Estimates for the New England Colonies about 1770" documents that by 1774 the colonists possessed a percentage of consumer durables remarkably congruent with that of Americans in the 1960s. Happily, Walsh straddles these two time bands in "Urban Amenities and Rural Sufficiency: Living Standards and Consumer Behavior in the Colonial Chesapeake, 1643-1777"; she emphatically points out the momentous transformation in the first half of the eighteenth century from what has been called a "state of artifactual pre-literacy" to what is known as "the consumer revolution."[85]

Possessions As Social Stratifiers

The definitive characteristics of this paramount transformation from relative homogeneity to dramatic differentiation in material life during the first half of the eighteenth century are almost contradictory. Although nearly all economic strata participated in improved life styles, the artifactual plenitude was enjoyed disproportionately by the rich.

While the consumer revolution eased everyday life across the board, it also led to personal possessions' serving as barriers between wealth groups.

Carr and Walsh summarize this signal shift in daily lives and its implications:

> By the 1750s there had occurred rapid and unprecedented increases in the production and purchase of all kinds of consumer goods. For the first time, groups well below the luxury-consuming elite were participating in this process.
>
> Furthermore, the appearance among a variety of people of new possessions and new ways of using them--for increased comfort, for display, for leisure, and for molding and supporting the on-going life of the family--suggest the emergence of a greater diversity of life styles than was before possible. Personal possessions were becoming both a reflection of and a spur to changing relationships between social groups, as small consumers as well as large turned to artifacts as a means for both improving their everyday lives and differentiating an increasingly complex social order.[86]

Before this change, according to Carr and Walsh, the relatively wealthy in St. Mary's County may have lived better than, but not really very different from, their poorer neighbors. After the change, the "standard of consumption . . . rose as fast at the bottom as at the top, even if the distance between rich and poor remained vast." More colonists enjoyed comforts and conveniences once restricted to the wealthy. "Life at the bottom had become less austere, life in middling families more comfortable, and the economic elite were adopting completely new ways of using personal possessions."[87]

Again, inventories from Maryland and Virginia show that homes of the wealthy--particularly town dwellers--set the pace for the increasing specialization of furnishings and accouterments used for working, relaxing and entertaining. The participation of many women in such "a sophisticated materialistic culture," Cary Carson and Walsh argue in "The Material Life of the Early American Housewife," constituted a widespread social phenomenon in which "the *lingua franca* of artifacts" operated.[88] In short, the consumer revolution permeated society.

This radical departure in patterns of behavior has been interpreted both as the culmination of a long evolution in the course of social and

On Probate Inventories 59

economic history as well as the overcoming of a temporary back-to-the-basics brought about by colonization. Carson speculates

> that it originated in bedrock alterations in English and European society beginning as far back as the fifteenth century perhaps. Certainly it could not have happened unless self-sufficient, food-producing peasants had become market-oriented, capitalistic farmers. It could not have happened until the large medieval family had become the so-called modern European family with fewer children left at home during the parents' peak earning years. It could not have happened unless reformation and secularism had spawned a pluralistic world in which individuals found a separate existence from church, state, and class.[89]

Yet, this mighty and ubiquitous historical trend--modernization--met with a significant if short-lived set back in a pioneer milieu like seventeenth and early eighteenth century St. Mary's County. Carr and Walsh acknowledge the difficulty of determining the causative role of local circumstances vis-à-vis pan-Atlantic material conditions and cultural attitudes. They are confident, however, that

> The colonists' standards of sufficiency, comfort, and of luxury were not simply more modest versions of the dictates of the mid-eighteenth century with which we are so much more familiar. They were different standards altogether. These attitudes and standards persisted for a long time and they were shared by most of the county's residents. What we find is simply a brief reversion to primitive and spartan conditions in a frontier situation; very few changes occurred in the material culture of St. Mary's County, except among the very rich, until well into the eighteenth century.[90]

But regardless of its pedigree, the prevailing patterns of consumption *before* the consumer revolution were uniformly rudimentary (often barely subsistence level), except for a "widespread weakness for silver," evidently prized as an aesthetic and pecuniary asset.[91] Immigrants often had to acquire the essentials, which--when inherited by the native-born--provided the basic necessities above which comforts could be accrued. With beds and pots already in hand, the acquisition of linens and ceramics became more feasible for the poor; with the inheritance of amenities, the rich were free to procure luxuries. The marked changes in consumption habits *after* the consumer revolution bring into being a recognizable world in the "modern" use and distribution of assets; thus, some 250 years ago, "greater diversity in life styles was becoming possible for whites at all wealth levels."[92]

Dimensions Of Race

An emphasis could be added to "whites" in the preceding summarizing statement that declares the advent of full-participation of all wealth levels in the consumer revolution. Although scholars working with inventories are scrupulous in indicating the particular perimeters of their data, the specifics can be overshadowed by the generalities in the overall conclusion. Canvassing the literature discloses the full extent of inclusion of the black population in the data and therefore in the conclusions; the challenge then arises of looking at inventories of black decedents in antebellum Boston both in relation to the representative methods and findings of the studies primarily concerned with white decedents in other times and places as well as in relation to the specialized issues and information inherent in examinations of non-mainstream populations.

Analyzed Decedents

Who precisely figures in the "who" in major scholarly endeavors using inventories? "All" often encompasses a defensible spectrum of decedents (especially when adjusted to reflect the range of age and class in the living population) without perforce including everybody.

Carr and Walsh state clearly that the 2,613 inventories extant for St. Mary's County from 1658 to 1777 "record all movable property of the dead men and women whose estates were administered through the probate court." They continue

> Nor were only rich men inventoried. Newly freed servants who owned only the clothes on their backs and their as-yet-unpaid freedom dues appear, and men too poor to form a household are a sizable inventoried group. There is ample opportunity to study the life styles of a variety of people.[93]

But they also make clear that their finding of burgeoning consumerism refers to the white inhabitants. While some blacks may figure among the 2,613 "men and women whose estates were administered through the probate court," manifestly the overwhelming preponderance of blacks were precluded from participation in the consumer revolution underway

On Probate Inventories

in 1750 by virtue of being themselves regarded as property. By 1755 one-third of the population was slave; a substantial proportion of the population was therefore excluded from the reckoning of generally improving material conditions.[94]

Jones stipulates that her "small, rigorously selected, statistical sample" relies upon randomly drawing "21 counties (or groups of counties in the South and in New York)" from a universe of "all the counties in existence in 1774 in all thirteen colonies." But the chances to be drawn were proportionate to the numbers of white "wealthholders" in each county. Whereas indentured whites were counted, free black males and 10 percent of free black females were not. Nonetheless, Jones notes the black presence in pre-Revolutionary America; of 435,000 possible legal holders of wealth among the 2.35 million people of the thirteen colonies (excluding Indians) figured almost four thousand free blacks. Of this 1 percent of the free wealthholders, the luck of the draw brought forth *one* inventory of a black decedent.[95] Therefore, of the 919 cases upon which the study is based, only 0.1 percent reflects the wealthholding experience of free blacks.

Main's discussion of correcting biases in colonial American probate records rests upon her examination of both "a complete set of inventories found in the microfilmed probate records, 1650 to 1719, of Suffolk and Hampshire Counties, Massachusetts" (unspecified number) and the probated decedents of "six counties in Maryland, 1670 to 1719" (3,467 inventories). Throughout this highly technical study, the population under consideration is restricted to adult free males, without any expressed attention to the race of the decedents.[96] In her volume devoted to life in early Maryland, Main focuses on the inventories of "all adult male decedents" encountered "in a complete collection of all records identified directly or indirectly as originating from six tidewater counties of colonial Maryland during the years 1656 through 1719," some 3533 inventories. While she manages astutely and sensitively to make palpable the living conditions of slaves through the inventories of slaveowners, she nowhere specifically addresses the material content of the lives of free blacks vis-à-vis other adult male decedents.[97]

Similarly, when investigating the distribution of wealth in four contiguous counties on the lower Western Shore of Maryland, Menard, Harris, and Carr work with the 1,735 inventories from 1658 to 1705 without any stated attention to the race of the property holders.[98] Identifying relationships between black and white wealthholding does not arise in this examination of changing patterns of wealth distribution among men and women in four wealth categories over almost fifty years.

Shammas, too, confines her comparative analyses to white decedents. In one study, 538 inventories "from three contrasting areas within the English realm--Worcestershire, East London, and Virginia" all probated between 1660 and 1677 speak to the material well-being of adult white men as well as adult white spinsters and widows in the mother country along with free adult white men in her overseas possession.[99] In another study, Shammas's investigation of the flowering of domesticity casts a spotlight on evidence from Oxfordshire, England, from 1550 to 1591 (253 inventories); from central and southern "Worcestershire, England, from 1669 to 1670 (272 inventories); and from Massachusetts in 1774 (294 inventories).[100] Since even the last group of inventories were those of white decedents, again the black experience remains unmeasured in the tracing of the evolution of the house into a home for the general population.

When Shammas looks at the labor association of black and white women in colonial America, she first draws upon the inventories of free adult white males and any unmarried free adult white females in the Chesapeake in fifty year intervals from 1660 to 1774. More specifically, ownership of female slaves and indentured servants is calculated for five counties in Virginia, 1660-76 (134 inventories); and for four counties in Virginia, 1724-28 (300 inventories).[101] Again, blacks as wealthholders are peripheral to the discussion. Yet, as in Main's examination of life in early Maryland, some understanding of the material content of the lives of both black and white women in the colonial Chesapeake is gleaned by Shammas from an adroit reading of the presence of housewifery stock in five counties in Virginia, 1660-76 (134 inventories); in central and southern parishes of Worcestershire, England, 1669-70 (275 inventories); and in ten counties in Virginia and Maryland in 1774 (141 inventories).[102]

But the more typical concentration on adult males occurs in D.K. Smith's exploration of inclusiveness and bias in colonial probate records. His testing of probate records for Hingham, Massachusetts, from 1718 to 1786, against a complete death register and real property lists for the same time and locale "yields a reliable estimate of the extent of underregistration," permitting identification of "the characteristics of those recorded in and those omitted from the probate records," i.e., the wealth bias in the probate records. Smith extols the rare inclusiveness of the death register--"listing, albeit on a separate page, the deaths of blacks and Indians in Hingham"--but provides no clear indication how these segregated populations fare in his conclusion about the primacy of wealth bias among probated male decedents.[103]

Similarly, when comparing rural and urban consumer behavior in York County, Virginia, and Anne Arundel and Somerset Counties, Maryland, from the 1640s through 1777, Walsh does not make clear if and how the approximately four thousand probate inventories encompass the black as well as the white population.[104] Her nuanced interpretation of inventories discloses the material elaboration of living standards over about 135 years for country vis-à-vis town dwellers in the tidewater Chesapeake, without mentioning the race of the inventoried colonists.

Black Lifestyles Through Inventories

The seemingly comprehensive studies of inventories are manifestly checkered in their stated and unstated attention to the experience of blacks. Nonetheless, some scholars do provide valuable information about--and provocative interpretations of--Afro-American lifestyles. Whether factually reconstructing slaves' living conditions or speculatively assessing cultural differences in standards of comfort, the scholarship does relay some sense of the material content of black lives that is accessible through examining inventories. A loosely chronological review of the literature will move from studies in which blacks appear as supporting actors to those which accord Afro-Americans center stage.

The evidence suggests that life for blacks was artifactually spare. "Only one bed, three pots, and two frying pans constituted virtually the entire housekeeping equipment" at work sites where slaves may have camped for a season, Main states in *Tobacco Colony*. She takes care to point out, however, that as harsh as living conditions were for slaves, for the most part servants, freedmen, and poor planters enjoyed little better. Food and clothing she judges to have been also uniformly humble. Given the overall rudeness of living conditions from 1656 to 1719, Main detects but one "troubling" inequity in black access to material goods--"the absence of sufficient bedding" to ward off coastal Maryland's winter months of raw cold.[105]

Shammas, too, highlights a materially rudimentary life-style for slaves in field work, "provided little more than clothing, bedding and a cooking pot" by planters in both the Tidewater and Piedmont areas of Virginia in the second third of the eighteenth century. Since production needs dominated white male decision-making in work assignments, household service--whether domestic chores like "childcare, cooking, laundering, and maintaining the house" or housewifery chores like "dairying, tending poultry and hogs, vegetable gardening, candle and soapmaking, spinning, and sewing"--was usually severely limited and confined to young or old female slaves unfit for field work.

Shammas deliberately counters the popular notion of slaves conveniently on hand to wait upon white owners; "it appears the average planter's wife had at most two female servants to do domestic and housewifery tasks for the 'family' of Whites and Blacks, and these slaves would probably be very young." Her comparison of housewifery utensils (butter and cheese making equipment, spinning wheels, brewing and cider equipment, as well as cows, hogs, and poultry) with ownership of female slaves in the 1774 Virginia and Maryland inventories reveals a positive relationship between owning a greater number of female slaves and possessing a spinning wheel and cheese and butter equipment.[106] Again, inventories of whites hint at the quality of material life experienced by blacks, in the meager everyday goods allocated to them and the elementary household technology operated by them.

What a contrast, then, with the life style discernible in the one inventory of a black decedent drawn into Jones's 1774 sample! "'Cyrus, a free Negro' in St. Andrews Parish in the Charleston District of South Carolina" not only owned five horses, he also mirrored "prevailing custom" among other wealthy Charlestonians in owning six slaves.[107] This seemingly literal as well as figurative "buying into" the values of the dominant culture contrasts emphatically with other evidence in the material record of patterns that are suggestive of distinctive Afro-American behavior. Preferences of late eighteenth and nineteenth century blacks in house type and tableware that can be affiliated with African cultural traits have been documented by archaeologists. At the same time, economic conditions rather than ethnicity may have been the operative factor; for instance, both poor blacks and poor whites probably owned mostly serving bowls because stews eaten from the communal dish were fast and simple.[108]

A parallel ambivalence in the material record is amply illustrated by Kathryn S. Smith's study of forty-one household inventories of blacks in the District of Columbia over forty-five years, 1831-76. As clues to the relative status of occupations, inventoried items overturn expectations associated with conventional occupational stratification hierarchies. While admitting the impressionistic and/ or mathematical suspect nature of her analyses, Smith ventures a conclusion that points to the intricate interplay of economic and ethnic factors in the material record of antebellum free blacks:

On Probate Inventories 65

> The unskilled and semi-skilled . . . do better in both wealth [total value of movable property] and status [clerical/ sales, petty proprietors, skilled, semi-skilled, and unskilled] than might be expected. . . . in Washington, DC, the unique circumstances of the government and service economy gave persons in occupations such as laboring, driving, and waiting more access to money and a comfortable life than in other places.[109]

In accord with mainstream indicators, Afro-Americans in the nation's capital in the second third of the nineteenth century appear to have abandoned artifactual pre-literacy, belatedly joining the consumer revolution. Their previous limited access to material assets may have originally been common to all in "a brief reversion to primitive and spartan conditions in a frontier situation"[110] to which almost everyone immigrated, willingly or unwillingly, "without any capital except the ability to survive and work."[111] Like free whites who persisted in living in accord with "standards of sufficiency, of comfort, and of luxury" that were linked to the values of 'the world we have lost' (i.e., before the advent of the consumer revolution in the mid-eighteenth century),[112] blacks had a cultural heritage of material simplicity.

> West Africans did not use tables, chairs, bedsteads, and so forth, nor did they use much metalware, so it is inappropriate to condemn the furnishings supplied to the slaves [by eighteenth century Maryland planters] as "inadequate."[113]

Nonetheless, even with this conceivably common bond in initial circumstances and parallel acceptance of domestic austerity, blacks and whites did not share equal access to acquiring property before, during, or after the consumer revolution. Yet whether it was enterprisingly self-sufficient slaves who had their own modest economy yielding "small amounts of money to spend upon consumer goods"[114] or sagaciously ambitious free blacks who identified tolerated careers yielding "a better time economically . . . than their concentration in jobs considered lowly would suggest,"[115] Afro-Americans have found niches in the occupational structure as well as accrued possessions that reflect the interaction of economic and ethnic forces.

The search for the black experience discernible through studies of probate inventories thus yields intriguing information. What becomes manifestly clear is that Afro-Americans' probate inventories remain enticingly underexplored. The probate records of black Bostonians in the 1840s now become the vehicle for delving into the issues of the efficacy of this source for understanding the material condition and cultural values of a hitherto presumed inarticulate population.

Part II

Analysis of the Probate Inventories

CHAPTER 4
A MULTI-ANGLED INQUIRY

To enter the everyday material world of antebellum black Bostonians, the archives in the Suffolk County Courthouse were searched to locate probate records for known members of the Afro-American community in Boston before the Civil War. Three sources guided the identification of documents for black decedents: Boston directories of the period, Carter Woodson's exegesis of the 1830 federal census, and a list of prominent black Bostonians (rosters 1 and 2). This controlled rather than random method yielded probate information about 113 decedents spanning from 1806 to 1895. Given the sources, it is not surprising that sixty-four of the decedents are clustered between 1830 and 1860, whereas only fifteen decedents preceded and thirty-four followed these three decades.

The pool of documents thus assembled makes no pretense about its inherent limitations. It is representative neither of all blacks who died nor of the entire living black population in antebellum Boston; its three sources are each clearly biased toward the more mature, stable, and affluent members of the Afro-American community. Therefore, attempting to extrapolate conclusions about all black Bostonians living or dead in the nineteenth century from these 113 probate records immediately registers as problematic; any argument about the material conditions of Boston's antebellum black community that is dependent upon documents that make no claim to being representative must be couched cautiously.

Yet this innate shortcoming can be turned to advantage--in effect, offering liberation from the numbers game that often dominates examinations of inventories. The "tainted" character of the method that was employed to create the pool of probate records encourages focusing on a chosen body of documents within that pool rather than indiscriminately studying all 113 decedents over the century. Moreover, a microcosmic approach ensures the sharpened focus appropriate for interpreting records that can engender mental recreations of the domestic environment of black Americans over a century ago.

For a variety of reasons, the probate records of the decedents from the 1840s were selected to receive the most extensive analysis (roster 3). The decade opened with the black community well-established in Boston, then continued with the socioeconomic repercussions of the Irish influx, and closed on the ominous note of the Compromise of 1850's strengthened fugitive slave law. As complete as possible an assemblage of documents for the selected twenty-three decedents there-

1850's strengthened fugitive slave law. As complete as possible an assemblage of documents for the selected twenty-three decedents therefore forms the core of the interpretation of probate records from Boston's black community before the Civil War.

A Case Study

Amy Jackson, widow, died in Boston on March 16, 1840. On October 19, a three-man committee--Thomas R. Sewall, Gustavius Andrews, and Charles B. Class--submitted its appraisal of her estate to Willard Phillips, Judge of the Court of Probate for the County of Suffolk "pursuant to the warrant to [them] directed from [his] Honor" (transcription 2.12). The committee valued Amy Jackson's estate at $2628.45--$2605 in real estate and $23.45 in personal estate. Another probate document--a bond and oath on the sale of real estate dated March 29, 1841--indicates that the real estate consisted of two pieces of property: "a lot of land with two small houses or tenements on it at the corner of Southac and Bultolph Streets . . . and another lot of land in May Street . . . with a dwelling house upon it" (transcription 2.17). The particulars "hereto annexed" on the October 1840 appraisement reveal that Amy Jackson's personal estate contained an array of household goods, ranging from "1 Lot wood & bark" to "3 Quilts & 1 Comforter" to "3 Thin Silver Spoons" (transcription 2.12).

These items can be relatively easily divided into three categories--"necessities," "amenities," and "luxuries."[1] Necessities include the bare essentials for everyday life--clothing and cleaning supplies, cooking and heating utensils, and minimal furniture (list 5.1). Amenities, while utilitarian, provide a degree of comfort--primarily bedding and linens, with the useful addition of a mirror and a storage unit (list 5.2). Luxuries are represented by silverware and books (list 5.3). Almost half of Amy Jackson's personal estate ($11.20 or 48 percent) was comprised of necessities; nearly the same amount ($11 or 47 percent) was made up of amenities; and only a small portion ($1.25 or 5 percent) consisted of luxuries.

Yet sparse as her personal estate may seem (and certainly of minor value in relation to her real estate holdings), it is actually possible to envision Amy Jackson living rather comfortably: clean and ironed clothes, well-made up bed, cooked meals served simply amid basic furnishings in a warm room. (There is a hint in the tubs and flat iron of her taking in wash.) Her luxuries--the niceties of three silver spoons and a Bible and three unnamed old books--seem appropriate for a widow who not only died testate, but also left two wills.

A Multi-Angled Query

In the first will, dated March 24, 1837, Amy Jackson left her estate to Mary Clark, the adopted daughter of her late husband, Thomas Jackson, and the wife of Thomas Clark, mariner, of Portland, Maine (transcription 2.1). But in the second will, signed on October 9, 1839, Amy Jackson named Eunice Senex, also called Venus Senex, nurse, the sole heir as well as executrix of her estate (transcription 2.6). Aside from the human interest aspect of disinheriting a relative (even if adopted) in favor of non-relative (even if in gratitude for nursing services), Amy Jackson's two wills present a puzzle in relation to her personal possessions. Both are signed "X, her mark." Thus, despite the books in her inventory, it is not safe to assume that Amy Jackson was literate. The two conventional indices--signature and books--contradict each other in her probate records. It may be that she once was able to sign her name or even write, but due to old age or failing health, was incapacitated. (Dr. Parker was paid $54.85 in August 1841 when the estate was finally settled.) Or, she may never have known how to sign her name and write but she may have known how to read the books she owned. Or she may not have ever been able to sign her name, write, or read--she may have inherited the books from her late husband Thomas or they may have been given to her.[2]

What adds to the complexity of understanding the issue of literacy are a few more twists to be found in the documents related to settling Amy Jackson's estate. The first convolution concerns the proving of one of Amy Jackson's two wills. On March 23, 1840, Phineas Blair as Public Administrator applied to the probate court for a letter of administration on the grounds that Amy Jackson died "intestate, leaving no heirs or kindred in this Commonwealth who by law can inherit her estate" (transcription 2.4). As a public administrator, Blair was an appropriate party to settle the estate of an intestate decedent with no legal heirs or kindred in Massachusetts. The directive to publish a notice in the *Boston Courier* for "two weeks successively" to alert "the next of kin, and all other persons interested" to appear at court on April 13 "to shew cause, if any you have, against granting" the requested letter of administration was a routine procedure (transcription 2.2).

On March 30, a week after Blair's application to administer Amy Jackson's estate, Eunice Senex presented to the court the October 1839 will that named her Amy Jackson's executrix and heir (transcription 2.5). The order to publish a notice in the *Liberator* for "two weeks successively" to alert "all persons interested" to appear at court on April 13 to "shew cause, if any they have, either for or against the probate" of the purported will was also a routine procedure (transcription 2.3).

Further complications arose before July 20 when Judge Willard Phillips ultimately proved, approved, and allowed Amy Jackson's October 1839 will. On April 13, "Mary Clark, claiming to be interested, together with her husband Thomas Clark appeared by Isaac Osgood, their attorney, and Phineas Blair, Public Administrator in and for said County, also appeared, and objected to said probate" (transcription 2.6). Apparently, a three-way conflict over Amy Jackson's estate unfolded. The Clarks based their claim on the March 1837 will, Eunice Senex on the October 1839 will, and Phineas Blair on the intestacy of a decedent with no heirs or kindred in Massachusetts.

After several continuations "from Court to Court," on July 20, "the allegations and testimony of the respective parties [had] been fully heard and considered." The witnesses to Amy Jackson's October 1839 will, S.E. Sewall, Gustavias Andrews, and Albert Bowman, had "made oath, that they saw the said Amy Jackson sign, seal, and heard her publish the same Instrument as her last Will and Testament," that she seemed to them to be "of a sound disposing mind and memory" and that they therefore signed the will as witnesses in her presence and in the presence of each other. Thus, Phineas Blair's bid for administration was dismissed (transcription 2.4), and Eunice Senex was legally recognized as the executrix (transcription 2.6).

But even more curiosities crop up in the probate records concerning the settling of Amy Jackson's estate. Two days before Eunice Senex is recognized in court as the rightful executrix, she signed a letter addressed to Judge Phillips, declining to act as executrix and requesting that Samuel E. Sewall--one of the witnesses to Amy Jackson's October 1839 will--be appointed administrator "to act in my stead" (transcription 2.7). This document was submitted to the court on July 20 to substantiate Samuel E. Sewall's petition for administration in which he states that "Eunice V. Senex, the executrix . . . has declined accepting said trust" (transcription 2.8). After the routine procedure of publishing a request for a letter of administration to allow objectors to appear in court, Sewall was decreed the administrator on August 17, 1840 (transcription 2.9).

Since it was not unusual for a woman to serve as the executrix--or administrix--of an estate (Hannah M. Benson first for her husband in 1831 and then for her brother in 1845),[3] it might seem that Eunice Senex withdrew out of trepidation in the face of the two wills and a public administrator jockeying to control the disposition of her benefactor's estate. In fact, the letter to Judge Phillips in which she requested that Samuel E. Sewall be named administrator in her stead

A Multi-Angled Query

was written in Sewall's hand. Although her signature was duly witnessed by a John St. Pierre, it is conceivable that a woman called "Eunice V. Senex" by court officials, but who signed her name "unis V Sinnix," may have been intimidated by the white male establishment. But an extremely unusual document has been preserved amid Amy Jackson's probate record--a request dated March 1, 1841, in what appears to be an untutored hand (transcription 2.16):

> Sir
>   I U V Senix want the property of Amy Jackson sold by the SE Sewall by the sixteenth of March which will be a year and one day since her Death if he is not disposed to do so thier is another gentleman that stands ready to take it and settle it right away
>   U V Senix
> please not to publish it in the Liberator for it is not so public a paper as some others
>   this paper is very limmeted in deed i want it put in the morning post and the dayley advertizer
>   unis V Sinnix

While it is not unusual for settling an estate to take a year, Eunice Senex seems to have galvanized Sewall into action; on March 29, 1841, he was officially licensed as administrator to sell Amy Jackson's real estate (transcription 2.17 and 11.18). In May and July he received sums for the two lots of land--$1000 from J.P. Coburn for Bultolph St and $1192.19 from John Thompson for 19 May Street (transcription 2.20). Thus Amy Jackson's real estate brought $2192.19 on the open market, as opposed to its appraised value of $2605.00. And the $7.90 "loss in selling personal property" recorded in the first account on March 1, 1841 (transcription 2.14) signifies that the $23.45 valuation placed on Amy Jackson's household possessions was also somewhat inflated.

But the very fact of the sale of Amy Jackson's estate directly conflicts with her seeming wealth at death in real estate and comfort in personal estate. Just relying on the inventory of her estate at her death, without examining the other probate records associated with settling her estate, gives a false impression. Amy Jackson clearly was not impoverished; she was, however, insolvent--unable to meet all just debts without sale of her property. And those debts consisted primarily of a claim of $1856.44 by Jonathan P. Hall (transcription 2.15), as well as the costs of settling the estate (i.e., $1.40 for the constable for summoning witnesses for the trial of probate of the will, $7.50 for the appraisers, and some $130 the administrator Sewall paid himself for his services) and for funeral expenses (transcriptions 2.14 and 2.20). In short, by the time all just debts had been met, Amy Jackson's appraised estate of $2628.45 had been reduced to $118.75 "to be paid according to the will" (transcription 2.20).

Amy Jackson's wealth was heavily encumbered; the records do not make it clear, but it may be safe to assume the $1856.44 claimed against her estate by Jonathan P. Hall was a mortgage note. Amy Jackson--or her late husband Thomas--may have followed what is considered the characteristic pattern of investing in real estate rather than accruing personal possessions. But the real estate was owned very precariously--even using the inflated appraisal of the inventory rather than the sale price, the equity Amy Jackson held in real estate at her death amounted to $748.56.[4] The irony is that this not inconsiderable sum amongst black Bostonians before the Civil War should be swallowed up primarily during settlement.

Yet unis V Sinnix--in keeping with her feisty note calling Sewall to task for his laggardly attention to settling the estate and demanding effective advertising for the sale of the real estate--did not choose to abide by the will once Sewall determined that $118.75 remained as the "Balance to be paid according to the will." On Oct 27, 1841, Eunice V. Senex "residuary legatee under the will" received $59.37, and on November 8 "Nathan Winslow, trustee of Mrs. Mary Clark by order of said Eunice V. Senex" received $59.37 1/ 2 (transcription 2.21).

Thus Amy Jackson's two wills were reconciled through the generosity of the heir of the second will toward the disinherited beneficiary of the first will. While the intriguing issue of Amy Jackson's literacy remains cloudy, the inventory of her estate, along with other probate documents, nonetheless manages to reveal her material conditions and to speak to the human interactions that can be linked to her life and death.

Patterns Of Human Interactions

The human interactions that can be linked to a decedent through probate records provide valuable clues to mapping out the structure of the black community's network in Boston.[5] When the names of the 1840s decedents, witnesses to wills, appraisers, and claimants are cross-referenced, many names reappear several times. Certain names reappear over time in association with many different decedents, while some names are interwoven with several others in a more complex pattern of human interaction.

A Multi-Angled Query

S.E. (or Samuel E.) Sewall and Phineas Blair are examples of the first category of multiple appearances of names in the probate records. Aside from his role in settling Amy Jackson's estate, Sewall was paid $5.00 from the estate of Emily Higgins, single-woman, in 1835; he was named guardian for the minor children of John E. Scarlett, clothesdealer, in 1845; he witnessed the will of Thomas Cole, hairdresser, in March 1847 and was paid $5.00 by the Cole estate in December of the same year.[6] Similarly, Phineas Blair, whose petition to administer Amy Jackson's estate was dismissed, posted bond for and administered the estate of John W. Brown, waiter, from 1840 through 1842; he was paid $8.25 for assistance in the administration and settlement of the estate of Chloe Russell, cook and widow, in 1841; he posted bond for and administered the estate of John Lewis Brent, alias John Lewis, hairdresser and barber, in 1844; he posted bond for, inventoried, and administered the estate of Calvin T. Hoyt, alias Charles Williams, mariner, from 1846 through 1848.[7] It seems relatively safe to assume from the evidence in the probate records alone that Sewall and Blair reappear over time in association with different decedents because settling estates was their business as lawyers and/ or public administrators.

The second category of multiple appearances of names in the probate records does not lend itself to such a straightforward explanation. The records of two decedents--John W. Brown and John E. Scarlett--disclose an interlocking and a crisscrossing pattern of interaction with other decedents that differs in degree and spirit from Sewall's and Blair's professional interaction with the black community. In the instance of John W. Brown, waiter, who died intestate in 1840 without heirs in Massachusetts to inherit his estate, Phineas Blair as Public Administrator petitioned successfully for administration and posted bond. But tracing the other names in Brown's probate records links him directly with members of the Afro-American community.

Chloe Russell, cook and widow, and Edward Labbottiere, hairdresser, posted bond in November 1840. In the "Schedule of Particulars" of Brown's inventory, dated January 25, 1841, it becomes evident that Chloe Russell was entitled to Brown's real estate during her lifetime. Moreover, a list of claims compiled by Blair and presented to Willard Phillips, Judge of Probate, on October 18, 1841, shows that Chloe Russell was owed $213.11 by Brown's estate. Next, the slightly increased sum of $214.15--in a revised list of claims submitted to Judge Phillips on April 16, 1842, by commissioners appointed to review claims against Brown's estate once it was declared insolvent--is acknowledged as due to "Edw Labbottiere assignee of C. Russell."

Then, Blair recorded in his third administrative account dated August 1842 that E. Labbottiere had been paid $8.00 in March "for 4 days going to Newport and Braintree for evidence before the auditor on claims under the mortgages." In addition, Blair charged Brown's estate $5.00 in April for "making a Deed to Labbottiere." Finally, in his fifth administrative account dated October 17, 1842, Blair declared Edw[d] Labbottiere as a recipient of $156.00, "cash paid under a decree of distribution on the Claims returned by Coms. of Insolvency." This sum of $156.00 represents about two-thirds of the $214.15 accepted by the commissioners in April 1842 as John W. Brown's just debt to "Edw[d]. Labottiere assignee of C. Russell," in keeping with the total amount of $370.91 available after settlement costs to meet claims of $410.45 against Brown's estate.

Turning to Chloe Russell's probate records, her will--written on October 12, 1840, and signed with her mark--reveals that aside from Lucy Stetson and Nancy Banks (her daughters by her first and third husbands, respectively), to whom she left one-half her wearing apparel and five dollars each, she also had a son--Edward Labbottiere--to whom she left the rest of her estate and whom she named executor. Labbottiere presented his mother's will to the court on March 21, 1842, when he also asked to administer her estate. Her will was proved on May 2 and on May 9 Labbottiere posted bond. Almost a year later and some five months after Blair declared payment of $156 to him, Labbottiere certified on March 22, 1843, that he had "rec[d] from the Adm[r] of the Estate of John W. Brown dcd, the sum of One hundred and fifty-six dollars," which comprised the inventory of his mother's estate. In simplified form, this string of interactions can be seen more readily as an interlocking pattern:

John W. Brown Estate
Administrative Bond (November 23, 1840)
    Chloe Russell
    E. Labbottiere
Inventory (January 25, 1841)
    Chloe Russell
List of Claims (October 18, 1841)
    Chloe Russell
Commissioners Return (April 16, 1842)
    Edw[d] Labbottiere assignee of C. Russell
Third Account (August 8, 1842)
    E. Labbottiere

A Multi-Angled Query

Fifth account (October 17, 1942)
    Ed^d Labottiere

Chloe Russell Estate
Will (October 12, 1840)
    Edward Labottiere
Executor's Bond (May 9, 1842)
    Edward Labbottiere
Inventory (March 22, 1843)
    John W. Brown
    Edward Labbottiere

In the instance of John E. Scarlett, clothesdealer, who died in 1844, S.E. Sewall served as the guardian for Scarlett's minor children. But again tracing the names in a series of probate records links Scarlett directly with other members of the black community. In 1840, along with John Robinson, clothing dealer, Scarlett posted surety for the administration of the estate of William S. Jinnings, trader. John T. Hilton, hairdresser, and John Rogers, gentleman/ clothing dealer, inventoried Jinnings's estate, while Scarlett was listed as a claimant for $20 against the estate. Upon Scarlett's own death in 1844, Hilton inventoried his estate. In 1847, Hilton also served as executor of the hairdresser Thomas Cole's estate, which he billed $25 and from which he received a legacy of $100. The first account of Cole's estate, moreover, records that $8 was paid to William Riley, gentleman/ clothing dealer. Next, Hilton served as a witness both to Riley's will and to the inventory of his estate in 1849, whereas Rogers posted surety in 1849 but withdrew as surety for the Riley estate a year later. And finally, a series of lists of debts dating from June 1850 to June 1851 from John Robinson's probate records show that John T. Hilton was owed $2. In simplified form, this string of interactions can be seen more readily as a crisscrossing pattern:

William S. Jinnings Estate
Administrative Bond (October 12, 1840)
    John E. Scarlett
    John Robinson
Inventory (December 28, 1840)
    John E. Scarlett
    John T. Hilton
    John Rogers

John E. Scarlett Estate
Inventory (October 28, 1844)
   John T. Hilton

Thomas Cole Estate
Order of Notice (June 14, 1847)
   John T. Hilton
Will (August 9, 1847)
   John T. Hilton
First Account (April 2, 1849)
   John T. Hilton
   William Riley

William Riley Estate
Executor's Bond (August 20, 1849)
   John Rogers
Will (August 20, 1849)
   John T. Hilton
Inventory (September 10, 1849)
   John T. Hilton
Surety Discharged (April 1, 1850)
   John Rogers

John Robinson Estate
List of Debts (June 17, 1850)
   John T. Hilton
List of Debts (December 9, 1850)
   J. T. Hilton
Claims of Creditors (June 9, 1851)
   J. T. Hilton

The Interlocking Pattern

Looking at the interlocking pattern of interaction detectable in the probate records of John W. Brown and Chloe Russell, it is not untoward to surmise that Chloe Russell, cook and widow, may have kept house for John W. Brown, waiter, during his wife's illness, thereby gaining her entitlement to his real estate during her lifetime as well as earning her the $213.11 claimed against his estate. Edward Labbottiere, as Chloe Russell's son and principal heir--which is spelled out in her will dated October 12, 1840--would appear to be a naturally interested party in the settling of Brown's estate.

Brown died on November 23, 1840; Chloe Russell on March 21, 1841. The inventory noting Russell's entitlement during her lifetime to Brown's real estate is dated January 25, 1841. What is a bit inconsistent is that the first list of claims against John W. Brown's estate is dated October 18, 1841, some seven months after Chloe Russell's death yet notes "Chloe Russell acct . . . $213.11." It is only in the commissioners return of claims against Brown's estate dated April 16, 1842, that "Edw Labottiere assignee of C Russell" is named as the claimant, as opposed to his deceased mother. According to the information in the third account, Labbottiere took an active role in the settlement of Brown's estate and was reimbursed for his efforts by Phineas Blair. By the time Blair submitted the fifth account on October 17, 1842, Edwd Labbottiere--without any mention of his mother, the original claimant on Brown's estate--was recorded as the recipient of $156.00. This was, of course, the same "One hundred and fifty six dollars" Labbottiere certified that he had received from the "Adm^r of the Estate of John W. Brown" and that constituted his mother's entire estate. In his first account, submitted to the court also on March 27, 1842, Labbottiere again records receipt of $156 in cash, as well as expenditures totaling $57.50 in October 1841 and March 1843, leaving a balance of $98.50 to be disposed of in accord with Chloe Russell's will.

Both the document certifying Labbottiere's receipt of $156.00 from the John W. Brown estate and the one listing Labbottiere's expenditures as executor, as well as the executor's bond, are in Phineas Blair's handwriting, with only the signatures in Labbottiere's own hand, thus explaining the payment to Blair of $8.25 "for assistance in the Adm^n & Settlement of the Estate." Most of the documents related to the settling of John W. Brown's estate are likewise in Phineas Blair's handwriting--from the petition for administration to the fifth account. Over the course of settlement--including the petition for sale of real estate to meet claims against the estate amounting to $510.45 and charges of administration amounting to $260.02--Phineas Blair paid himself $120.00. With Brown's estate Blair exercised his duties and prerogatives as a public administrator; since evidence about deeds and mortgages needed to be gathered, commissioners of insolvency remunerated, and real estate auctioned, settling John W. Brown's estate proved costly. But Brown's assets consisted primarily of real estate and notes, and the only avenue for reimbursement open to his creditors was through probate, even if its cost reduced the amount of money they eventually received. With Chloe Russell's estate, Blair literally lent a hand to Labbottiere, the executor under his mother's will, most obviously by drawing up many of the documents. Moreover, Chloe

Russell died solvent and her assets were totally liquid, thereby containing costs and simplifying settlement. One complex and the other simple, the two sets of probate records nonetheless reveal an interlocking pattern of interaction among John W. Brown, Chloe Russell, and Edward Labbottiere.

The Crisscrossing Pattern

Looking at the crisscrossing pattern of interaction detectable in the probate records of William S. Jinnings, John E. Scarlett, Thomas Cole, William Riley, and John Robinson, it is not untoward to surmise that Jinnings (a trader), Scarlett (a clothes dealer), Cole (a hairdresser), Riley (a gentleman/ clothing dealer), and Robinson (a clothing dealer) moved in the same circles in the black community, especially since John T. Hilton (a hairdresser) and John Rogers (a clothes dealer)--whose names also appear in these probate records--were in comparable socioeconomic circumstances. It does not appear, however, that the interest of Scarlett et al. in settling estates sprang primarily from the financial benefits they might gain as principal heirs or their assignees--even though Scarlett claimed $20 against Jinnings's estate, Hilton billed Cole's estate for $25 as well as was bequeathed $100 by Cole, Riley was paid $8 by Cole's estate, and Hilton was owed $2 by Robinson's estate. Rather, the evidence suggests that their involvement was based on their being well-acquainted with one another and their standing in the community, as well as their knowledge of the market value of real and personal property.

Bequests to mutual self-help organizations and churches bespeak the commitment Cole and Riley apparently felt for community institutions and tend to substantiate suppositions about their leadership role within the community. Further support for these inferences can be drawn from noting that another name--Richard G. Wait--threads its way through the probate documents that display the crisscrossing pattern of interaction. Wait inventoried the estates of David Walker, clothing dealer, in 1830; James Gould, laborer/ bootblack, in 1831; of Cesar Fletcher, laborer, in 1832; as well as William S. Jinnings in 1840. (Scarlett posted surety for Walker's estate and Robinson helped to inventory Fletcher's estate.)[8] Wait, like Sewall and Blair, was an outside professional who assured the impartiality of court-ordered procedures, carried out in tandem with friends and neighbors of the deceased.[9] That these community members were indeed friends and neighbors can be deduced from the probate records. The clearest references to friendship occur in Thomas Cole's will, dated March 27, 1847 (transcription 1.1). Both in his bequests and in his choice of executors, Cole demonstrates the strength of non-kin relationships. He bequeathed $100 each to John T.

Hilton and to his son, Thomas Hilton. Moreover, he "nominate[d] and appointe[d] [his] friends the said John T. Hilton and Alfred G. Howard, executors of this [his] last will and testament." Alfred G. Howard, hairdresser, who posted bond and acted as executor for Cole's estate, was also a legatee of $75 and a claimant of $25 from Cole's estate (transcriptions 1.2, 1.4, and 1.8).

In addition, Cole bequeathed "Three Hundred dollars, my feather bed which formerly belonged to my mother, all my sheets, counterpanes, pillowcases, one dozen towels, and my best china tea set" to Mrs. Elizabeth Riley (transcription 1.1). It is true that the first account records that Elizabeth Riley was paid $13 on July 20 and $60 on August 23, 1847, the latter specifically "for nursing," but these payments for services rendered were separate from her legacies of "furniture &" (valued at $27.50) and of $300 in cash (in two installments of $150 each) dated November 28, 1849 (transcription 1.8). Thus it appears that Mrs. Elizabeth Riley--the wife of William Riley, gentleman/ clothesdealer--was both friend and nurse to Thomas Cole. Aside from the considerable legacy of $300, the character of the items that he stipulated Mrs. Riley should receive (especially the descriptive language of the bequest--"my feather bed which formerly belonged to my mother . . . my best china tea set") tends to suggest she warranted his high regard. The complexity of their relationship is further emphasized by the fact that Ann Jennett--or Jenette--Jackson, her daughter by her first marriage, was paid $20 by Cole's estate on January 29, 1849 (transcription 1.8). It is clear that Cole deliberately distributed his wealth in accord with his loyalties to community members (for instance, the Rev. John T. Raymond and Mrs. John T. Raymond, separately) or organizations (for example, the Bay State Lodge of the Grand United Order of the Odd Fellows, number 114). There is but one mention of a relative, in a bequest to his nephew (and namesake) Thomas Cole Richardson of $300, entrusted to Hilton and Howard, as executors, to invest in a savings bank until Richardson came of age.

Cole was financially in a position to be generous to friends and community. He held no real estate at his death; in fact, the first account lists $25 paid on September 8, 1847, to Edward Blake for rent (transcription 1.1). His personal property, valued at $2690.84 in the inventory of his estate, consisted of $171.51 in household goods and business stock, with $2519.33 in cash (transcription 1.5). But according to the first account submitted by John T. Hilton and Alfred G. Howard, Cole's wealth was enhanced when the sale of his personal estate realized a gain of $215.44, bringing his total estate to $2906.28 (transcription

1.8). Thus, even after the "sundry payments, as stated in schedule B," as well as $100 "Allowance to Executors settling estate thus far," there remained $436.53 (corrected sum) "to be appropriated agreeably to the provisions of the Will of said Testator" by the executors, Hilton and Howard, i.e. "to such charitable objects as they may see fit," "such charitable religious, and benevolent objects as my said Executors may approve" (transcription 1.1).

Insofar as being neighbors, the decedents and those whose names appear in their probate records frequently worked or resided in close proximity to one another. William Riley, John Robinson, John Rogers, and John E. Scarlett--all clothing dealers at the time of their deaths--had business addresses on Brattle Street. More important, however, Cole lived at 9 Southac Street, the corner of Garden and Southac (later called Phillips); William Riley owned real estate on Southac Street and Southac Court (later Phillips Street and Phillips Court, or 68 and 70 Phillips Street); John Robinson owned real estate on the corner of Bridge Place and West Cedar Street; and John E. Scarlett owned real estate at 17 Belknap Street.[10] The properties on Southac (or Phillips), West Cedar, and Belknap are all within a few blocks of one another, on Beacon Hill, in Ward 6.

Comparative Analysis Of Associated Decedents' Estates

The various probate documents--wills, lists of claims, administrative accounts, etc.--indicate that the decedents in the crisscrossing pattern of interaction were well-acquainted with one another and of comparable standing in the community. Focusing exclusively on the inventories of their estates both further associates and individualizes the five key figures in the crisscrossing pattern of interaction: William S. Jinnings, trader, who died in, 1840; John E. Scarlett, clothing dealer, who died in 1844; Thomas Cole, hairdresser, who died in 1847; William Riley, gentleman/ clothing dealer, who died in 1849; and John Robinson, clothing dealer, who also died in 1849.

The total value of their estates at death can be compared, as well as the value of their real estate, their personal estate, their business stock, cash, and household goods. Dividing the five estates into these six categories sometimes requires no more than duplicating the groupings recorded in the inventories. For example, Scarlett's record clearly sets forth real estate and personal estate, with the latter broken down into "Household Furniture &," "Second hand Clothing &," and "Cash." Moreover, "Household Furniture" and "Second hand Clothing" are each itemized "as per Schedule on file." In the case of Cole's estate,

A Multi-Angled Query

however, the division between household goods and business stock is not nearly so clearcut (transcription 1.5). But, "errors excepted" (as is stated on the "List of Claims not Paid" against the Jinnings estate), the six categories of the five decedents in the crisscrossing pattern of interaction can be compared and contrasted. A quick overview shows that the five estates ranged in value from $430 to $4306.25; two of the five decedents had no real estate, one had $3000 worth; the two decedents with considerable personal estates died with large amounts of cash, notes, or savings rather than business stock or household goods, while household goods in no instance represented the major category of wealth at death.

The appraised value of the household goods of these five decedents nonetheless suggests a variation in overall expenditures on personal possessions. From a low of $20 to a high of $237.16, the monetary value of household goods at death comprised 5 percent of Jinnings's estate ($20 of $430), 5 percent of Scarlett's estate ($73.75 of $1410.25), 5 percent of Cole's estate ($136.14 of $2690.84), 1 percent of Riley's estate ($56 of $4306.25), and 18 percent of Robinson's estate ($237.16 of $1299.39). Robinson's estate of $1299.39 consisted predominately of $944.23 worth of real estate (73 percent), with the remaining $355.16 in personal estate being divided between $118 worth of business stock (9 percent) and $237.16 worth of household goods (18 percent). Since Robinson had no cash, notes, or savings, his sizable holdings of household goods constituted a substantial proportion of his estate. Cole, who owned $136.14 worth of household goods (5 percent), on the other hand, died with $2519.33 of his estate on deposit in two banks and in cash (94 percent), but with no real estate. And, although Scarlett's $73.75 worth of household goods parallelled Cole's expenditure in this category in terms of total estate (5 percent), his assets at death consisted primarily of real estate worth $1264.69 (90 percent), with $51.81 in business stock (4 percent) and $20 in cash (1 percent). Jinnings possessed but two kinds of wealth when he died. His $20 of household goods (5 percent) was in keeping with Scarlett's and Cole's holdings in relation to the value of their total estate, but his $410 of business stock (95 percent) dominated his assets. Last, Riley, whose $4306.25 of wealth at death consisted in large measure of $3000 worth of real estate (70 percent) and of $1180 on deposit in two banks and in cash (27 percent), had $70.25 worth of business stock (2 percent), with only $56 worth of household goods (1 percent).

Therefore, while Riley's and Robinson's estates resembled each other in proportion of real estate to personal estate, they radically deviated in proportion of household goods to total estate. Similarly,

Cole, Jinnings, and Scarlett held the same proportion of household goods to total estate, but Cole and Scarlett had diametrically opposed holdings in real estate vis-à-vis personal estate--or more accurately--in real estate versus cash, while Jinnings had neither real estate nor cash, only business stock, as the balance of his inventoried assets. The numbers thus reveal some interesting variations among the estates of these five decedents, even if in three estates the value of household goods was 5 percent and if in two estates the value of real estate was about 70 percent. The differences are most striking when one category of wealth constitutes 90 percent or more of the total estate: business stock for Jinnings, real estate for Scarlett, and cash for Cole.

Comparative Analysis Of Associated Decedents' Household Goods

A closer look at the particulars of these household goods--analyzing them into "necessities," "amenities," and "luxuries"--can further refine an understanding of the commonalities and differences among the decedents in the crisscrossing pattern of interaction. Unfortunately, neither the inventories of William S. Jinnings nor William Riley are suitable for this three-part analysis of household goods into categories of comfort. In the former instance, but one item is listed--"Wearing apparel of the dec'd"--and in the latter case, all items are lumped together--"Household furniture." With some ingenuity, however, the inventories of Cole, Robinson, and Scarlett do lend themselves to this system of classification (transcription 1.5). Decisions were made consistently, even if with a bit of uncertainty on occasion.[11] Necessities were identified by their plain utility: a collection of basic furnishings (lists 2.1, 9.1, and 10.1). Amenities often proved problematic: a potpourri of useful accessories (lists 2.2, 9.2, and 10.2). Luxuries were so designated by virtue of their transcending the utilitarian: an assortment of elegant appointments and signs of literacy (lists 2.3, 9.3, and 10.3).

A quick quantitative analysis allows comparison of the appraised value of Cole's, Robinson's, and Scarlett's holdings in each category of comfort at death vis-à-vis household goods and total estate. The numbers tell a fairly straightforward story without associating the decedents with one another in any significant manner. Cole, whose total estate was the wealthiest, possessed luxuries ($66.93 or 2.4 percent) approximately equal to necessities plus amenities ($69.21 or 2.4 percent), whereas Robinson, whose total estate was the least wealthy, possessed double the amount of luxuries ($162.00 or 12 percent) to

A Multi-Angled Query

necessities plus amenities ($75.16 or 6 percent). Scarlett, meanwhile, whose total estate was closer in wealth to Robinson's than to Cole's, possessed a minimum of luxuries ($14.00 or 0.9 percent) to necessities plus amenities ($59.75 or 4.1 percent). Robinson's holdings in luxuries represented not only two-thirds of his household goods but also one-eighth of his total estate. For Cole, on the other hand, luxuries may have represented about half his household goods but only one-fiftieth of his total estate. And for Scarlett, luxuries represented one-fifth of his household goods, but a mere one-hundredth of his total estate. Thus, Robinson, with the lowest total estate, dramatically exceeded Cole and Scarlett in the proportion of his total estate comprised of luxuries. By the same token, it is noteworthy that Cole, whose total estate was valued at approximately twice that of Robinson's and Scarlett's, held the smallest proportions of necessities and amenities to total estate than did either of the other two decedents. For Cole amenities plus luxuries ($93.43 or 3.3 percent) do not dramatically overwhelm necessities ($42.71 or 1.5 percent). But for Robinson, amenities plus luxuries ($197.50 or 15 percent) dominate necessities ($39.66 or 3 percent). While for Scarlett, amenities plus luxuries ($40.25 or 2.7 percent) very moderately surpasses necessities ($33.50 or 2.3 percent).

Scarlett, in fact, had the "proper," temperate hierarchy of necessities to amenities to luxuries, in that it was inversely graduated from greater to lesser. Neither Cole nor Robinson showed such "propriety"; the hierarchy was not only reversed--luxuries in the ascendent position--but also the delineation of the progression from necessities to amenities to luxuries jackknifes rather than proceeds more or less diagonally (graph 1). It has been argued that when necessities vis-à-vis amenities and luxuries account for a diminished proportion of household goods, the standard of living has risen. In other words, once the basics are in place, the acquisition of amenities and luxuries becomes feasible.[12] Consequently, the proportion of wealth tied up in necessities falls because item-for-item the basics are often appraised for small sums in contrast to amenities and necessities. Do the estates of these three decedents fit this model? A closer examination of the specific necessities, amenities, and luxuries held by Cole, Robinson, and Scarlett can help to ascertain their standard of living as expressed in these categories of comfort.

Toward Envisioning The Domestic Environment

Organizing each decedent's household goods into a typology of consumer durables allows for comparative analysis that may further twentieth-century comprehension of Cole's, Robinson's, and Scarlett's material life. When necessities are organized into six generic sets that would seem to comprise the bare essentials for everyday life--sleeping, eating, clothing oneself, keeping warm and clean, with a modicum of furniture--the gaps leap out. While all three decedents possessed beds and bedding, plain furnishings, and kitchenware at death, none possessed the wherewithal--buckets or tubs--for cleaning. Admittedly some ambiguously labelled crockery could conceivably have been used for cleaning. Although Scarlett and Robinson owned heating and/ or cooking stoves and accouterments, Cole had none. Scarlett and Cole died owning wearing apparel; Robinson died without any clothing. Many explanations can be advanced for these curious absences, including the distribution of these possessions to family and friends before death in the case of Robinson's apparel, to the lack of need for heating and cooking accouterments in the case of Cole who rented quarters, to the gender-specific uses of cleaning apparatus in all three cases.[13]

Looking at this breakdown of necessities in terms of their dollar worth and the interrelationship of generic sets offers a slightly different perspective on the three decedents' simplest personal possessions. The monetary value assigned to Scarlett's necessities descended from his beds ($12.00 or 36 percent) to apparel ($10.00 or 30 percent) followed by kitchenware ($6.00 or 18 percent), heating and cooking fixtures ($3.00 or 9 percent), and then plain furnishings ($2.50 or 7 percent). The appraised value of Cole's necessities was dominated by his apparel ($34.96 or 82 percent), with beds next ($6.25 or 15 percent) and then plain furnishings ($1.00 or 2 percent) and kitchenware ($.50 or 1 percent). The worth of Robinson's necessities ranged from heating and cooking fixtures ($15.00 or 38 percent) to kitchenware ($11.50 or 29 percent) to plain furnishings ($7.66 or 19 percent) and finally to beds ($5.50 or 14 percent). The accumulation of essentials, with the exception of uniformity in no ownership of cleaning apparatus, appears at first extremely idiosyncratic when depicted graphically (graph 2). Cole and Robinson, for whom beds and bedding represented virtually the same proportion of their necessities, diverged increasingly in every other generic set--particularly in apparel. Scarlett in no generic set coincides with the other two decedents, with the closest conjunction occurring with Cole's estate in the generic set of plain furnishings.

Turning to the actual possessions themselves provides yet another picture of the differences and similarities among the decedents' bare essentials for everyday life (lists 2.1, 9.1, and 10.1). All three had bedsteads, beds and/ or bedding, but Scarlett's inventory lists bed-associated items that can be understood to constitute three units of furniture for sleeping ("2 Bedsteads Bed & Bedding," "Cot Bedstead, Bed &c"), Cole's inventory lists one ("Bedding," "Bedstead"), and Robinson's three ("2 Bedsteads," "One trundle Bedstead"). Among their plain furnishings, all three had tables--but Robinson had two to Scarlett's and Cole's one. Moreover, Robinson had eighteen chairs, while Scarlett had six and Cole none. Robinson had no provisions among his plain furnishings for storage; Scarlett owned one trunk and Cole four trunks as well as two chests. Of the three, only Scarlett had basic lighting devices. As to heating and cooking fixtures, Scarlett's inventory lists a cook stove, while Cole's inventory makes mention of no facility for heating or cooking, in strong contrast with Robinson's inventory, which lists fireplace fittings, two old stoves, and a cooking stove. There is reference to kitchenware most obviously among Robinson's necessities when knives and forks are listed, but his inventory, like the others, also lists crockery and either glass or unbreakable ware that can be presumed to have been used for eating or food preparation.

If the aforesaid were to be the only household goods that each decedent possessed at death, their life style would have been equally rudimentary. Cole may have had some elegant clothing (hence the high value placed on his apparel) or even many different pieces of clothing of the customary variety; similarly, Scarlett's clothing may have consisted of a few unusually valuable pieces or numerous inexpensive items. Regardless, apparel--while an important generic set among their necessities ($10.00 or 30 percent for Scarlett; $34.96 or 60 percent for Cole) and a sizable category of wealth in relation to household goods (14 percent for Scarlett; 26 percent for Cole) was in both cases only a minor category in relation to total estate (0.7 percent for Scarlett; 1 percent for Cole). Once apparel is removed from consideration, the configuration of items constituting the bare essentials for everyday life as found in the inventories of Cole, Robinson, and Scarlett can be mentally recreated. One to three beds, a table or two, a slew of chairs or none, numerous or no storage units, several simple sources of lighting or none, one or more or no fixtures related to heating and cooking, and some items associated with food preparation and/ or consumption--those were their basics.

But Cole, Robinson, and Scarlett possessed more than necessities at death. When their amenities are organized into six generic sets that would seem to comprise the utilitarian with a degree of comfort--softer beds and seating, furniture meant for a specific use, linens and floor coverings, with accouterments for attending to one's appearance and the time of day--the gaps are as readily apparent as they were in the generic sets of necessities. While all three decedents possessed specialized furnishings and mirrors at death, only Cole and Robinson owned feather bedding, a commonly sought-after and achieved improvement in life style.[14] Both Scarlett and Robinson had some floor coverings, whereas Cole had none; yet Cole and Robinson both owned linens and/ or curtains, but Scarlett owned none; and, finally, Scarlett and Cole each possessed a timepiece, while Robinson did not. The absence of any particular amenity--other than feather bedding--does not seem peculiar since an amenity by definition connotes a broader spectrum of choice.

Looking now at this breakdown of amenities in terms of their dollar worth and the interrelationship of generic sets offers a clearer view of the decedents' slightly finer personal possessions. The monetary value assigned to Scarlett's amenities descended precipitously from specialized furnishings ($13.25 or 51 percent) to mirrors and timepiece ($5.00 or 19 percent each) and then to floor coverings ($3.00 or 11 percent). The appraised value of Cole's amenities was dominated by feather bedding ($15.00 or 57 percent), with linens and curtains next ($5.75 or 22 percent), then timepiece ($3.00 or 11 percent) and mirrors ($2.00 or 7 percent), and finally specialized furnishings ($.75 or 3 percent). The worth of Robinson's amenities ranged from feather bedding ($12.00 or 34 percent), to specialized furnishings ($8.50 or 24 percent), to mirrors ($7.00 or 20 percent), to linens or curtains ($6.00 or 17 percent), and last floor coverings ($2.00 or 5 percent). The accumulation of amenities, when depicted graphically, appears at first glance as idiosyncratic as the necessities the three decedents possessed at death (graph 3). Scarlett and Robinson--for whom mirrors represented virtually the identical proportion of their amenities--seem to have diverged in every other generic set except floor coverings. Cole and Robinson approach conjunction only in linens and curtains; Cole and Scarlett only in the timepiece set. And the one generic set other than mirrors in which all decedents held possessions--specialized furnishings--varies strikingly when proportion of amenities is considered.

Now, consideration of the actual possessions themselves helps to visualize the differences and similarities among the three decedents' comfortable but utilitarian household goods (lists 2.2, 9.2, and 10.2). All three had mirrors, but Cole had one, Scarlett two, and Robinson three. All three had specialized furnishings, but of a varying sort. Seating that conveys a sense of ease and/ or prestige includes the "7 Flag. Bot Chairs" and the "sofa" owned by Scarlett, the "Rock^g chair & Cush " owned by Cole, and the "Settee," the "Rocking chair," and the "Old sofa" owned by Robinson. Storage units that bespeak some sophistication in workmanship include Scarlett's "Old Bureau" and Robinson's "Common Bureau." Tables that are designated for special uses include a "Work Table" and a "Dining Table" in Scarlett's estate, as well as the "Table" associated with the previously mentioned "Old sofa" in Robinson's estate. Scarlett's "Light Stand," Robinson's "Entry Lamp" and Cole's "Velise & bag" as well as "Port Folio & Sund " complete the miscellany of items that fall under the rubric of specialized furnishings. As to simple floor coverings, Scarlett possessed "Carpet & Backing" while Robinson had "One Old Carpet." On the other hand, only Cole and Robinson owned feather bedding as well as household linens and curtains--"2 White counterpanes," "1 Doz. Towels," "6 window curtains," and "11 Coverlids" in the latter instance. And finally, the inventories of Scarlett and Cole list "Timepiece" and "Time piece," respectively.

These amenities do introduce a note of greater homeyness and convenience. A mental recreation that adds the comfortable but utilitarian to the bare essentials for everyday life conjures up a configuration of items from the estates of Cole, Robinson, and Scarlett that shows them enjoying a less austere standard of living. Mirrors and specialized furnishings--particularly seating, but also tables intended for different uses, storage units worthy of the designation bureau, as well as an odd assortment of possessions that were meant to serve specific purposes--join with nondescript carpeting, some linens and maybe curtains or feather bedding to soften the strictures of the basics. Even the prosaic term "timepiece" denotes a workaday object, comparable to the other amenities in lifting its owner's material life from rude sufficiency to unadorned decency.

But, again, Cole, Robinson, and Scarlett possessed more than necessities and amenities at death. When their luxuries are organized into six generic sets that would seem to comprise the elegant and/ or superfluous as well as belongings connected with literacy, again the gaps are as striking as they were in the generic sets of necessities and amenities. Even though all three decedents possessed china and/ or silver, literacy belongings, and decorative items, Cole had no fine furnishings while Scarlett died owning neither jewelry/ clocks nor musical instruments. But perhaps with luxuries--which connote even a broader spectrum of choice than amenities--it is their similarity rather than dissimilarity that can be seen to be the more telling comment upon the standard of living for these three decedents.

In any event, looking at the breakdown of luxuries in terms of their dollar worth and the interrelationship of generic sets allows for a sharpened picture of Cole's, Robinson's, and Scarlett's finest consumer durables. The monetary value assigned to Scarlett's luxuries rises rapidly from decorative items ($.50 or 4 percent) to china/ silver ($3.00 or 21 percent) and fine furnishings ($3.50 or 25 percent). The appraised value of Cole's luxuries starts with decorative items ($1.68 or 3 percent), climbs slowly up to china/ silver ($5.00 or 7 percent), next quickly rises to jewelry/ clocks and musical instruments ($15.00 or 22.4 percent each) then jumps up to literacy belongings ($30.25 or 45.2 percent). The worth of Robinson's luxuries ranged from literacy belongings ($1.00 or 0.6 percent), moving up first to china/ silver ($5.00 or 3 percent) and then to decorative items ($10.00 or 6 percent), before ascending to musical instruments ($20.00 or 12 percent) and jewelry/ clocks ($25.00 or 16 percent), and finally rocketing up to fine furnishings ($101.00 or 62.4 percent).

The accumulation of luxuries, when depicted graphically, has the same wayward appearance under casual inspection as the necessities and amenities the three decedents possessed at death (graph 4). But, in point of fact, there may be more congruence in luxuries than in the other two categories of household possessions. For Cole, Robinson, and Scarlett, decorative items represented approximately the same proportion of luxuries; but, more important, for Cole and Robinson china/ silver relatively closely converged in proportion, as did literacy belongings for Cole and Scarlett. Moreover, Robinson approaches Cole in jewelry/ clocks and, to a lesser degree, in musical instruments. While it is true that some of the necessities or amenities similarly approached in proportion--Cole's and Scarlett's plain furnishings or Scarlett's and Robinson's floor coverings, for instance--the occurrence of such similitude in luxuries implies a rather narrow spectrum of choice (graphs 2, 3, and 4). Of course, the wildly divergent should not be overlooked; Robinson far surpassed the other two decedents in his holdings of fine furnishings.

Finally, then, consideration of the actual possessions themselves helps to distinguish the differences and similarities among the decedents' elegant and/ or literacy-related possessions (lists 2.3, 9.3, and 10.3). All three had visual images of one kind or another--Scarlett, "3 Small Pictures"; Cole, "Lot of framed prints &c"; and Robinson, "3 Pictures & frames." All three also owned china and/ or silver--"10 Silver tea Spoons" in Robinson's estate, "6 Small Silver Spoons" in Scarlett's estate, and a "White Tea Set" in Cole's estate. Two of the decedents possessed time keeping devices that evidently exceeded in status the humble timepiece--a "Gold watch & key &c" for Cole and "1 Mantle clock & case" for Robinson. Among the fine furnishings, Scarlett's "Card Table & Cloth" qualifies as a possession for strictly leisure-time usage, while Robinson's sixteen-piece suite of mahogany furniture (including a card table), "1 Music Stool," "24 yards woollen carpeting," and "2 Astral Lamps" suggests the deliberate acquisition of stylish appointments. As to the musical instruments, both Cole's and Robinson's inventories list a "Piano Forte," with Cole's listing a "Flute" as well.

All three had belongings usually associated with literacy, but they vary from decedent to decedent. Scarlett's household goods included a "Writing Desk" and a "Book case," but no books. Cole's estate contained a "Lot of Books" as well as a "Map of U.S." Robinson's inventory, on the other hand, simply cited a "desk." Since Cole died testate, his signature appears in his probate documents, lending weight to the assumption that he was in fact literate. The sheer monetary value placed on the unfortunately vaguely worded "Lot of Books" further strengthens this assumption. Cole's books alone figured only second in appraised value among all generic sets of his household goods, thereby--along with a didactic map--making literacy belongings a surprisingly sizable portion of his consumer durables (22 percent of household goods). In contrast, neither Scarlett's nor Robinson's literacy belongings were comprised of books, even though Scarlett's holdings included a book case. Both, however, were owners at death of furniture that could be interpreted to signify the ability to write. Scarlett's "Writing Desk" and Robinson's "desk" find corroborating evidence of signature literacy--as inconclusive as it may be for proving real literacy--in the pool of probate documents. Both died intestate, thus leaving no will to bear a tell-tale signature or "X, his mark." But, in the full array of the crisscrossing decedents' probate records, Scarlett and Robinson signed an administrator's bond as sureties in 1840, during the settling of Jinnings's estate.

Cole's, Robinson's, and Scarlett's luxuries contribute a touch of taste and quality to a mental recreation of a domestic environment thus far incorporating only the bare essentials for everyday life softened but slightly by the comfortable yet utilitarian. Pictures or prints, a china tea service or silver spoons, perhaps some furniture that indicates socializing and sophistication or a timekeeping device that transcends the practical--when added to musical instruments and the tangible paraphernalia of literacy--produce an image of a human habitation that admits, albeit sparingly, of personal expression.

Once the full complement of the three decedents' personal effects--necessities, amenities, and luxuries--is reexamined, there are some quirks that dissipate any easy conclusions about the conditions and/or rationale for the acquisition of various items. For instance, Cole possessed both a pragmatic "Time piece" and a flashy "Gold watch &

key &c"; Scarlett owned "5 Com Lamps & 2 Brass Candlesticks" but only one "Light Stand," as well as the previously noted "Book case" but no books; Robinson's inventory lists seven tables of one kind or another, as well as twenty-eight chairs all told, not counting the seating capacity of a settee, a rocker, two sofas, and a music stool (transcription 1.5). The sometime hodgepodge character of the inventories can be lost in excerpting and abstracting their contents for the purposes of comparative analysis; so, too, the truly idiomatic nature of the individual decedent's accumulation of ordinary to extraordinary consumer durables can be overshadowed by generalizations.

Ostensible Versus Real Wealth

The inventories of the household goods of Thomas Cole, John Robinson, and John E. Scarlett--when examined in accord with this system of progression from necessities to amenities to luxuries--leave an impression of reasonable, even rosy, material conditions. Feather beds, mahogany furniture, china tea sets--all contribute to a sense of gentility and security. Moreover, these decedents had holdings in business stock and real estate or cash. Like Amy Jackson, they clearly were not impoverished. Yet two of the three--also like Amy Jackson--died insolvent, unable to meet all just debts without sale of their property. Cole's estate, after all legacies and payments, showed a surplus of over $400 to be distributed by the executors to charity (transcription 1.8). But Scarlett's and Robinson's probate records reveal that their seeming prosperity was heavily encumbered.

In Scarlett's case, on October 28, 1844--some eight months after the court named his widow the administrix of his estate--Margaret Scarlett submitted a petition for a widow's allowance in conjunction with the filing of the inventory of her husband's estate by N.C. Cary, Phineas Capen, and John T. Hilton. The inventory appraised Scarlett's personal estate at $145.56, and Judge Phillips allowed the widow $145.56, not to be taken "as assets . . . for the payment of debts or charges of administration." In effect, Scarlett's personal estate (household goods, business stock, and cash) was decreed a "reasonable allowance" for his widow.

On October 28, Margaret Scarlett also petitioned for her dower, or thirds, in her husband's real estate. A month later, after publishing a copy of the petition "three weeks successively in the newspaper called the Morning Chronicle," her petition was granted and three commissioners were appointed "for the purpose of setting off and assigning to the said Margaret Scarlett her dower in said real estate according to law." On April 7, 1845, the commissioners--Frederick W. Sawyer, Richard Urann, and Phineas Capen, "all of said Boston, Esquires, three disinterested persons"--returned their report, which appraised the four pieces of property comprising John E. Scarlett's real estate and assigned Margaret Scarlett the land and house at 11 South May Street, valued at $1200, with a mortgage of $324.88 held by Samuel E. Sewall.

This document was signed by the commissioners; it also was signed by S. E. Sewall, who on that same day had been appointed the legal guardian of John E. Scarlett's minor children, at the request of their mother. Sewall had earlier taken an active role in Margaret Scarlett's obtaining her widow's allowance; he next submitted on her behalf a petition for sale of real estate on April 21. Since Scarlett's just debts at the time of his death amounted to $2701.57, the charges of administration were estimated to be $75, and the widow's allowance had been set at $145.56, the value of the personal estate of $145.56 was some $2776.57 shy of being sufficient for the payment of these debts and charges. Margaret Scarlett requested therefore to be "licensed to sell so much of the . . . real estate as may be necessary." The appraised value of the real estate cited in this document--$3246.43--corresponds to the appraised value stated in the inventory of Scarlett's estate, without taking mortgages or Margaret Scarlett's dower into account.

About four months later, on July 2, the advertisement for the sale at auction of Scarlett's four pieces of real estate that had occurred on the preceding June 18 was filed with the court. If this property sold for its inventoried value, then it realized $3246.43. But Scarlett, according to the petition for sale of real estate, died owing $2701.57 in just debts; there was also the $75 in administrative costs to levy against the proceeds of the auction. While not mentioned in that document, Margaret Scarlett's dower of $875.12 in equity in 11 South May Street would have to be subtracted from monies received from the auction before debts could be paid. Therefore, $3651.69 was needed, $405.26 more than the value of the real estate as appraised by Cary, Capen, and Hilton on Scarlett's inventory.

Possibly the real estate sold at prices closer to the values set by the commissioners who assigned Margaret Scarlett her dower; Sawyer, Urann, and Capen appraised the four pieces of property at $3865.69, and even with the higher mortgages they recorded against the two South May Street properties, they calculated $1804 in equity versus the $1265.69 in equity the inventory presents. Conceivably, then, the auction could have produced a surplus of $214. The worst case scenario thus would find that Scarlett had died insolvent, with $405.26 negative net worth, and the best case scenario would find that he had died insolvent, with $214 positive net worth.

In any event, here was a man who ostensibly owned two pieces of land with houses, as well as portions of two other houses with their land, who possessed home furnishings and business stock and some cash, but whose estate could not be held intact for his widow and minor children. Through astute management of the probate process, however, Margaret Scarlett--with the assistance of Samuel Sewall--was able to forestall destitution. Her widow's allowance rescued the household furnishings, business stock, and cash from creditors, while her widow's dower retrieved the equity in one piece of real estate. Nonetheless, the difference between John E. Scarlett's apparent wealth at death--$3391-.99 on the inventory of his estate--and his actual wealth after settlement--the $1020.69 Margaret Scarlett salvaged through invoking her rights as a widow, plus $214 or minus $405.26--should not be ignored.

John Robinson's affluence at death was similarly deceptive. Not only was his $3000 worth of real estate heavily mortgaged, but also his total estate was subject to numerous debts beyond the usual funeral expenses and administrative costs of settlement. Robert Morris, Esquire, and Jonas W. Clark, trader, at the request of Robinson's heirs, petitioned and were named Robinson's administrators in November 1849. On March 11, 1850, the inventory of Robinson's estate showed $2055.77 in mortgages to be deducted from his $3000 in real estate. Then on May 20, Morris and Clark filed a petition for sale of real estate, stating that Robinson's just debts amounted to $3352.12, whereas his personal estate was worth only $355.16, $2996.96 short of the necessary sum to meet the demands of his creditors. A list of debts accompanying this document included $1250 for "Note & Mortgage to Dr. Parkman," $112 for "Interest on do 1 year & 6 mos," $850 for "Note & mortgage to Ralph Haskins," and $51 for "Interest on do--1 year" or $2263 total in mortgages and interest accrued against Robinson's $3000 of real estate since his death eight months before. But Morris and Clark did not next arrange for the sale of Robinson's real estate under the license that had been granted to them on June 17. Instead, some six months later on December 9, the two administrators filed a representation of insolvency with the court, asking that "commissioners may be appointed to receive and examine all claims of creditors." The list of debts they appended for the most part duplicates the first roll call of claimants, with some inexplicable omissions and additions. Of the $3584.89 now claimed against the estate, $2506.68 is cited as the "Amount of Sundry mortgages and interest." Accordingly, William Minot and Owen G. Peabody were appointed and on June 9,

A Multi-Angled Query

1951, they submitted a "Claims of Creditors" that replicated many of the names on the two previous list of claims but failed to mention mortgages or interest. Although the exact sums often varied--for instance, "Mrs. Hayden's bill, for Services &c" was $426.60 in June 1850, but Ellen Hayden was owed $543.35 in December 1850 and $594.96 in June 1851--and some items are omitted--for example, a "Tax Bill" for $28.80 and "Taxes of shop in Brattle Street" for $18 only appear in the first list of debts--all three reckonings, aside from mortgages and interest, amounted to about the same indebtedness--$1089.12 in June 1850, $1078.21 in December 1850, and $1091.30 in June 1851.

Thus, Robinson died insolvent--unable to meet all just debts without sale of his property. The equity he held in real estate at his death was reduced even further--as interest continued to accrue--over the year and eight months that passed while his estate was settled. Finally, on September 8, 1851, Morris and Clark submitted their account. The "Am^t. of sale of John Robinson's interest in Real Estate on West Cedar St" along with the amount of his "interest in personal property" yielded $719.74. Of this, $183.20 was paid out to cover the undertaker, the auctioneer, the appraisers, the newspaper for advertising, shop rent, taxes, and the commissioners Minot and Peabody. The administrators allowed themselves $50 for their services, thereby leaving $486.54 to satisfy the remainder of Robinson's creditors.

To understand the significance of this figure, it is necessary to retrace the paper trail of Robinson's probate records. His two real estate holdings were originally inventoried at $3000 less $2055.77 in mortgages and interest. By the time his estate was settled, mounting interest had increased the debt against his real estate to $2506.68, thereby reducing his equity from $944.23 to $493.32, if property values had remained constant. But, *if* property values had risen somewhat by the time his real estate was sold and *if* the wording "John Robinson's interest in Real Estate on West Cedar St" that appears in the first account actually referred to his equity in both the "brick house in Bridge Place & Land" and the "wooden[house] corner of Bridge Place & West Cedar St & land" recorded in his inventory, then the $569.32 figure represents his ultimate actual wealth in real estate--the price paid in June 1851 for the two properties by the buyer(s) (presumably more than the March 1850 $3000 appraisal) minus the full $2506.68 in mortgages and interest.

While this is better than $493.32 (the amount of his equity had property values not risen), $569.32 still falls short of Robinson's $944.23 equity at death. Moreover, his "interest in personal property"--appraised at $355.16 in March 1850--appears to have realized only $150.42 when sold. His ostensible estate of $1299.39 yielded $719.74 on the auction block, and--once $233.20 in selected debts (primarily funeral expenses and the costs of settling the estate) were paid--$486.54 remained to offset about a $1000 of claims. Thus, a man who had owned two houses with their land, who possessed a suite of mahogany furniture and business stock, died insolvent, with a net worth of negative $604.76.

Robinson's estate may be interpreted as embodying the paradigm of high debt accompanying high assets.[15] He clearly was considered credit-worthy, although it is difficult to imagine more than his strong standing in the community as a businessman that would have justified confidence in his ability to meet all his debts. No doubt his owning two houses and possessing fine furnishings lent his efforts to build up an estate legitimacy in the eyes of his creditors. Possibly, had he lived longer, the income from his business would not only have met his--and his heirs', Susan M. and Richard Robinson's--daily needs, but also would have retired the mortgages outstanding against his property and pulled him out of debt. But, upon close examination, Robinson's estate simply cannot escape the specter of financial overextension.

The estates of Cole, Robinson, and Scarlett therefore present three very different pictures when their probate records are studied to determine their actual versus inventoried wealth. Cole was in a position to assign bequests in household goods or cash, to satisfy his creditors, to cover his funeral expenses, and to pay for estate settlement costs, and still have some $400 left over. Scarlett's death necessitated his widow's invocation of her rights in order to retain his personal estate as well as the equity in one of his four pieces of real estate; Margaret Scarlett managed to shelter herself and their minor children from a worst reduction in material circumstances via the protection probate afforded widows, but most likely was left insufficient money to meet all claims against her husband's estate. And finally, the settling of Robinson's estate in essence precipitated the collapse of his fictive prosperity. The overall impression--no longer as rosy as the one conveyed by focusing exclusively on the decedents' household goods--now registers as startlingly tenuous. Scarlett's and Robinson's wealth--like Amy Jackson's--seems almost evanescent, erased by liabilities.

Perhaps, however, their wealth--while no longer signifying their own (or their heirs') financial advancement--may be viewed as community financial growth. In a paradoxical parallel to Cole, they may have--albeit through their debts and not their bequests--redistributed their wealth to the community. Cole's amassed assets went to several community organizations, as well as to his friends and a family member (transcription 1.1). Were Scarlett's and Robinson's creditors members of the black community, so that upon their death their wealth stayed within and thereby enriched the community? The crisscrossing pattern partially emerged from just such payments among decedents and/ or their friends: Scarlett was listed as a claimant for $20 against William S. Jinnings's estate, Cole's estate paid William Riley $8, and Robinson owed John T. Hilton $2. However, these hints at intracommunity financial dealings involve such minuscule sums that they support neither a notion of mutual exchange--"what goes round comes round"--nor a concept of overall communal rather than individual monetary advancement.

Scarlett's, Robinson's, and Amy Jackson's estates make clear that the big money was in mortgages. Who held the mortgages and thus not only regained their investment but also earned interest when the decedents' real estate was auctioned? In the case of Scarlett, according to the commissioners who assigned his widow her dower, the property at 9 South May Street was subject to two mortgages held by William Livermore Junior of Groton and the property at 11 South May Street was subject to a mortgage originally held by William Whiting but afterwards assigned to Samuel Sewall. In Robinson's case, the June 1850 list of debts specifies that Dr. Parkman and Ralph Haskins both held mortgages on his real estate. Finally, a March 1841 list of claims cites that Amy Jackson's estate owed Jonathan P. Hall $1856.44, which very likely constituted a mortgage with interest against her $2605 worth of real estate. In all these particular instances, those who held the mortgages and thereby controlled the financial power of the capital seem not to have been members of the black community.

The process of this multi-angled inquiry--a case study of one decedent, two sample investigations of the patterns of human interactions detectable in probate records, a model comparative analysis of the value and contents of the estates of associated decedents, an experimental exercise in mentally recreating historic material conditions, an exploratory examination of ostensible versus real wealth--has made abundantly clear how intricate a source even a single packet of probate records for one decedent can be when allowed to speak. Complications arise exponentially in accord with increasing the number of documents, but the evidence gleaned from the foregoing variegated inquisition can serve as a useful gauge for the worthiness of the conclusions that can be drawn from the larger pool of probate records for Boston's black community before the Civil War.

CHAPTER 5

AN IN-DEPTH INVESTIGATION

Broadening the pool of documents to include the probate records of all twenty-three 1840s decedents makes it possible to understand the world of the black population during this one decade more fully. The estates of Amy Jackson, Thomas Cole et al. thus now become pieces in a larger picture puzzle, which when assembled conveys a more complete image of the material environment typically experienced by Afro-Americans in antebellum Boston.

For two of the 1840s decedents, however, insufficient evidence has been preserved for the purposes of analysis. In the first instance, the only document in the probate record consists of a widow's petition for her dower rights. When John Brooks, a laborer, died intestate in 1843, he possessed real estate. Unfortunately, the description of the property--"a piece of land and tenement, situate in Westerly part of said Boston" on Cypress Street near Vine Street--states no value. In the second instance, the documents in the probate record only pertain to the administration of the estate. When Arthur Jones, a barber, died intestate in 1841, he was in debt. Unfortunately, although the barber William H. Ross--a creditor of Jones's estate--was officially appointed to conduct an inventory, the forms remain incomplete.

The probate records of twenty-one decedents thus lend themselves to analysis. With this modest sampling, it is possible to address the issue of occupation and its relationship to the amount and make-up of the estates. Often an individual decedent's specific occupation may be noted; however, a decedent can also be cited generically as a semi-skilled laborer if his occupation implies a certain amount of skill and/or stability (rigger, waiter) or as a businessman if his occupation connotes a degree of enterprise (hairdresser, clothier). A simple system of rank ordering the decedents in accord with the appraised values of each of the categories of wealth spotlights some patterns among the deceased while cloaking others.

When the total estates of the twenty-one decedents for whom sufficient evidence has been preserved are listed in rank order from poorest to wealthiest, the appraised values range from $28.01 to $9710.06. Only one clearcut point emerges from this exercise: other than for mariners, there is no easily-identified relationship between the total estate and the occupation of the decedent. Not only do two semi-skilled laborers (a teamster and a soapboiler) supercede businessmen (clothing dealers and hairdressers) in appraised wealth of total estate at skilled laborers (a teamster and a soapboiler) supercede businessmen (clothing dealers and hairdressers) in appraised wealth of total estate at death, but also different levels of wealth resist any straightforward association with specific occupations. In other words, while two semi-skilled laborers may rank twentieth and twenty-first, three others (a chimneysweep, a rigger, and a waiter) rank fourth, sixth, and eleventh in total estate. Two clothing traders do show up next to each other twice--thirteenth and fourteenth, as well as eighteenth and nineteenth in total estate--but for the most part occupations of conventionally high social standing are cheek-by-jowl with those of seemingly low status.

Yet in this veritable melee, three decedents quite obviously constitute a discrete unit. Their occupations, the circumstances of their deaths, and their low wealth level were similar. John Smith alias Freeman Smith, Calvin T. Hoyt alias Charles Williams, and John Brown were all mariners who died aboard ship in 1845, 1846, and 1847, respectively. Their captains reported their wages (and proceeds from sale of effects in the case of John Brown) to Phineas Blair, Public Administrator. While Brown's estate amounted to twice that of his fellow seamen (because of the aforementioned sale of his effects?) and even though the next wealthier estate amounts to less than $40 more than Brown's, these three mariners still form together a distinct social stratum--moreover, an echelon of society often lost to historical understanding by virtue of transience, poverty, and illiteracy.[1] Ship captains apparently kept account of and honored the earnings of a deceased crewmember; when there was no known next of kin, the sum was turned over to a public administrator. The irony is that, while these black seamen can thereby be included in understanding their community, the value of their estates was then "lost" in official bureaucracy, subjected to many years of administrative fees, until exhausted (in the cases of Smith and Hoyt) or substantially reduced, when it was paid into the coffers of the Treasurer of the Commonwealth of Massachusetts (in the case of Brown). Nonetheless, the total estates of John Brown, John/Freeman Smith, Calvin T. Hoyt/Charles Williams suggest that mariners traveled light, holding little or no property (real or personal), and that they were essentially worth no more than their current job's paycheck.

Rank ordering the real and personal estates of the twenty-one 1840s decedents, however, reveals immediately that it was much more common for blacks of all occupations in Boston to hold personal rather than real property. Eleven of the twenty-one in the sample possessed no real estate at death, while only one possessed no personal property. Somewhat less readily discernible is the fact that the ten decedents who held real estate are among the eleven who ranked the highest in total wealth--and in almost the same order of appraised value; Thomas Cole, conspicuous by his lack of real estate holdings (he was ranked seventeenth in value of total estate), tops the list for value of personal estate. Since the rank ordering of the decedents by appraised value of real estate parallels their rank ordering by appraised value of total estate, something of the same absence of an easily-identified relationship between this variable and specific occupations prevails.

But despite the impressive fact that almost 50 percent of these decedents owned real estate, it is important to note that some blacks in 1840s Boston were less likely than others to manage this socioeconomic foothold. All three mariners, two of the three women, two of the four laborers, and two of the five semi-skilled laborers held no real estate at death. Thus, while two businessmen also died without possessing real estate, Thomas Cole was markedly and William Jinnings was somewhat more prosperous than the other nine decedents without real estate, ranking seventeenth and eighth in appraised value of their total estates.

For the most part, then, semi-skilled laborers and businessmen predominated in possessing real estate at death, but the former's holdings vary from the low of $243 to the high of $9567.20, while the latter's holdings climb from a low of $700 to a high of $5500--and a laborer appears right in their midst with $2019.29 in real estate at death.

This same laborer, John Lewis Brent alias John Lewis who pops up sixteenth in appraised value of real estate, turns up as the sole decedent holding no personal estate at death. Two businessmen (a gentleman/clothing dealer and a hairdresser) rank twentieth and twenty-first, but businessmen are also to be found in the second, eighth, twelfth, thirteenth, and fifteenth positions. Semi-skilled laborers are likewise scattered--seventh, ninth, eleventh, sixteenth, and eighteenth. Women rank third, tenth, and nineteenth in appraised value of personal estate at death. Again, only mariners constitute a discrete unit in which occupation can be associated with specific assets at death. Fourth, fifth, and sixth in rank order of personal estate, John/Freeman Smith, Calvin T. Hoyt/Charles Williams, and John Brown exceeded the holdings of a laborer, a hair renovator, and a widow; however, John Lewis Brent alias John Lewis, James Howe, and Amy Jackson possessed real estate which raised them substantially above the mariners in value of total estate at death.

Can occupation be associated with assets in the three different divisions of personal estate--business stock; cash, notes, and savings; and household goods? From the preceding discussion, it would seem likely that mariners will hold neither business stock nor household goods. But women would seem very likely candidates to die with household goods and without business stock. By the same token, it would not be untoward to expect businessmen to possess business stock as well as cash, notes, and savings, while semi-skilled laborers might need to own the tools of their trade. Excepting the mariners, it would be reasonable to assume that everyone would possess the wherewithal of domestic life.

A minority of decedents, in fact, owned business stock at death, and--as expected--those who did were businessmen or semi-skilled laborers. Nonetheless, three semi-skilled laborers and a businessman figure among those without any business stock at death. One of the semi-skilled laborers, however, was John W. Brown, a waiter, whose occupation does not require work implements. The lack of the tools of their trade is less easily explained for the estates of Charles Biner, teamster, and Peter Williams, rigger, both of whom would seem to have needed some equipment. None of the three women nor the three laborers--like the mariners--held indisputable business stock at their deaths. Clothiers ranked seventeenth, nineteenth, twentieth, and twenty-first, outnumbering and/or outranking both the two semi-skilled laborers and the two hairdressers among the eight decedents with business stock in their personal estates.

Fourteen decedents, on the other hand, had cash, notes, and savings at death. Indeed, Thomas Cole's rank as seventeenth in appraised value of total estate rests primarily upon his holdings in savings and cash, which place him twenty-first in cash, notes, and savings at death. James H. Howe (the other hairdresser for whom sufficient documentation has been preserved) died with no liquid assets. Other businessmen fared erratically when accruing money: John Robinson, like James H. Howe, had no cash, notes, and savings, while John E. Scarlett and Peter Gray book-end the three mariners, as eighth and twelfth in liquid assets. Laborers rank fifteenth and eighteenth; semi-skilled laborers fourteenth, sixteenth, and seventeenth; women thirteenth and nineteenth. But decedents filling these occupations also died without any money, most notably Primus Hall, the twenty-first ranked in appraised value of total estate, the bulk of which consisted of real estate holdings.

The mariners--whose total estates equaled their personal estates, which in turn simply consisted of cash--cannot be understood deliberately to have accumulated the sums that constituted their wealth at death. For the other eleven decedents, a degree of conscious choice can hesitantly be assumed. Were decedents with certain occupations more given to depositing savings in the bank, lending money, or keeping cash reserves? Businessmen had money on hand in varying amounts--from Peter Gray's $15.00 to William Riley's $180.00; otherwise, the only other decedent to have cash at death was a widow. Moreover, Chloe Russell inherited the sum that constituted--like the mariners--her total estate. Decedents for whom notes represented a portion of their personal estate represent three occupations: a businessman, a single woman, and two semi-skilled laborers. For one laborer, Joseph Sprague, the note mentioned in his probate records comprised his total estate. Conversely, two businessmen, the singlewoman, two semi-skilled laborers, and a laborer died with savings on deposit in banks. In no instance did savings represent the sole category of wealth at death, although bank deposits did predominate in three estates--those of Thomas Cole, hairdresser; Edward Lawson, laborer; and Peter Williams, rigger.

The routine assumption that, barring mariners, most 1840s black Bostonians--and especially women--would possess household goods at death must be reexamined in light of findings that show otherwise. A businessman, a widow, and two laborers--according to the inventories of their estates--owned no household goods. Other decedents with those occupations were recorded, of course, to have furniture, clothing, pots and pans, clocks, etc. Businessmen (ranked twentieth and twenty-first, as well as seventh, ninth, thirteenth, fifteenth, and eighteenth) constitute seven of the fifteen decedents with household goods; semi-skilled laborers (ranked eighth, twelfth, fourteenth, seventeenth, and nineteenth) follow closely by comprising five of the fifteen decedents with household goods. The remaining three consist of two women (ranked tenth and eleventh) and one laborer (ranked sixteenth).

Is the lack of household goods to be credited? Like the proposed reasons for lack of probate,[2] explanations of the absence of certain items in inventories are numerous and sensible.[3] How plausible are any of these explanations in relation to the three 1840s decedents, other than mariners, without household goods? Moreover, is it certain that all three died without owning any of the stuff of everyday life? Each deserves attention.

It seems, at first reading, that the documentary evidence for lack of household goods is straightforward in all three cases. The inventory of the estate of John Lewis Brent, alias John Lewis, laborer, states unequivocally that he died with no personal estate. The declaration of the contents of the cook/widow Chloe Russell's estate by her son, Edward Labbottiere, certifies that she died only possessing cash. The crossed-out references to "the value of personal estate" in the administrative account pertaining to the estate of Joseph Sprague, laborer, indicate that personal property did not contribute to his wealth at death.

Thus, for all three decedents, the supposition of no household goods would seem indisputable. But a closer reading of the probate records makes it possible either to detect or to infer the ownership of the stuff of everyday life, even when unrecorded in inventories purporting to catalogue completely the deceased's "real estate, goods, chattels, rights, and credits," the usual charge to the appraisers.

To take the last instance first, Joseph Sprague, laborer, died intestate in May 1841. A thorough review of the administrator Timothy B. Wood's first account, filed in August 1842, permits the following reconstruction of events:

1. Joseph Sprague held a $600 "note, secured by Mortgage," against Jonas W. Clark.
2. Sprague and his wife died, leaving two minor children, Lucy H. and Joseph A. Sprague.
3. The administrator Wood received the $600 that Sprague had lent to Clark.
4. Wood paid $98.25 in funeral and administrative costs and then turned the balance of $501.75 over to Clark, guardian of the two Sprague children.

According to this reconstruction, Joseph Sprague exhibits the characteristics of a family man of some substance, rather than the attributes of a single laborer who happened to die with someone owing him $600. Since Sprague had the financial reserves to lend money, it is highly unlikely that his family's domestic environment was totally barren. The notation of "no Inventory having been returned to Court" leads to the speculation that the purpose of probate in this instance was to regularize Jonas Clark's dual roles--as Sprague's debtor and as Sprague's children's guardian. Once the funeral and administrative costs were paid out of the $600 that Clark owed Sprague, Clark--as guardian of Sprague's daughter and son--received on behalf of his wards the balance of what he had previously borrowed on his own behalf. The listing of the decedent's personal estate apparently was considered of secondary importance; it seems reasonable to surmise, however, that Joseph Sprague did own household goods at death, although their kind and value must remain indeterminate.

In the case of Chloe Russell, cook/widow, who died testate in March 1841, the information in the inventory of her estate directly contradicts the language to be found in her will. Edward Labbottiere, her son and executor, certified that her estate consisted of the "sum of One hundred and fiftysix dollars and that no other goods or estate belonging to her said estate have come to my knowledge or possession". But Chloe Russell had bequeathed half her clothing to each of her two daughters in her will dated October 12, 1840. The fact that her wearing apparel constituted legacies may account for its not being cited as part of her estate;[4] in other words, Chloe Russell owned household goods in the form of clothing, but since she had designated her daughters as the recipients of her garments, her son was under no obligation to list them as part of her estate. It is somewhat more curious, however, that there is no mention of Labbottiere's honoring his mother's bequest of $5.00 each to her two daughters in his administrative account. Chloe Russell most certainly died possessing more than $156 cash, but the precise value of her wearing apparel cannot be determined.

As for John Lewis Brent alias John Lewis, laborer, who died intestate and with no known heirs in 1844, the discrepancy between his sizable real estate holdings and his lack of personal estate is striking. How could someone who had acquired around $2000 in real estate equity die without owning a single item of personal estate? As with the Joseph Sprague estate, a full accounting of all the deceased's possessions may have been a secondary consideration. A $950 mortgage on Centre Street and a $330 mortgage on No. 2 Grove Street, together with debts of $373.87, needed to be settled. Regardless of whatever assets in personal estate John Lewis Brent may have held at death, evidently liquidation of his real estate holdings was deemed necessary to produce the $1654.58 required to retire his mortgages and to satisfy his creditors. Accordingly on March 8, 1845, the two pieces of real estate were auctioned and a long paper trail of administrative accounts from June 1845 to October 1851 traces the official management of the estate and subsequent transferral of the remaining $593.87 to the Treasurer of the Commonwealth of Massachusetts. John Lewis Brent alias John Lewis no doubt owned household goods, but--in view of his wealth in real estate--legal documentation by-passed his personal estate, thereby leaving its nature and worth impossible to determine.

Thus for the three decedents whose inventories showed no household goods, strong arguments can be made for believing that they nonetheless owned the stuff of everyday life. Inventories of some estates focused on whatever must have been regarded as the decedents' most valuable asset--a note, inherited cash, or real estate. Such personages might die insolvent, unable to meet all just debts without sale of property, but they were unlikely candidates to have died devoid of the normal material accessories of daily life.

Perhaps, more boldly, it can be asserted that even the mariners--seemingly worth only their current paychecks--probably died owning personal property apart from cash. The clue lies in Phineas Blair's certification of having received from John Brown's captain a sum representing not only the balance of the deceased's wages but also the proceeds from the sale of his effects. While no such reference to "effects" occurs in the otherwise comparable documents about the estates of John/Freeman Smith and Calvin T. Hoyt/ Charles Williams, the fact that one mariner had marketable possessions--no doubt bought by his shipmates--suggests that seamen should not automatically be classed among the totally dispossessed. As with the unmentioned household goods of the cook/widow and the two laborers, the particulars of the mariner's effects--a trunk? a knife? a watch?--simply cannot be determined. Despite this uncertainty about the precise make-up and the appraised value of household goods for the six decedents for whom household goods are not specifically itemized, no longer can any occupation be associated absolutely with absence of domestic and personal possessions.

Occupation And Assets

In fact, examination of the relationship between an occupation and the proportion of a decedent's estate tied to different assets shows that there is little uniformity, except for the mariners, among the decedents with the same livelihood--accepting, of course, the figures from the inventories as accurate reflections of the deceased's actual possessions. Real estate comprised 90 to 100 percent of the total estate of one laborer, two semi-skilled laborers, three businessmen, and one woman. Personal estate, on the other hand, constituted the full 100 percent of the total estate of the three mariners, two of the three laborers for whom there is documentation, two of five semi-skilled laborers, two of the seven businessmen for whom there is documentation, and two of three women. Business stock, representing 1 to 10 percent of total estate, appears in the inventories of one semi-skilled laborer and four businessmen, but also represents 95 percent of the inventoried property of one businessman. Cash, notes, and savings as 100 percent of the recorded estate can be associated with the three mariners, one laborer, and one woman. Similarly, a businessman and a woman died with 94 and 99 percent, respectvely, of their assets in cash, notes, and savings, while a laborer and two semi-skilled laborers had between two-thirds and four-fifths of their total estate in money. Conversely, only one decedent--a semi-skilled laborer--had 90 percent of his estate tied up in household goods; one laborer, one semi-skilled laborer, and one businessman had household goods approximating one-fifth of their es-

An In-Depth Investigation 107

tate's value, although for four businessmen household goods represented only 5 percent of their total estate.

Consumer durables, then, for the most part comprised a minor portion of the total estates of the twenty-one 1840s decedents from Boston's Afro-American population, no matter what their occupation. Nonetheless, juxtaposing the three least and the three most wealthy who died with household goods listed in their inventories leads to a contrasting understanding of the material life of antebellum black Bostonians. As overall wealth rises, the proportion of expenditure on household goods falls. If the first observation seems to suggest that the vast majority of the decedents achieved or chose a similarly low level of consumption to meet their domestic needs and desires, the second finding appears to demonstrate that the wealthier of the deceased were not required to devote so large a portion of their assets to acquiring the stuff of everyday life. But the numbers may tell an incomplete story. To take the two most extreme cases, only looking at the actual contents of their inventories can provide the opportunity for discerning if the personal possessions of the chimneysweep Henry Robinson, whose $87.01 1/2 worth of household goods represented 90 percent of his total estate's value of $96.96, corresponded to those of the soapboiler Primus Hall, whose $72.74 worth of household goods represented 0.7 percent of his total estate's value of $9710.06.

As it happens, the estates of Henry Robinson and Primus Hall qualify for this variety of analysis, since their inventories figure among the eleven in which household goods appear and are itemized. As noted previously, of the pool of probate records for Boston's black community in the 1840s, the documentation for one decedent (Arthur Jones, barber) was left incomplete while that for another (John Brooks, laborer) remains unclear. Also, as has been detailed above, the inventories of six other decedents (the three mariners, John Brown, John/Freeman Smith, and Calvin T. Hoyt/Charles Williams; as well as two laborers, John Lewis Brent alias John Lewis, and Joseph Sprague; and the cook/widow Chloe Russell) include no household goods, even if their actual absence is arguable.

To these eight decedents must be added four more for whom the documentation does contain references to household goods but the citations are unfortunately insufficiently differentiated for the purposes of analysis. In the inventory of the estate of Charles Biner, teamster, "Household furniture, Plate, Pictures, Wearing apparel of dec^d, Fuel & Sundries" all were assigned the lumpsum value of $170.00. In the personal estate of Peter Gray, trader, his "Silver Lever Watch" and his "Wearing Apparel" are appraised individually, but his "Household

Furniture" received but one overall valuation of $235.00. The trader William Riley's inventory shows a generalized citation of "Household furniture," in his case worth $56.00. And, finally, the personal estate of Lucinda Smith, singlewoman, included a "Trunk and Clothing" appraised at $15.00, with the trunk and the garments treated as one item.

Therefore, of the twenty-three 1840s decedents, twelve estates must be excluded from attempts to recapture accurately but imaginatively the domestic environment experienced by diverse members of Boston's antebellum black community. While the eleven inventories that lend themselves to analysis into the three categories of necessities, amenities, and luxuries, as well as to generic sets within those categories of comfort, do include the estates of the criss-crossing decedents (Thomas Cole, John Robinson, and John E. Scarlett), their household goods can now be seen in the broader context of the personal possessions of fellow community members of different occupations, wealth, and even gender. Did any of these differences signify in ownership of types of household goods?

Selected 1840s Decedents' Household Goods

Rank ordering the decedents by the appraised value of their holdings of necessities, amenities, and luxuries indicates remarkably consistent positioning based on the sum of money each expended in the three categories of comfort, despite sizable differences in the monetary worth of the eleven decedents' necessities, amenities, and luxuries (lists 1.1-11.3). Expenditures for necessities varied from James Howe's $.81 to Edward Lawson's $67.75, amenities differed from John W. Brown's and William S. Jinnings's zero dollars to John Robinson's $35.50, and luxuries soared from John W. Brown's, William S. Jinnings's and Peter Williams' zero dollars to John Robinson's $162.00. Not only did the appraised values of luxuries differ quite dramatically from least to most, but also marked leaps occur between eighth-ranked John Scarlett's $14.00 and ninth-ranked Henry Robinson's $51.06, as well as between tenth-ranked Thomas Cole's $66.93 and top-ranked John Robinson's $162.00. The progression from least to most is considerably more gradual in the categories of necessities and amenities, where increments of $5.00 to $10.00 are the norm. Such a smooth ascent suggests that there was not a radical gulf between the haves and have-nots in their holdings at death of necessities and amenities.

Yet, despite this hint at equity among the decedents when considering their ownership of domestic basics and comforts, the preponderance of the eleven occupy either the same or very nearly the same position in two or three of the rank-orderings. Three of the decedents--John W. Brown, Thomas Cole, and John Scarlett--twice rank in the same position and then, in the third ordering, rank but one position higher or lower. Another decedent, James H. Howe, ranks first, third, and fourth in the three categories. And three other decedents--Primus Hall, Henry Robinson, and John Robinson--twice rank in the same position and then, in the third ordering, rank three positions higher or lower. In other words, for only two decedents--Edward Lawson and Peter Williams--does the ranking bolt about with differences of seven or eight positions, and even in their cases, two of the rankings are within two positions higher or lower.

Therefore, for the most part, the 1840s decedents maintained stable positions vis-à-vis one another in their holdings of all categories of personal possessions. Those who ranked low in one category tended to rank low in all three and vice versa, and those in middling positions can be found across the board in that range. Of course, the two ringers disrupt this tidy summary, particularly since the rankings for Edward Lawson and Peter Williams put each of them in top or second positions in one category yet at the rock bottom or near bottom in another. Moreover, these two decedents' rankings proceed roughly inversely: Lawson starts at the top in necessities, drops to the low middle in amenities, and then rises to the middle in luxuries, while Williams starts at the low middle in necessities, rises to the near top in amenities, and drops to the bottom in luxuries.

Such incongruities also intrigue when an attempt is made to correlate rankings of the eleven 1840s decedents in value of total estate and value of household goods with rankings in value of their necessities, amenities, and luxuries. Only with John Scarlett does there seem to be a direct correlation between a rank of eighth in total estate and rankings of seventh, eighth, and eighth in the three categories of comfort. Somewhat close are tenth-ranked Thomas Cole in total estate, who ranks ninth, ninth, and tenth in necessities, amenities, and luxuries, and top-ranked Primus Hall in total estate, who ranks tenth, seventh, and seventh in the three types of household goods. Henry Robinson, the lowest ranked of the decedents in value of total estate, holds the rankings of sixth, sixth, and ninth in necessities, amenities, and luxuries. And then come the two ringers, Peter Williams and Edward Lawson, who rank second and third respectively in total estate, yet the former ranks tenth in amenities and the latter ranks eleventh in necessities. Finally, John W. Brown, the sixth-ranked decedent in value of total estate, bottoms out as second to lowest in necessities, with no amenities or luxuries. William S. Jinnings, who also possessed no amenities or luxuries, at least ranked fifth in necessities. In short, there appears to be some degree of correlation between total estate and the three kinds of household goods only among the wealthier decedents; of the four highest ranking, three--John Scarlett, Thomas Cole, and Primus Hall--evidence a measure of connection between their ranking in overall wealth and their rankings in necessities, amenities, and luxuries.

Conversely, there is some degree of correlation between value of household goods and value of necessities, amenities, and luxuries at the bottom, the middle, and the top of the spectrum when the eleven 1840s decedents are rank ordered by value of household goods. James H. Howe and John W. Brown--two decedents with the lowest dollar amounts of household goods--also rank low in the value of the three types of personal possessions; in fact, their rankings of first and second in household goods directly correspond with their first and second rankings in necessities. At the top of the spectrum, eleventh-ranked John Robinson ranks eleventh in both amenities and luxuries; tenth-ranked Thomas Cole ranks ninth in both necessities and amenities; and, then, seventh-ranked John Scarlett ranks seventh, eighth, and eighth in necessities, amenities, and luxuries. If a correlation between value of household goods and worth of the three categories of comfort seems to belabor the obvious, then discrepancies would not occur between the rankings of four decedents--Peter Williams, Primus Hall, Edward Lawson, and Henry Robinson in household goods and their rankings in one or more of the types of personal possessions. Hall, sixth-ranked in household goods, may be seventh-ranked in amenities and luxuries, but he is also tenth-ranked in necessities. Similarly, Henry Robinson, ninth-ranked household goods, does rank ninth in luxuries, but he also ranks sixth in both necessities and amenities. Then fifth-ranked Peter Williams combines a fourth-ranking in necessities, a tenth-ranking in amenities, and a third-ranking in luxuries, while Edward Lawson, eighth in household goods, ranks eleventh, fourth, and sixth in necessities, amenities, and luxuries. And, of course, William S. Jinnings, third-ranked in value of household goods, ranks fifth in necessities and second in amenities and necessities. Thus, the critical factor in these instances of discrepancy between rankings in value of household goods and rankings in worth of the three categories of comfort seems to be uneven expenditure among the three categories. When rankings in necessities, amenities, and luxuries show differences of three or more (even if one of these rankings, as in the case of Henry Robinson, correlates directly with the decedent's overall ranking in value of household goods), the skewing appears to "misposition" the decedent in regard to dollar worth of

An In-Depth Investigation

personal possessions. In other words, the distribution of the decedents' holdings in the categories of comfort provides a more subtle gauge of their material life vis-à-vis one another than the lumpsum value of their household goods; Edward Lawson may rank eighth in dollar amount of household goods at death, but his $80.00 included more assets in necessities than did eleventh-ranked John Robinson's $237.16 of household goods.

Can the distribution of holdings in necessities, amenities, and luxuries be associated with occupation? While this modest sample of the Afro-American population in Boston before the Civil War does not permit large-scale pronouncements, tentative conclusions can be proposed. The eleven 1840s decedents, when classified according to their occupation, consist of one laborer and one woman, four semi-skilled laborers and five businessmen. Of the two occupation types in which comparison is possible, the rankings of holdings in the three categories of comfort ricochet up and down the scale, but the businessmen do present a slightly stronger picture. First, they rank higher (six and above) more often than the semi-skilled laborers, and, second, a decedent's high rank in one category of household goods is consistent with his ranking in the other two categories. For semi-skilled laborers, the exceptionally high ranking--in necessities for Primus Hall, in amenities for Peter Williams, or in luxuries for Henry Robinson--appears to be a fluke, whereas for businessmen, the low rankings in necessities, amenities, and luxuries for James H. Howe and William S. Jinnings--appear to make *them* the fluke. Edward Lawson, the sole laborer, seems to fit the model of the semi-skilled laborer for whom a ranking in a particular category of household goods appears disproportionate, while the widow Amy Jackson more closely adheres to the model of the businessmen for whom rankings are usually consistent across the board. However, only one of the four semi-skilled laborers had the edge on Edward Lawson, while Amy Jackson was considerably outranked by three of the five businessmen. In short, conforming to the model for another occupation type did not necessarily mean parity in overall wealth.

An examination of both the proportion of total estate and the proportion of household goods devoted to necessities, amenities, and luxuries adds another dimension to the businessman's position of superiority. If only the dollar amounts are considered businessmen did not always own at death household goods of greater value than decedents in other occupations. But when their proportions of total estate and household goods are contrasted with those of decedents in the other occupations, it becomes evident that businessmen had relatively small percentages of their assets tied up in consumer durables. The clothes dealer John Robinson's 12 percent of total estate (68 percent of household goods) represented by luxuries is far exceeded by the chimneysweep Henry Robinson's 53 percent of total estate (59 percent of household goods) represented by the same category. Not all the decedents of other occupations, however, had large portions of their total estates comprised of household goods; the widow Amy Jackson and two semi-skilled laborers, John W. Brown and Primus Hall, died with each category of comfort consisting of less than 1 percent of their total estate. But the three of them, like the businessmen James H. Howe and William S. Jinnings had inordinately low proportions of their total estates in household goods because the appraised value of their personal possessions was considerably less than the appraised value of the other property that constituted their total estates. They simply did not own much in the way of household goods. The decedents in the most attractive situation, then, would be the three businessmen for whom the appraised value of household goods represented moderate portions of their total estates yet whose holdings in necessities, amenities, and luxuries provided the full complement of basics, comforts, and refinements.

Thus far the evidence suggests that businessmen in antebellum Boston's black community enjoyed advantaged material conditions in their everyday life. Suppose the three categories of household goods were considered in more detail, would a more nuanced understanding emerge? Dividing the eleven 1840s decedents' holdings of necessities, amenities, and luxuries into sets that refer more specifically--albeit still generically--to their actual possessions encourages a correspondingly more concrete sense of the individual decedent's domestic environment. Looking briefly at the generic sets within each category reveals a good deal of variation. Plain furnishings appears in all but one inventory; there are two or more decedents who owned nothing in every other generic set. Fewer decedents (two) owned cleaning apparatus than literacy belongings (seven). Four had no beds or bedding but seven had decorative items; two of the seven decedents with decorative items were among the four without beds or bedding. Plain furnishings represented from 69 percent--James Howe's $.56--to 1 percent--Henry Robinson's $.33--of a decedent's holdings in necessities, although the appraised values ranged from Primus Hall's $8.95 to Henry Robinson's $.33. Literacy belongings constituted from 92 percent--Primus Hall's $3.50--to 0.6 percent--John Robinson's $1.00--of a decedent's holdings in luxuries, although the appraised values ranged from Thomas Cole's $30.25 to James Howe's and Amy Jackson's $.50. Peter Williams died with $16.00 worth of feather bedding, 52 percent of his amenities, while Amy Jackson's $4.00 worth of feather bedding constituted 37 percent of her amenities. Decorative items, appraised at $46.12 1/2, comprised 90 percent of Henry Robinson's luxuries, while Thomas Cole owned $1.68 in decorative items, comprising 3 percent of his luxuries.

When the eleven 1840s decedents are classified according to their occupations, an interesting overall pattern can be detected. In the category of necessities, decedents of different occupations may match--whether in high or low sums--the other decedents in a given generic set. For instance, both Edward Lawson, a laborer, and Primus Hall, a semi-skilled laborer, lead the other decedents in virtually equal amounts of bed and bedding, whereas Amy Jackson, a widow, and Peter Williams, a semi-skilled laborer, have similar respectable amounts of plain furnishings. Individual businessmen can show in several generic sets--heating and cooking fixtures, kitchenware, and apparel--the highest monetary value, but also can show no holdings in those same generic sets, thereby being equaled or surpassed by decedents of other occupations. In other words, among decedents of the two occupation types for which comparison is possible, as well as among decedents of different occupation types, the discerned diversity in the generic sets of necessities cannot readily be associated with occupation.

In the category of amenities, however, a shift away from this scattershot pattern can be perceived. Now conjunction among decedents most often happens between the semi-skilled laborers and the businessmen. For instance, Thomas Cole, a businessman, and Peter Williams, a semi-skilled laborer, each have about the same amount of feather bedding; Thomas Cole and Primus Hall each died owning about the same monetary value of mirrors. Edward Lawson, laborer, and Amy Jackson, widow, however, do exactly match the other decedents on occasion (mirrors for the former, linens and curtains for the latter), just as decedents with no holdings in a particular generic set may be a laborer, three semi-skilled laborers, and three businessman (feather bedding) or three semi-skilled laborers, three businessman, and a widow (floor coverings) or representatives from all four occupation types (time-pieces). The semi-skilled laborers and businessmen seem to converge the most frequently and--except for floor coverings--at higher levels of value than the other two occupation types, but businessmen usually appear to have been more likely to possess given amenities, even if the dollar worth may be less than a particular semi-skilled laborer's feather bedding or another's timepiece. Two businessmen owned feather bedding, only one semi-skilled laborer owned any; four businessmen had specialized furnishings, only three semi-skilled laborers had any;

two businessmen possessed floor coverings, only one semi-skilled laborer possessed any; three businessmen died with mirrors, only two semi-skilled laborers died with any; three businessmen had timepieces, only two semi-skilled laborers had any. Businessmen can therefore be increasingly associated with a lifestyle that was comfortably functional.

Businessmen again usually were more likely to possess given luxuries, even when the dollar amount may be less than the appraised value of a laborer's and a semi-skilled laborer's decorative items or that of two semi-skilled laborer's literacy belongings. Again, two businessmen owned fine furnishings, only one semi-skilled laborer owned any; three businessmen had china and silver, no semi-skilled laborers had any; two businessmen possessed jewelry and clocks, only one semi-skilled laborer owned any; four of the five businessmen died with both literacy belonging and decorative items, only two semi-skilled laborers died with any of each; two businessmen had musical instruments, only one semi-skilled laborer had any. The laborer and the widow were not without a couple of luxuries--china and silver as well as decorative items for the former; china and silver as well as literacy belongings for the latter--which placed them ahead of two semi-skilled laborers and one business man (none of whom had luxuries) and equal to one semi-skilled laborer and one businessman (both of whom had literacy belongings and decorative items). The propensity to acquire possessions related to literacy and/or objects suited for decoration cut across all occupation types, but businessmen were at the forefront in frequency, if not always the dollar amount. In fact, with the odd exception of the semi-skilled laborer Henry Robinson's large holdings of decorative items, a businessman usually was more likely to own luxuries than decedents in other occupations and these luxuries were more likely to be of greater monetary value than those of decedents with different occupations. Therefore, in gradual progression--from necessities to amenities to luxuries--businessmen generally consolidated their advantaged position.

Their preferable condition receives further confirmation from looking at the proportions represented by the various generic sets within the three categories of comfort. In necessities, for instance, plain furnishings can correspond with 1 to 29 percent for semi-skilled laborers and with 2 to 69 percent for businessmen, with 5 percent for the laborer and 33 percent for the widow among the eleven decedents. The 1 percent translates into $.33 and the 29 percent into $2.00; the 2 percent into $1.00 and the 69 percent into $.56; the 5 percent into $3.25 and the 33 percent into $3.70. In other words, a small range of money may translate into a broad range of proportions referring to generic sets within the category of necessities. The correspondence between the dollar value of the generic set and its associated proportion becomes clearer within amenities for businessmen and semi-skilled laborers. For example, in mirrors 20 percent refers to $7.00 and 2 percent refers to $.50. But, again, the correspondence is sporadic, since $2.00 in mirrors for a businessman can represent 7 percent of his amenities, while $2.10 in mirrors for a semi-skilled laborer can represent 13 percent of his amenities. Nonetheless, businessmen have only one instance of marked contrast between the dollar value of the generic set and its corresponding percentage of his amenities--James Howe's 89 percent of specialized furnishings which translates into $2.00 But two semi-skilled laborers, Primus Hall (with 65 percent representing specialized furnishings worth $10.77) and Henry Robinson (with 94 percent representing a timepiece worth $12.00), show parallel--although less inflated--discrepancies. In short, a small range of money does not translate into as broad a range of proportions in amenities as in necessities.

In luxuries, businessmen are least likely of the decedents to display percentages that contrast markedly with the dollar value of the particular generic set, although it happens when $.50 corresponds to 50 percent of James H. Howe's luxuries for both his literacy belongings and his decorative items, while $.50 can represent 4 percent, in the case of John Scarlett's decorative items. The decedents of the other three occupation types who owned luxuries either split them between two generic sets (the laborer Edward Lawson's 80 percent holdings in china and silver and 20 percent holdings in decorative items) and/or possessed disproportionate amount of one generic set (the semi-skilled laborer Henry Robinson's 90 percent holdings in decorative items, 0.9 percent of fine furnishings, 5 percent of jewelry and clocks, 4 percent of literacy belongings, and 0.1 percent of musical instruments). Only in one generic set, and with one occupation type, is there any consistency in proportion of luxuries (and, in fact, consistency in proportion of any of the generic sets of the three categories of household goods): literacy belongings and businessmen. While the dollar amounts diverge emphatically, the percentages converge--45.2 percent for Thomas Cole and 50 percent for both James H. Howe and John Scarlett. Of the two semi-skilled laborers who owned books and desks, etc., Primus Hall far exceeded the businessmen in the proportion of his luxuries given over to literacy belongings, but his peer who died with possessions related to literacy only had 4 percent of his luxuries given over to paraphernalia used for reading or writing.

In the final analysis, businessmen for the most part again seemed to improve their lot in relation to the other decedents as the focus proceeds from necessities, to amenities, to luxuries. The obvious explanation, of course, lies in the fact that, while two of the five businessmen start and stay behind the other 1840s decedents, the laborer and the woman ultimately fall behind, and two of the four semi-skilled laborers drop out completely when the three categories of household goods are divided into generic sets.

Selected 1840s Decedents' Domestic Environments

Returning to the question raised earlier on, and moving from the generic to the specific, what of the actual contents of the inventories of the eleven 1840s decedents? Can differences be discerned in the style of life achieved or chosen by this small sample that can be associated with occupation? The five businessmen include the three criss-crossing decedents--Thomas Cole, hairdresser, John Robinson, clothing trader, and John Scarlett, clothesdealer--whose household goods have been closely examined for their similarities and dissimilarities (lists 2.1-2.3, 9.1-9.3, and 10.1-10.3). A mental image of their domestic environment was gradually constructed from the array of the particular possessions that comprised the generic sets in each category of comfort:

- Necessities--one to three beds, a table or two, a slew of chairs or none, numerous or no storage units, several simple sources of lighting or none, one or more or no fixtures related to heating and cooking, and some items associated with food preparation and/or consumption.
- Amenities--mirrors and specialized furnishings (particularly seating, but also tables intended for different uses, storage units worthy of the designation bureau, as well as an odd assortment of possessions that were meant to serve specific purposes), along with nondescript carpeting, some linens and maybe curtains or feather bedding and a timepiece.
- Luxuries--pictures or prints, a china tea service or silver spoons, perhaps some furniture that indicates socializing or sophistication or a timekeeping device that transcends the practical, along with musical instruments and the tangible paraphernalia of literacy.

William S. Jinnings, owning only wearing apparel at death, quite clearly did not conform to the lifestyle of his peers. But James H. Howe does not radically disrupt this configuration of material life. Of necessities, he owned several chairs, a fixture related to heating or cooking, and a couple of simple lighting sources; of amenities, he possessed a storage unit worthy of the name bureau, specialized seating, and a plain timepiece; of luxuries, he died with a tangible indication of literacy and one picture (lists 4.1-4.3). Perhaps the major difference between the nature of Howe's household goods and the characterization of the other three businessmen's domestic environment lies in the lack of any comfort other than that implied by the sofa; all the personal possessions in his inventory convey a sense of the durable and the spartan, regardless of their categorization as necessity, amenity, or luxury. James Howe's limited repertory of household goods thus principally deviates from that of his fellow businessmen by virtue of austerity; conceptually, he conforms to the model.

The four semi-skilled laborers--John W. Brown, waiter, Primus Hall, soapboiler, Henry Robinson, chimneysweep, and Peter Williams, rigger--present a less coherent model from which to develop the sense of a common setting for their daily life. Moreover, one decedent had no luxuries, while one had neither luxuries nor amenities, thereby both exaggerating and diminishing the significance of the luxuries--and to a lesser degree, of the amenities--that were owned at death by semi-skilled laborers (lists 1.1-1.3, 3.1-3.3, 8.1-8.3, and 11.1-11.3). Regardless, Henry Robinson's household goods would be likely to generate incongruities no matter to which occupation type he were to be assigned. How he--a chimneysweep by trade--came to own such a marvelous cacophony of *objects* stimulates conjecture (especially given the large assortment of clothing that figures among his necessities) that Robinson conceivably "rescued" cast-off apparel and saved exotica that he found in the course of his work. His peculiar luxuries (sea shells, a statue, swords, a hubble bubble) suggest either a cabinet of curiosities that may have served primarily for amusement or--along with the often unusual apparel (military garments, bonnets, epaulettes)--a junkshop that may have provided a second source of income.

A mental image of the domestic environment can nonetheless be formulated, however imperfectly, through a compilation of the particular possessions that constitute the generic sets in each category of comfort for semi-skilled laborers:

- Necessities--up to four or no beds and tables, over two dozen chairs or none, three or more storage units or none, usually no lighting source, possible fixtures and/or items related to heating or cooking, and clothing.

- Amenities--two or no mirrors, occasionally specialized furnishings (bureaus, tables for different uses, and seating of various kinds), and maybe curtains or feather bedding or carpeting or a timepiece.
- Luxuries--numerous decorative items and the tangible paraphernalia of literacy, possibly along with musical instruments.

On the whole, the semi-skilled laborers appear to have lived leaner than businessmen when acquiring the attributes--both symbolic and real--of conspicuous consumption: china and silver, musical instruments, fine furnishings, or jewelry and clocks that transcended the practical.

What is interesting to note is that Edward Lawson, the laborer, and Amy Jackson, the widow, seem to resemble one another when their domestic environments are envisioned (lists 5.1-5.3 and 7.1-7.3). Amy Jackson had the wherewithal to live in relative comfort--all the plain furnishings necessary for the conduct of daily life (bed, tables, chairs, chest), the basic equipment requisite for heating, cooking, eating, and cleaning, as well as clothing; the important measures of comfort to be had in a mirror, feather bedding, and a plenitude of linens; and finally the unostentatious refinements of a few silver spoons and four books, among them a Bible. So, too, Edward Lawson would seem to have enjoyed a comparably well-arranged lifestyle--furniture to meet most everyday needs (bed, table, chairs), the apparatus necessary for warmth and food preparation and consumption, as well as clothing; along with the practical non-essentials of a mirror and carpeting; and finally the small-scale enhancements of a half-dozen silver spoons and a number of pictures. Jackson and Lawson certainly did not own a surfeit of household goods; however, what they did have endowed their material life with the dignity of balance--sufficiency, decency, and even a touch of elegance.

Indices Of Literacy

Amy Jackson, however, differed from Edward Lawson in that she--like two semi-skilled laborers and four of the five businessmen--died possessing literacy belongings (roster 4). Four of the 1840s decedents had books listed in their inventories; the widow Amy Jackson's holdings are the most specific--"1 Bible & 3 old books" (transcription 2.12). The two semi-skilled laborers, and the one businessman are simply credited with owning an indeterminate number of unidentified books (transcription 1.5). Four of the 1840s decedents had furniture pertaining to literacy listed in their inventories. One of them, a semi-skilled laborer with books, had a "Broken desk," while two of them, businessmen without books, each had a desk, and the fourth, another businessman without books, had both a "Writing desk" and a "Book case." The businessman James H. Howe--although himself intestate--did affix his signature in November 1830 as a witness to the will of the waiter Henry Benson and in July 31 as an appraiser to the inventory of Benson's estate; evidence of his signature tends to fit in with his owning a desk at death.[5] When such rather sketchy signs of literacy are correlated with other clues from the probate records, the strongest candidates for commanding the ability both to read and to write would appear to be a semi-skilled laborer and a businessman. Primus Hall, the soapboiler, had books and a desk (even if broken), and he died with a signed will. Moreover, Primus Hall affixed his signature in the early 1830s to the list of debts presented to him as executor of the bootblack James Gould's estate.[6] Thomas Cole, the hairdresser, had books and a map of the United States, and he died with a signed will. It is striking that the appraised value of his books alone--$30--far exceeded that of any other 1840s decedents' literacy belongings. Moreover, Cole bequeathed "all [his] books to the Adelphic Union Library Association," which can be interpreted as further substantiation of his being literate--and as a sign of his supporting literacy in the community (transcription 1.5). Two other businessmen, both of whom died intestate, moved in the same circle as Thomas Cole; their ownership at death of furniture pertaining to literacy--along with their signing an administrative bond as sureties in the settling of fellow businessman William S. Jinnings's estate--suggests that John Robinson and John Scarlett were literate. Given the serious barriers to determining genuine literacy that have previously been noted, the actual proficiency of the 1840s decedents--individually and collectively--remains too problematic to draw any firm conclusions based soley on the evidence in the probate records (roster 5). Owning books and being able to sign one's name do not necessarily signify literacy today, either.

Inventoried Assets Versus Net Worth

The ground is somewhat firmer underfoot when investigating the 1840s decedents' real versus ostensible wealth. A decedent's inventoried assets can shrink or even evaporate in the face of his or her liabilities. In fact, of the eleven 1840s decedents under discussion, only four died solvent; moreover, of the six insolvent decedents for whom the documentation is clear, three ended up with negative net worth. The details have been recounted for these outcomes for the widow Amy Jackson, as well as for three of the businessmen--Thomas Cole, John Robinson, and John Scarlett. Amy Jackson's assets were virtually erased by her liabilities. John Robinson's estate was overwhelmed by his creditors' claims, and John Scarlett's inventoried wealth was considerably reduced by his debts although the documentation is unclear about whether his estate ultimately had positive or negative net worth. Thomas Cole alone was solvent; his executors' account (when the errors are corrected) indicates that of the $2439.03 which remained after paying debts, funeral expenses, and administrative costs, $436.53 was left above the $2002.50 in bequests.

The two remaining businessmen--James H. Howe and Williams S. Jinnings--both died insolvent, the former clearly with positive net worth and the latter possibly with negative net worth. Given Howe's inventoried wealth of $707.58, a positive net worth of $59.43 does not particularly draw attention to itself. The administrative records, however, introduce both complexity and mystery. As would be expected, James Howe's real estate was sold in order to retire a $200 mortgage and satisfy creditors; according to the first account, the property on Kennard Avenue brought in $1180.00 cash from John Rogers, some $280 above its appraised value. Thus, Howe's estate would seem to have about $980 in equity from his real estate. When added to his $7.58 in personal property, however, there would still be only $987.58 to satisfy some $1433.82 in debts and administrative costs. So how did Howe end up with $59.43 positive net worth when he should have ended up with $446.24 negative net worth? The answer lies in uninventoried savings on deposit in the amount of $305.67 plus no record of retirement of the mortgage to offset the $1180 realized on the sale of his real estate plus the full value of his personal estate--all of which yield $1493.25. This sum represents Howe's assets during settlement, $59.43 more than the $1433.82 in debts and administrative costs levied against his estate.

William S. Jinnings's likely ultimate negative net worth of $1336.98 came about through the accumulation of debts amounting to $2236.44. In January 1841, his father and brother, administrators of his estate, record in the first account that $1053.32 1/2--rather than the $430 stated in the December 1840 inventory--constitutes his assets. This figure represents the $410 listed as Jinnings's personal estate in the inventory (without taking into account the $20 added for the value of the "Wearing apparel of dec^d"), $566.10 gained on the sale of his personal estate (which was apparently undervalued in the inventory), and $77.22 1/2 in sums collected and received (without further explanation of the source). At the same time, $158.75 is shown as the administrators' expenditures, leaving a handsome balance of $901.57 1/2. But the list of claims also compiled and filed with the court by his administrators in January 1841 indicates that $2236.44 in debts were outstanding against the estate of their son and brother. Jinnings was declared insolvent and commissioners appointed to "receive and examine the claims of creditors against [his] estate." Curiously, only one creditor appears on the commissioners return in September 1841, claiming a mere $2.11. It is difficult to believe that the twenty creditors recorded by Jinnings's father and brother, claiming a formidable $2236.44, simply failed to submit their claims to the court-appointed commissioners--particularly since William S. Jinnings died owing his brother $1567.85, Charleston $4.86 in taxes, and Boston $5.50 in taxes. Moreover, Jinnings's court-declared insolvency was based on the list of claims drawn up by his father and brother, and the sole claimant recognized by the commissioners does not appear on this list. The most likely explanation is that William S. Jinnings died with $901.57 1/2 in assets to meet $2238.55 in liabilities, leaving him with minus $1336.98 net worth.

Two semi-skilled laborers, John W. Brown and Primus Hall, also died insolvent, one with negative and the other with positive net worth. Liabilities and administrative costs wiped out John W. Brown's inventoried wealth of $800, leaving his estate with a negative net worth of $139.54, as has previously been described. In the case of Primus Hall, assets of $9710.06 at death were reduced to $3563.99 after settlement. On June 13, 1842, a list of debts totaling $4120.11 was presented to the court in conjunction with a petition for sale of real estate that stated the Primus Hall's $141.86 in personal estate was insufficient to meet these debts and to cover the $300 of estimated administrative costs.

Jonas W. Clark, Hall's executor, petitioned to be granted a license to sell a portion of Hall's $9567.20 worth of real estate, specifically the West Cedar and Southac Streets property in Boston, but not the property situated in Mill Row (variously located in Cambridge, on Hall's inventory and his widow's petition for dower--or in Charleston, on Hall's will--or in Somerville, formerly Charlestown, in this document--or Somerville, in the widow's dower). Primus Hall had bequeathed his wife Ann the Milk Row property in a will dated March 4, 1842; three days later he added a codicil that also left the West Cedar and Southac Streets property to her. But Ann Hall, like Margaret Scarlett, invoked her rights as a widow in order to salvage as much of her late husband's real estate as possible before the sale of the West Cedar and Southac Streets property.

On July 25, she waived the provisions made for her in his will and claimed her dower of his estate. Accordingly, on August 15, three commissioners assigned to her "a small wooden two story house on the northeast corner of the estate on Southack St for the widow's right of dowery . . . also the Mill Row estate . . ." Since a widow's dower was understood to be a third of her husband's real estate, Ann Hall was probably awarded about $3189 in land and buildings--or one-third of the $9567.20 worth of real estate listed on Primus Hall's inventory. This would include the $1100 appraised value of the Milk Row property, thereby indicating that "the northwest corner" of the West Cedar and Southac Streets property the commissioners assigned to her was worth about $2089. Moreover, a year later, on August 25, 1843, Ann Hall petitioned for an allowance, "having renounced the provisions in her late husband's will, and taken her dower in the real estate, and having supported since the decease of her husband two children"; Judge Phillips decreed that she be allowed $82.86 out of her husband's personal estate. Therefore, Ann Hall managed to retain the Mill Row property, worth $1100, and a corner of the West Cedar and Southac Streets property, probably worth about $2089 together, as well as $82.86, so that only the remaining portion of her husband's total estate was subject to the claims of creditors and administrative costs.

These latter sums are spelled out in Jonas W. Clark's first executor's account, submitted on the same day that Ann Hall requested and was granted her widow's allowance. Aside from Ann Hall's allowance of $82.86 and $182.43 in executor's services, etc., $5327.29 in payments were recorded by Clark. The long stretch of payments mentions fourteen instances of "note & interest" as well as references to "interest on mortgage," "note & mortgage," and discharging mortgages," suggesting that Primus Hall borrowed extensively and that his real estate was not owned outright. On the other side of the ledger, aside from the $141.86 in inventoried personal estate, Jonas Clark recorded that he had received sums equaling $5742.78: $5450.43 from the sale of Hall's real estate in Boston (presumably minus the northwest corner assigned to Ann Hall), along with $253.89 in rents, $12.00 from John Rogers "for damages for not taking land," $7.50 from John L. Roberts "for an old building," and $18.96 from three purchasers "for soap." Subtracting the sums paid from the sums received leaves $292.06; when this is added to Ann Hall's dower and allowance, Primus Hall's estate, after settlement, shows a net worth of $3563.99, $6146.07 less than his inventoried wealth.

The laborer Edward Lawson's estate presents no convolutions. He died solvent; his estate of $366.00 easily met his just debts of $171.00 since the $366.00 consisted of $286.00 cash on deposit. It can be safely assumed that the $195.00 "allowed the widow by order of court" probably included the $80.00 worth of Edward Lawson's inventoried household goods; Elizabeth Lawson thus retained $115.00 of her husband's savings, as well as received $25.00 for her services as administratrix. While the reduction of liquid assets by about half was certainly not a negligible financial event, the settlement of Edward Lawson's estate shows primarily funeral and medical expenses, along with administrative costs. The fact that otherwise there is only one payment of $8.00 to Joshua Bennett for "Rent" and one payment of $11.25 to Otis Hayden for an unspecified "Bill" indicates that Edward Lawson lived within his means.

The 1840s decedents under discussion, therefore, ranged in inventoried assets from $96.96 to $9710.06 and in net worth after settlement from negative $1336.98 to positive $3563.99. If the actual wealth of these eleven decedents is compared with that of nine other decedents from the 1840s for whom the documentation permits such an analysis, then the figures reveal a similar spectrum. Inventoried assets range from $28.01 to $9710.06, net worth after settlement from negative $1336.98 to positive $5836.50. Businessmen can be found at the bottom (William Jinnings and John Robinson) as well as at the top (William Riley and Peter Gray) of the economic ladder when their actual wealth is calculated. Nonetheless, of the four with greatest net worth after settlement, three are businessmen (Thomas Cole, William Riley, and Peter Gray). Moreover, all three died solvent, and their assets far exceed those of all the other decedents, except for the semi-skilled laborer (Primus Hall) whose estate at death was the wealthiest but was reduced through insolvency to the third greatest in net worth. Indeed, it was his widow's skillful maneuvering that accounts for the bulk of this sum.

While probate was itself a bureaucratic procedure, the particulars of the settlement of each decedent's estate--like the contents of that estate--disclose individual circumstances and choices.[7] Therefore, as has been shown, each probate packet merits close scrutiny not only for what it can document about the material conditions and values of the antebellum Afro-American community in Boston, but also for what it can reveal about specific black Bostonians who died in the 1840s. Any conclusions about wise or occupation-determined management of assets can be made only in guarded terms. For example, while one was a laborer and the other a businessman, both Edward Lawson and Thomas

Cole rented living quarters but both died solvent. The evidence suggests that inventoried affluence can disappear as real estate--a conventional sign of socioeconomic achievement--goes to the auction block to retire mortgages and satisfy claimants, who may have considered the decedents with real estate more credit-worthy than those without real estate. Nonetheless, decedents like Primus Hall and John Robinson seem to have managed their finances, if not exactly with virtual abandon, at least with some disregard for the day of reckoning. On the other hand, perhaps they embody an admirable enterprise that counterbalances the commendable circumspection of an Edward Lawson, thereby demonstrating the range of responses of even an extremely focused sample of antebellum black Bostonians to their social and economic milieu.

Through a methodical examination of the probate records of twenty-three decedents, distinct individual personalities emerged and customary communal behavior surfaced. Stories that lay dormant between the lines of these official documents told themselves to the scrupulous reader. The foregoing in-depth investigation of probate records from a previously presumed inarticulate population, then, sets the stage for contrasting findings from this primary source with the scholarship on black social history and probate inventories.

Part III

The Literature Vis-a-Vis the Probate Records

CHAPTER 6
RESONANT READING

How much of the preceding analysis of the probate records of black Bostonians in the 1840s confirms--and how much calls into question--information and conclusions based on other sources? First, to summarize the findings:

A case study of one decedent illustrated both the necessity of using the entire probate record (not just the inventory) and the intricacy of tapping a single probate record as a source. The complete documents for Amy Jackson told an intriguing story. A comfortable domestic environment and considerable real estate assets at death were virtually wiped out by "just debts" and administrative costs; meanwhile, a complex drama of human relations was enacted, conveying the spirit of the strong-minded legatee, unis V Sinnix, an ordinary member of the black community.

Two sample investigations of patterns of human interactions detectable in probate records brought to life the network of relationships--kin and non-kin--that animated the black community. The documents for John W. Brown and Chloe Russell revealed an interlocking pattern. Brown and Russell, non-kin, appeared in each other's probate records because Brown owed Russell money and left her a life interest in his real estate; Russell's son, Edward Labbottiere, also figured in both sets of documents, as an interested party in his mother's claim against Brown's estate. On the other hand, the documents for Thomas Cole, William S. Jinnings, William Riley, John Robinson, and John E. Scarlett presented a crisscrossing pattern. This coterie of non-kin decedents turned up in each other's probate records, weaving a web of interaction that embraced many community members, living and dead.

A model comparative analysis of the value and contents of the estates of associated decedents revealed similarities and differences in the holdings and life styles of community members of like standing. The inventories of the estates of the five businessmen--Cole, Jinnings, Riley, Robinson, and Scarlett--showed striking variation--from zero to large assets in real estate or cash and from negligible to sizable amounts of household goods. In general, the household goods of three of the associated decedents--Cole, Robinson, and Scarlett--projected an image of relatively consistent domestic environments. Individually, however, their personal possessions at death preserved the panoply of idiomatic acquisition.

their personal possessions at death preserved the panoply of idiomatic acquisition.

An exploratory examination of ostensible versus real wealth pointed up the tenuousness of affluence in the black community. Again, whether looking at the probate records for a single decedent (Amy Jackson), for three decedents (Thomas Cole, John Robinson, and John Scarlett), or for eleven decedents (the four already listed plus John W. Brown, Primus Hall, James H. Howe, William S. Jinnings, Edward Lawson, Henry Robinson, and Peter Williams), the inventories often depicted a prosperity which was appreciably undermined or nearly erased once probate was concluded. More than half died insolvent; when their estates were settled, their inventoried assets generally were substantially reduced.

An experimental exercise in mentally recreating historic material conditions conjured up portraits of no-longer-extant domestic environments. Whether looking at the probate records for a single decedent (Amy Jackson), for three decedents (Thomas Cole, John Robinson, John Scarlett), or for eleven decedents (the four already listed plus John W. Brown, Primus Hall, James H. Howe, William S. Jinnings, Edward Lawson, Henry Robinson, and Peter Williams), the inventories permitted imaginative reconstructions that show gradations of life style, even within a quite limited range of consumption.

A three-fold inquiry into occupation and its relationship to the amount and make-up of the deceased's estate disclosed that businessmen for the most part enjoyed advantaged material circumstances. The estates of twenty-one decedents were rank-ordered, first in their entirety and then in their key divisions, disclosing that there was little consistent correlation between occupation and wealth at death or between occupation and the various components of that wealth. The household goods of eleven decedents were then analyzed into necessities, amenities, and luxuries and rank ordered, showing that these categorized expenditures provided a better gauge than household goods as a whole to variation in the material conditions of decedents of different livelihoods. In fact, a close look at the particulars showed that, whereas occupation could not be readily associated with generic sets of necessities, it could be correlated with generic sets of amenities and even more so with generic sets of luxuries. Most often, businessmen equaled or exceeded their compatriots, having owned the full complement of consumer durables at death yet not having had to tie up an inordinate proportion of their wealth in personal possessions.

These findings are the product of attentive scrutiny of the probate records of twenty-three black decedents in antebellum Boston. The factual data now can serve as the basis for revisiting the themes identified in the review of black social history, as well as for reexamining the issues raised in the literature on probate inventories as historic sources. Upon occasion, reference to other primary source material--the federal census, public documents, Boston directories--helps to clarify or substantiate the usefulness of probate records as tappable resources about hitherto allegedly inarticulate populations. The focus, however, remains on weighing the evidence actually available in the probate records against current scholarship.

The Probate Records In Relation To Inventory Scholarship

A good number of the findings cited in the above summary bear upon issues raised in the literature on probate inventories as historic sources. First and foremost, this study of a modest number of probate records of the black community in Boston during the 1840s has demonstrated that for both quantitative and qualitative information the complete probate record is a far better source than a household inventory plucked from its context, i.e., the full array of whatever documents comprise the entire probate packet. An examination of the complete probate packet ensures against misunderstanding the true value of a decedent's estate, brings more characters on the stage, clarifies the conundrum of omissions, provides multiple clues about literacy, and reveals personal ties that undergird the black community's social fabric.

Establishing Actual Wealth

Large scale studies that work with several thousands of inventories to determine degrees of economic inequality or to identify levels of consumption among various population groups in the past can misconstrue historic reality when inventoried or ostensible wealth is not adjusted to reflect probated or actual wealth. Although decedents may seem to have commanded considerable assets during their lifetime and their financial house of cards may not have collapsed until after settlement, their affluence has to be regarded as conditional when it can be shown to dissolve in the face of outstanding debts. The clothing trader John Robinson's estate--ostensibly worth $1299.39 according to the inventory but actually worth negative $604.76 after probate--represents a persuasive example; if the former figure were to be taken as an accurate account of Robinson's wealth, then an extremely false impression of his prosperity would contribute not only to a mistaken assessment of his individual affluence but also to faulty computations of the aggregate wealth of the black community (table 51).

Enhancing The Human Dimension

Reference to all the available probate documents can add a human dimension to the enumeration and appraisal of property that occurs in an inventory. Not that inventories alone are totally devoid of biographical and cultural clues: they usually state the decedent's occupation, provide insight into his or her tangible surroundings, and--by setting forth the names of three appraisers--hint at his or her association with other people. Yet an almost egocentric focus on inventories alone--and therefore the decedents alone--forestalls the broader understanding to be derived from engaging with as many as possible of the personages whose names are found in the probate records. Caught thus in the net are not only the appraisers, but also spouses and children, relatives and friends, executors and administrators, legatees and heirs, debtors and creditors. The hairdresser Thomas Cole's probate records represent a convincing example. If only the inventory of his estate is examined, no particular vibrancy of interpersonal relations is discernible. Other than the cryptic notation--"Mrs. Riley legacy"--bracketing the first two lines of the "Household furniture, &c.," the document only reveals that Phineas Capen, a justice of the peace who frequently acted in his official capacity for the black community, along with Benjamin P. Bassett and Edwin F. Howard, both well-connected members of the black community, served as the appraisers (transcription 1.5).

The other documents in his probate packet, however, not only explicate the obscure notation about Mrs. Riley and her legacy, but they also place Thomas Cole amid a large cast of characters: the Rev. and Mrs. John T. Raymond; the Bay State Lodge of the Grand United Order of the Odd Fellows, number 114; Eunice R. Davis; the Deacons of the First Independent Baptist Church in Belknap Street; a nephew, Thomas Cole Richardson, son of Mrs. E. Richardson; Thomas Hilton and his father, John T. Hilton; Alfred G. Howard; the Adelphic Union Library Association; and so forth, just in the will alone (transcription 1.1).

Whereas Cole's inventory sheds minimal light on his personal and social relations with other people, his will indicates that he accorded women their individual identities ("for her sole and separate use"), that he accepted philanthropic obligations readily ("for the relief of the sick, poor, and destitute"), and that he wanted to share his own good fortune with a nephew and a friend's son when they each came of age. In addition, Cole's will partially decodes the elliptical "Mrs. Riley legacy"; the items bracketed in his inventory are described as particularly precious gifts to Mrs. Elizabeth Riley, who also is to receive $300 cash. Only consultation with the executors' account of amounts paid, however, offers some clarification of Cole's relationship with Mrs. Riley, the wife of a fellow businessman with whom he was well-acquainted (transcription 1.8). Two payments to Mrs. Riley, one specifically "for nursing" suggests the source of Cole's esteem and his motivation for bequeathing her his most cherished possessions. If all the information about people that lurks in probate records were not pieced together, then the vitality of human intercourse that they encapsulate would be seriously diminished.

Explicating The Missing

Careful inspection of the complete probate record packet can help to unravel mysteries that the inventories themselves create when they are divorced from their paper context. A major scholarly dilemma crops up when the list of the decedent's personal estate sometimes omits what would seem to be a basic necessity. The absence of clothing, for instance, plays havoc with confidence in the trustworthiness of inventories as complete catalogues of decedents' possessions at death. Some cogent explanations have been advanced for these omissions--widow's portion, bequests, soft-hearted appraisers, ahistorical definition of the basic necessities--that satisfy on a large scale.[1] But, on a small scale, the lapses have a distinctly capricious air.

The estate of the laborer John Lewis Brent alias John Lewis represents a good example. The inventory shows his owning $2,019.29 in real estate, but absolutely nothing in personal estate. The inventory itself offers a slight hint at solving the riddle of this apparent gulf between the decedent's real and personal estate; at the bottom of the page, along with the particulars about the property, two mortgages are declared. Thus, the $2,019.29 signifies not clear holdings in real estate, but rather equity in real estate appraised at $3,300. Further investigation of the probate documents shows that John Lewis Brent alias John Lewis died owing not only $1,280.71 in mortgages, but also $373.87 in debts. The personal possessions of an intestate decedent with no known heirs were evidently of little moment to Phineas Blair and the other public officials who administered John Lewis Brent's estate. The real estate needed to be auctioned to retire the mortgages and pay the debts; the probate process simply regulated this business matter. The total absence of any personal estate on John Lewis Brent's inventory should be viewed skeptically; it is highly unlikely that someone with $2000 in real estate equity possessed nought else. Thus, neither the failure to enumerate his movable property can be regarded as mere whimsy on the part of the appraisers, nor can the absence of personal estate be wholly credited. If inventories with curious omissions were accepted at face value, then questionable quantitative findings would distort qualitative judgments about historic property ownership.

Looking For Literacy

Regarding probate records--rather than inventories alone--as constituting the source can help to answer a question for which there is often little hard evidence. The extent and degree of literacy among historic populations for whom personal papers are not extant generally eludes documentation. The listing in inventories of books and/or furnishings that pertain to reading or writing certainly can be cited as suggesting literacy. But such evidence remains inadequate for establishing literacy. Of the other types of documents commonly found in probate packets, wills would seem to be the most valuable for determining literacy. The presence of a signature as opposed to an "X" can be submitted as signaling the ability to write. But such evidence remains inconclusive for proving literacy.

The widow Amy Jackson's and the businessman James H. Howe's probate records represent excellent examples. Amy Jackson's inventory shows her owning four books at death--"1 Bible & 3 old books"--which, especially in conjunction with her other genteel domestic possessions and substantial real estate holdings, easily promote the impression that she was literate (transcription 2.12). The fact that Amy Jackson died testate, therefore, simply adds a strong reason for supposing that she probably knew how to read and write. But both her first and second wills are signed with "X's" (transcriptions 2.1 and 2.6). Whether from infirmity or inability, the lack of a signature directly contradicts the ownership of books. Amy Jackson's literacy therefore must remain speculative.

James H. Howe's inventory indicates that he owned a desk at death, which--in association with his advantaged occupation and his comfortable real estate holdings--readily fosters the notion that he was literate. The fact that James Howe died intestate, however, quickly subtracts a strong reason for supposing that he probably knew how to read and write. But James Howe's signature can be found in probate records, just not in his *own* packet. In the early 1830s, his signature appears both as a witness to the will and as one of the three appraisers for the inventory of Henry Benson, his sister's husband.² Similarly, the signature of this sister, Hannah M. Benson, appears as executrix in her husband's and as administrix in her brother's probate records.

The ironic yet obvious fact is that, other than at the bottom of a will, the least likely signature to be found in a packet of probate records would be that of the deceased. Whatever the value of signatures in determining literacy, they have to be tracked primarily within probate records of other decedents. Moreover, an assessment of the frequency of the ability to read and write in the black community requires examining probate records with attention to clues about literacy that transcends rote calculations and simplistic deductions about books or desks or signatures.

For instance, a crucial piece of evidence may be in the probate records of another decedent. Take Amy Jackson's documents; whereas the evidence for *her* ability to read and write may always be contradictory, there seems little doubt about the literacy of the amanuensis of her nurse and legatee, Eunice Senix. Mistakes in spelling and punctuation indicate that u V Sinnix relied on a somewhat unpolished scribe, but these errors only enhance the power of this document to speak to the literacy of ordinary people. Amid the rhetorical wording common and necessary to probate records, Eunice Senix's request seems refreshingly unstylized and unvarnished. This note stands as the most striking piece of evidence about literacy in the black community that surfaced in the complete pool of documents. There were some lists of debts that may have been in the hand of a decedent's relative, but for the most part handscript documents or portions of documents were executed by public officials like Phineas Blair.

Multiple clues--located in the deceased's probate records or in his or her documents, as well as in those of other decedents--increase the probability of accurate assessments of literacy. But, most commonly, pronouncements about reading and writing skills when based on probate records alone have to be couched speculatively. The question of literacy demands recourse to other sources for trustworthy answers.

One such source is the federal census, which in 1840 inquired about literacy, but confined its inquiry to "number of white persons, over 20 years of age in each family who cannot read and write." Ten years later, the query was reframed to identify "persons over 20 years of age who cannot read and write" in each household, and 13.6 percent of black Bostonians were recorded as illiterate. Nonetheless, the other 86.4 percent of the Afro-American community should not be regarded as having been genuinely proficient in reading and writing.

It would be misleading to assume that literacy in the mid-nineteenth century meant anything more than rudimentary knowledge of reading and writing. Many of those judged literate were, in fact, functional illiterates, able to write little more than their names and, in some cases, unable to read and comprehend a newspaper.[3]

The 1850 census does not, of course, address the literacy--rudimentary or otherwise--of black Bostonians who died in the 1840s. It does, however, record as literate eight community members--George Washington, Jonathan Cash, Jonas W. Clark, John P. Coburn, Emiliano Mundrucu, Coffin Pitts, John Rogers, and Robert Morris--who formed a peer group that interacted with the 1840s decedents Thomas Cole, Primus Hall, James H. Howe, William S. Jinnings, Edward Lawson, William Riley, John Robinson, and Joseph Sprague (roster 6). The members of this peer group can be linked directly or indirectly through the probate records with the foregoing 1840s decedents. All eight, according to the 1850 census, were able to read and write. Moreover, among the three households with children between the ages of six and sixteen, ten of the twelve children had attended school within the previous year, and none of the wives were recorded as unable to read and write. This 100 percent female literacy contrasts markedly with the instances of signature illiteracy among women to be found in the 1840s decedents' probate records (roster 7). The two testate women--Amy Jackson and Chloe Russell--both signed their wills with "X's"; four of the nine widows signed documents with "X's"; and, of the other six women--daughters, kin, and non-kin heirs--who were signatories to various probate procedures, one was obliged to use an "X." Thus, out of seventeen women, seven were incapable of writing their own names.

The high rate of literacy for the eight individuals in the peer group as presented in the 1850 census also contrasts with findings from the probate records (roster 8). Given the grand sweep of literacy indicated by the census, the probate records offer much more complex evidence. The lawyer Robert Morris, who died in the early 1880s, quite obviously was fully literate; multiple clues in the probate records attest to his ability to read and write at an advanced level, even if his occupation were not a profession demanding linguistic sophistication. The clothesdealer Emiliano Mundrucu most likely was literate; he owned a wide range of books when he died in 1863--among others, a three volume *History of Washington*, a large Bible, the *Memories of Napoleon Bonaparte*, *Uncle Tom's Cabin*, and two volumes on the *History of the*

Russian War, as well as "1 sett of Shakespeares works"--but the probate records show nothing more to verify his literacy. And what to make of Jonathan Cash--recorded as able to read and write in the 1850 census--yet unable to sign his name on Edward Lawson's administrator's bond in 1841? The attribution of literacy in the census seems dubious. In fact, probate records, even with their generally inconclusive evidence, do offer more clues than the census does for making assessments of literacy--the ownership at death of books and/or furnishings related to literacy, as well as signatures. The census simply records a self-reported ability to read and write and therefore lacks sufficient credibility to serve as a satisfactory alternative guide when probate records fail to provide definitive information.

A more trustworthy source than the federal census--one with internal verification--can, however, be compared with findings from probate records. The *Black Abolitionist Papers*, a microfilm collection of some 14,000 original documents from 1830 to 1865, constitutes a virtual catalogue raisonné of black anti-slavery activism in which some 1840s decedents took part.[4] If the probate records give mostly mixed messages about literacy and the census gives disputable evidence, then an assemblage of documents that includes unequivocal proof of reading and writing skills can corroborate assessments that otherwise must remain speculative if based solely on probate records.

The case of the businessman Thomas Cole represents a prime example. The owner of a "Lot of Books" valued at $30 and a "Map of U.S." valued at "25c," Cole died testate, leaving his books to the Adelphic Union Library Association and affixing his signature to his will and codicil--all fairly strong reasons to suppose that Cole could read and write. Supposition about his writing skills can be replaced with certainty, however, on the basis of extant personal documents that preserve both Cole's penmanship and his politesse. A letter of introduction shows that his writing skills were by no means limited to a handsome signature.

M.[aria] W.[eston] Chapman
Faneuil Hall

    December 20*th*/45
    Madame Chapman
Geo. Latimer
will render you
any services you
wish to-day.

Thos Cole[5]

Moreover, sundry orations and letters printed in newspapers of his day make clear that Cole's command of the language was that of a well-read man, capable of referring to the Bible, to the Constitution, and to historic precedent, as well as of showing familiarity with the political issues of the day.

For instance, in 1837 he addressed the New England Colored Temperance Convention:

> We shall add speed to the car of abolition, and sustain those mighty advocates who are agitating the country in behalf of the downtrodden slave and the rights of humanity; and demonstrate to the world that we have intellectual faculties capable of the highest cultivation, and progressive improvement in all the arts and sciences, and polite literature of the age--as has been proved already in many instances that might be adduced. Mankind, however they may differ in complexion or features, are precisely alike in that immortal part which alone distinguishes them from the animal creation.[6]

And in 1840 he wrote to the editor of the *Colored American*:

> Let us here after remember, that although we may despairingly imagine that we can gain nothing by petitioning for "liberty and equality," and the use and exercise of the right of suffrage, there may be much to lose by refusing them. Is this the time to turn away and despair of obtaining our inalienable rights? Surely not. Now, if ever, is the time when there is most occasion and necessity for us united to come forward, and use all lawful efforts to promote our own elevation to all the rights and privileges of our common humanity.[7]

Thus Cole's handwritten notes and his newspaper articles prove what can only be surmised about his literacy skills from the probate records. Most important, however, the necessity of seeking confirmation from other sources for a decedent like Cole, whose probate documents contained multiple clues, suggests that conclusions about literacy drawn solely from inventories--or even probate records--are subject to question.

Tracking Personal/Communal Networks

Requisite for proving literacy, other primary sources only reiterate evidence about black community organization and values clearly discernible in the probate records of the 1840s decedents. Unquestionably, probate records reveal a complex network of communal interaction. Thomas Cole, again, can serve as a suitable example. His probate documents capture his intersecting with other members of the black community; plotting out the intersections produces a web of relationships. Even when only four key people--John P. Coburn, John T. Hilton, Alfred G. Howard, and Coffin Pitts--are selected from Cole's probate records for tracking throughout the complete pool of probate records, the circle widens impressively. Numerous members of the antebellum black community then become indirectly linked to Cole through the two executors and two posters of surety directly named in his probate records.

The search through the probate records for every instance in which Coburn, Hilton, Howard, and Pitts appear as actors produces a first circle of community members whose names can then be traced in these same documents to produce a second circle of people who knew each other and whose names can in turn be tracked to produce yet a third circle of community members who were acquainted. In essence, these connected circles can be conceived of as ever-widening ripples, with everyone linked to Cole and to each other in varying degrees over a period of three decades.

The first circle includes seven different people associated with Coburn, Hilton, Howard, and Pitts, with one person--Robinson--associated with three of the initial four and another--Riley--associated with two of them:

John P. COBURN = 1847, surety for Thomas COLE
 1842, surety for Primus HALL
 1849, surety for John ROBINSON
 1863, witness for Emiliano MUNDRUCU

John T. HILTON = 1847, executor for Thomas COLE
 1840, inventory for William S. JINNINGS
 1844, inventory for John E. SCARLETT
 1849, witness and inventory for William RILEY
 1851, creditor of John ROBINSON

Alfred G. HOWARD = 1847, executor for Thomas COLE

son of Peter HOWARD

Coffin PITTS = 1847, surety for Thomas COLE
    1849, surety for William RILEY
    1849, surety for John ROBINSON

The second circle includes six more people:

Primus HALL
    1831, bond for David WALKER
    1842-43, Hall's executor and creditor--Jonas W. CLARK
    1843, Hall's creditor--John ROGERS

John ROBINSON
    1840, surety for William S. JINNINGS
    1849, Robinson's administrator--Robert MORRIS
    1849, Robinson's administrator--Jonas W. CLARK

Emiliano MUNDRUCU
    1831, partner and creditor of Joseph BANTISTA
    1863, Mundrucu's witness--Jonas W. CLARK

William S. JINNINGS
    1840, Jinnings' inventory--John ROGERS
    1840, Jinnings' surety--John E. SCARLETT

John E. SCARLETT
    1830, surety for David WALKER

William RILEY
    1849, Riley's witness--Henry L.W. THACKER

The third circle includes two new people, with the reappearance of three people from the first circle--Hall, Howard, and Riley--as well as one person from the second circle--Walker:

John ROGERS
    1846, paid estate--James H. HOWE
    1849, surety for William RILEY

Jonas W. CLARK
    1831, bond for David WALKER

1842, guardian for minor children of Joseph SPRAGUE
1845, surety for James H. HOWE

Robert MORRIS
1854, witness for Peter HOWARD

Thus, radiating out from Thomas Cole at the center, a network embraces nineteen different members of the Afro-American community, appearing and reappearing in each other's probate records in roles ranging from executor to creditor (roster 9). The width and breadth of this phenomenon, although predicated on tracking only four of some twenty-six people named in Thomas Cole's probate records (not counting the members of the Bay State Lodge of the Odd Fellows and the brethren of the First Independent Baptist Church), depicts effectively the ties that bound the black community together. Questions about the rationale for mutual help and the wellspring of communal solidarity therefore find convincing answers in probate records; other sources merely complement these findings by showing patterns of interactions whose intersections can be plotted out to produce a parallel web of relationships.

Public documents like those collected in the *Black Abolitionist Papers* amply illustrate a joining together of the community inspired by black activism. Again, Thomas Cole represents a fine example. His interests encompassed not only advocating temperance and the exercise of voting rights but also opposing African colonization and separate schooling for black children. Cole, an adherent of William Lloyd Garrison, spoke out fiercely against slavery. Moreover, he frequently mobilized the Afro-American community in efforts of self-determination, whether in taking care of its own orphans, rescuing a black newspaper, celebrating emancipation elsewhere, or holding conventions for group decision-making. According to the *Black Abolitionist Papers*, Cole's activism brought him into contact with at least twenty-one other community members, many for different causes, over about a decade and a half. His name can be found in sixteen documents, each one of which also contains the name(s) of one to ten of twenty-one other race leaders who were active in community affairs:

1831 = Anti-American Colonization Society[8]
    John T. HILTON
    Coffin PITTS
    Robert ROBERTS
    Thomas DALTON

Samuel SNOWDON
James G. BARBADOES
1831 = For establishment of a black college[9]
George PUTNAM
Henry L.W. THACKER
Primus HALL
John T. HILTON
Peter HOWARD
Thomas DALTON
Robert ROBERTS
Samuel SNOWDEN
James G. BARBADOES
1833 = Support for William Lloyd Garrison[10]
George PUTNAM
James G. BARBADOES
Samuel SNOWDEN
John T. HILTON
1833 = Silver cup to Garrison[11]
John T. HILTON
Peter HOWARD
George PUTNAM
Primus HALL
Henry L.W. THACKER
Samuel SNOWDEN
Emiliano F.B. MUNDRUCU
1837 = Mourning Elijah P. Lovejoy[12]
William S. JINNINGS
James G. BARBADOES
John T. HILTON
1838 = For temperance[13]
John T. HILTON
1839 = For Samaritan Orphanage[14]
William S. JINNINGS
Benjamin P. BASSETT
John T. HILTON
Primus HALL
1839 = Temperance dinner in honor of anniversary of emancipation in British West Indies[15]
John T. HILTON
1839 = New England Colored Temperance Society[16]
Benjamin P. BASSETT
1840 = Support of *Colored American*[17]

William S. JINNINGS
1840 = National Convention of Colored Inhabitants of the United States of America[18]
John T. HILTON
William C. NELL
James G. BARBADOES
Samuel SNOWDEN
Benjamin P. BASSETT
1840 = Welcome back to Garrison[19]
James G. BARBADOES
John T. HILTON
1841 = Regrets to soiree in honor of David Ruggles[20]
John T. HILTON
William C. NELL
1842 = Celebration of anniversary of emancipation in British West Indies[21]
John T. HILTON
George WASHINGTON
John B. COBURN
1843 = Call for a national convention among free people of color[22]
John T. HILTON
George WASHINGTON
Coffin PITTS
Benjamin P. BASSETT
William C. NELL
1844 = Petition to school board protesting separate school for colored children[23]
William C. NELL
Jonathan CASH
William RILEY
John P. COBURN
Coffin PITTS
John ROBINSON
Jonas W. CLARK
John ROGERS
George WASHINGTON
Thomas DALTON

The name that appears the most frequently is that of John T. Hilton, twelve times over the course of fourteen years (roster 10). Ten names of community members familiar from the personal network developed from Cole's probate records include those of John P. Coburn, Primus Hall, John Robinson, Emiliano Mundrucu, William S. Jinnings, William Riley, Peter Howard, John Rogers, Jonas W. Clark, and Henry L.W. Thacker. It is not surprising to find that these men had earned activist credentials comparable to Cole's. Of the 1840s decedents, Primus Hall was an established race leader by virtue of his housing the school for black children in his home around the turn of the century,[24] and William S. Jinnings cultivated high visibility in the 1830s as the Boston agent for the New York-based newspaper, *The Colored American*.[25] John P. Coburn, a clothesdealer, and Henry L. W. Thacker, a waiter, supported the formation of the black military company, the "Massasoit Guards," in the early 1850s.[26] Peter Howard's barbershop, conveniently located in the heart of the black residential community, served for over two decades as a center for the dissemination of information, ranging from entertainment to employment opportunities; moreover, it provided cover for fugitive slaves.[27] Jonas W. Clark, a clothes dealer, regularly outfitted fugitives and took a leading role from 1844 to 1855 in the ultimately successful campaign to abolish separate schooling for black children.[28] Pre-eminent among these prominent activists, however, figured John T. Hilton, a hairdresser, whose influence touched the black church, the African Masonic Lodge, and the public schools. Hilton, an avowed integrationist, presided over meetings, offered resolutions, delivered speeches, and chaired committees, all dealing with major community concerns.[29] The importance of Hilton, along with Howard and Cole, can best be understood when it is pointed out that the three of them were members of a key abolitionist group--the Boston Vigilance Committee, founded in 1842. While integrated at double the proportion of blacks in Boston's population, this organization of 168 members had only eight Afro-Americans among its ranks.[30] Thus there was reason for continual interaction in the civic sphere. These men not only participated in each other's personal lives, but they also obviously collaborated on deliberate endeavors to express their collective view and mold their shared destiny.

This communal spirit may explain the selection (or volunteering?) of two of the appraisers for Cole's estate. Benjamin P. Bassett had a history of cooperating with Cole in matters of community betterment; Edwin T. Howard was the son of Peter Howard, who the public documents show joined with Cole in favoring the establishment of a black college and in admiring Garrison. Edwin T. Howard was also the brother of Alfred G. Howard, Cole's friend, executor, and heir. It is curious, however, given both their father's relationship with Cole and their own roles in the settlement of Cole's estate, that the documents in the *Black Abolitionist Papers* show neither Edwin T. nor Alfred G. Howard as engaged alongside Cole as activists.

But these public documents do show the activism of one of Cole's beneficiaries, the Rev. John T. Raymond, even if not directly in conjunction with Cole:

1842 = Friends of Liberty appeal on behalf on George Latimer[31]
       Samuel SNOWDEN
       William C. NELL
1844 = Meeting protesting jailing of Charles T. Torrey[32]
       John T. HILTON
1846 = Reception for Garrison and Buffum[33]
       William C. NELL
       Samuel SNOWDEN
       John T. HILTON

The Rev. Raymond's activism, while not directly intersecting Cole's, does overlap. Hilton, Snowden, and Nell can be associated with both Raymond and Cole. This shared cadre of fellow activists more than likely guaranteed considerable interaction between Raymond and Cole, who, therefore, can hardly be seen to have moved in distinctly separate spheres. Raymond is thus drawn into Cole's network.

The public documents can also strengthen the web of relationships already developed through Cole's probate records (roster 9). John Robinson was associated with three of the four members of Cole's first circle--John P. Coburn, John T. Hilton, and Coffin Pitts--and was himself associated with Robert Morris and Jonas W. Clark. Since Coburn can also be associated with Primus Hall and Emiliano Mundrucu; Hilton associated with William S. Jinnings, John E. Scarlett, and William Riley; and Pitts associated with William Riley, etc., a radiating web of personal interaction can be developed that centers on Robinson. Although Robinson does not appear in Cole's probate records, he does intersect with Cole in one instance of activism (roster 10). The 1844 petition to the Boston school board that protested separate schooling for black children was signed by Cole, Robinson, Nell, Riley, Coburn, Pitts, Clark, and Washington, among others. Here Robinson's relationship with Riley, Coburn, Pitts, and Clark--sketched out previously through tracking intersections in probate records--can be seen to include the united rejection of school segregation.

But, according to the *Black Abolitionist Papers*, Robinson's activism was not confined to one instance:

1838 = Anti American Colonization Society[34]
    John T. HILTON
    Coffin PITTS
    John E. SCARLETT
1848 = Against Thomas Paul as Smith School master[35]
    Coffin PITTS
    Benjamin P. BASSETT
1848 = Against Thomas Paul as Smith School master[36]
    Jonas W. CLARK
    Emiliano MUNDRUCU
    George WASHINGTON

Thus, like Cole, Robinson interacted with Coburn, Hilton, and Pitts in both the personal and public domains. Their paths crossed those of Benjamin Bassett, Emilio Mundrucu, William C. Nell, and George Washington. Robinson and Cole were opposed to African colonization; Hilton shared their opposition, joining with Cole and Pitts, among others, in 1831, and with Robinson and Pitts in 1838. The two kinds of linkages--personal and public--can seemingly be tracked ad infinitum, and black activists' solidarity on public issues can therefore be understood to be profoundly grounded in their interdependence in personal matters.

This universe of mutually-reinforcing civic and private interaction was further strengthened by geographic proximity, of both home and business locales. The 1840s decedents and members of the personal and/or public networks associated with Thomas Cole, the Rev. John T. Raymond, and John Robinson crossed paths literally as well as figuratively. Real estates references found in the 1840s decedents' probate records can be plotted on a 1838 map of Boston, showing a concentration of sites (chart 2 and figure 2). In the days of the walking city,[37] it is likely that the residents of the Beacon Hill area in particular saw each other regularly on their daily rounds.

The federal censuses from 1830 and 1840 reiterate this finding (charts 3 and 4; figures 3 and 4). Analyzing residence by wards reveals that the 1840s decedents and network members tended to live in the same part of Boston, Wards 5 and 6, which were immediately adjacent to each other. The range of occupations indicates that socioeconomic standing did not create residential enclaves.[38] Meanwhile, the Boston directory listings for 1830, 1835, 1840, and 1845 zoom in for a somewhat closer look at this residential intermingling, since--like the real estate references in the probate records--streets rather than wards are cited for the 1840s decedents, as well as for network members (charts 5, 7, 9 and 11; figures 5, 6, 7, and 8). The visual evidence makes clear again the concentration of residence, in tandem with socioeconomic integration.

Moreover, the Boston directories often list business as well as home locales (charts 6, 8, 10, and 12; figures 5, 6, 7, and 8). Clothing dealers clustered on Brattle Street, while the remainder of those with work addresses were mostly sprinkled over a commercial area of the city within an easy commute by foot to and from the principal black residential sections. Not only within their neighborhoods, then, but also walking back and forth to their jobs, as well as during the work day, the 1840s decedents and network members probably maintained continuous contact and exchange. The censuses and the directories, therefore, complement information in the probate records about geographic proximity, making clear that the black community existed as an interactive physical entity. No doubt sharing common ground nurtured a communal attitude among Boston's Afro-Americans that embraced residential and business neighbors whose names do not appear among those noted. The many-layered infrastructure of the black community found in public documents, censuses, directories, and probate records consistently suggests inclusion rather than exclusion.[39]

Ultimately, the innumerable strands of personal and public intersections among Afro-American leaders in antebellum Boston produced a tightly-woven social fabric that offered a degree of stability and a sense of belonging for the community as a whole. Although the preponderance of people tracked through the public documents comprising the *Black Abolitionist Papers* were businessmen, an occasional semi-skilled laborer, like the soapboiler Primus Hall or the waiter Henry L.W. Thacker, or a laborer, like George Washington, occupied leadership roles (roster 9). More important, the events and endeavors described in public documents frequently involved a sizable turnout of the black citizenry, so that those whose names have been tracked did not by any means operate in isolation from the community.[40]

For example, the support for William Lloyd Garrison that was expressed by Thomas Cole, George Putnam, James G. Barbadoes, Samuel Snowden, and John T. Hilton occurred at a "Public Meeting of the Colored Inhabitants of Boston and Vicinity" held in the "African meeting-house in Belknap-street" on March 19, 1833. Resolutions were adopted, $25.00 was contributed, and, according to the article in the *Liberator* describing the event, "The assembly was large and respectable, and manifested the most perfect harmony of sentiment and decision of purpose."[41] Some ten years later, in 1843, a call went out from John T. Hilton, Thomas Cole, George Washington, Coffin Pitts, Benjamin P. Bassett, and William C. Nell, among others, for a "Great gathering of the People of Color" to be held in the "Baptist meetinghouse, Belknap-street, on Thursday evening" July 20, "at half-past 7 o'clock, at which time and place the colored citizens, without regard to age or sex, are earnestly invited to attend." The announcement went on to request "most respectfully" the presence of the "true friends of liberty and of the colored man" and closed with a rousing charge:

> Who will not be present at such a meeting? Will any stay behind? Come, then, one and all, both small and great. Come, ye noble band of abolitionists, who for some 13 years have fought like Spartans for the triumph of Liberty.
>
> To this call let there be one general rush, and a hearty response. Let those who always buckle on their armor at the sound of Freedom's triumph, be there--and whosoever will, let them come.[42]

The network of race leaders that radiated out from Thomas Cole thus did not hold themselves aloof. In fact, public interactions that cut across socioeconomic differences mirrored personal associations that extended deep and wide into the community. Black activists of higher standing in antebellum Boston not only can be linked with each other through their own probate records, but can also be connected with a broad spectrum of ordinary people. Three examples demonstrate the normalcy of this behavior. In 1831, the bootblack and laborer James Gould died; Primus Hall served as executor of his estate, overseeing the sale of Gould's real estate--appraised at $500--to meet debts amounting to $488.92.[43] In 1835, the single woman Emily Higgins died; Robert Roberts, her landlord, served as executor of her estate, overseeing the consolidation of her assets of $152.80 to meet her liabilities of $152.80.[44] In 1842, the laborer Joseph Sprague died; Jonas W. Clark was named guardian of his two minor children.

James Gould, Emily Higgins, and Joseph Sprague may not appear by name in public documents as framers of resolutions or officers of organizations, but surely they can be taken to be included in the "one and all, both small and great" who rallied to the causes--anti-colonization, pro-temperance, anti-slavery--spearheaded by the black leadership. The unity of the Afro-American community on many public issues can be understood to be the spirit of cooperation evident in personal matters simply writ large. Both the *Black Abolitionist Papers* and probate records, by preserving the complementarity of public and personal interactions, indicate that privacy and individualism were pursued less than mutual aid and collective progress. Thus, the black voice that speaks through probate records not only conveys this prizing of communal sharing and solidarity, but it also proclaims a valuing of cultural self-determination that is affirmed by the public documents.

In sum, then, the evidence available in this pool of probate records suggestively addresses issues raised in the literature on probate inventories as historic sources. Seemingly technical concerns like determining real wealth or explaining suspect absences take on their true significance for understanding substantive matters like the amount of aggregate affluence and the make-up of individual property. Gleaning information about unknown to renowned players in the historic human drama becomes a sleuthing adventure: who knew whom, who possessed entree to liberating literacy,[45] who knit up the community. Relevant findings from the probate records of twenty-three black decedents from Boston in the 1840s therefore can be usefully compared to the literature on probate inventories.

The Probate Records In Relation To Social History Scholarship

This close study of probate records from Afro-American decedents in 1840s Boston also sheds varying amounts of light on the dominant themes in black social history. The evidence from this modest pool of documents somewhat contradicts conventional wisdom about the significance of occupation in the historic black community and also brings into question general observations about the preference for investment in real rather than personal property among Afro-Americans in the past. Moreover, the probate records show themselves to be an extremely suggestive resource about diversity in the black community, about intraracial interaction, about the security of the black couple-headed household, about the discharge of communal obligation among Afro-Americans, about working black women, about Afro-Americans' belatedly joining the consumer revolution, and about black home ownership.

Occupation And Material Condition

Since blacks were shut out of the mainstream, their socioeconomic hierarchy had a logic of its own that finds expression in the probate records. Occupations like hairdresser or used clothing dealer--which would be held in low esteem and which would rarely be lucrative in the broader society--could be at the top of the ladder in the Afro-American community because these livelihoods afforded steady employment and frequently depended only on black patronage. Findings from the probate records bear out the materially advantaged circumstances of such businessmen. They were in the most attractive situation because the appraised value of their household goods represented moderate portions of their total estates, yet their holdings in necessities, amenities, and luxuries provided the full complement of basics, comforts, and refinements (tables 30-33). And, indeed, businessmen--in gradual progression from necessities, to amenities, to luxuries--consolidated their preferable position (tables 34-39).

In other words, whereas specific occupations cannot be readily associated with possessing given necessities, businessmen were more likely to possess given amenities and luxuries at death than the 1840s decedents of other occupations. For instance, two of the five businessmen--Thomas Cole and John Robinson--owned feather bedding, while only one semi-skilled laborer--Peter Williams--did; similarly, three of the five businessmen--Thomas Cole, John Robinson, and John E. Scarlett--possessed china or silver, while none of the semi-skilled laborers did. That is not to say that feather bedding and silver or china were out-of-reach for even laborers or women, since the laborer Edward Lawson owned "6 Small Silver Tea Spoons" and the widow Amy Jackson owned "1 Feather Bed & pillows" as well as "3 Thin Silver Spoons." But overall, businessmen seem to have enjoyed a higher standard of living, acquiring fancy furniture, elaborate time-keeping devices, decorative pictures, musical instruments, and books. The environment conjured up for businessmen, then, included embellishments that may hint at buying into a life style set apart from those who possessed but the bare necessities. Yet, while a businessman's relative affluence and high status was reflected to a degree in his possessions at death, the nature of his consumption does not appear to have differentiated him radically from community members of different livelihoods.

Intraracial Social And Civic Intercourse

Diversity within commonality also seems to describe the highly tenuous conclusions that can been drawn from the 1840s probate records about intraracial interaction. To begin with, the probate records themselves contain no internal evidence regarding the decedent's color--white, black, or mulatto. Death records and city directories do specify race, but--like the 1830 and 1840 federal censuses--only distinguish between white and colored. In 1850, however, the census called for the recording of color in a column to be left blank for white or to be marked with a "b" for black or an "m" for mulatto. According to the census, mulattoes comprised 21 percent of Boston's Afro-American population at mid-century. Moreover, they "were generally more skilled, held more property, and were a bit less residentially separated from the white society than the darker members of their race."[46]

Of course, these findings do not include any of the 1840s decedents. But among those figuring in the analysis would have been the peer group that intersected with Thomas Cole, Primus Hall, James H. Howe, William S. Jinnings, William Riley, John Robinson, and Joseph Sprague. The peer group included eight community members who can be located in the 1850 census--Jonathan Cash, Jonas W. Clark, John P. Coburn, Robert Morris, Emiliano Mundrucu, Coffin Pitts, John Rogers, and George Washington (roster 10). Five of these eight men formed key strands in both the personal and the public relationships that knit up the black community (rosters 9 and 10). Of the six who participated in Thomas Cole's personal network--Jonas W. Clark, John P. Coburn, Robert Morris, Emiliano Mundrucu, Coffin Pitts, and John Rogers--the census states that four were black and two mulatto. Of the seven who took part in Cole's public network--Jonathan Cash, Clark, Coburn, Mundrucu, Pitts, Rogers, and George Washington--the census records that four were black and three mulatto. Therefore, one-third of the men from Cole's personal network who can be located in the 1850 census were recorded as mulattoes. Similarly, slightly over two-fifths of the men from Cole's public network who can be located in the 1850 census were recorded as mulattoes. Overall, the eight members of the peer group were 37.5 percent mulattoes, a disproportionate number given the 21 percent comprising Boston's Afro-American community in 1850.

Nonetheless, the peer group *was* mixed, thereby prompting the surmise that intraracial interactions were commonplace in the black community in the 1840s. Mulattoes appear with greater frequency in the peer group than their numbers in the population warrant probably as an outgrowth of what might be termed escalating biases, i.e., relying on two sources--the census and probate records--that already favor the most stable and successful elements in the population. Thus, mulattoes are doubly overrepresented. In any event, the peer group of mulattoes and blacks that crossed paths within Thomas Cole's extended networks shows that diversity and commonality went hand-in-hand in both personal and public relationships tracked through probate records and the *Black Abolitionist Papers*. As far as can be determined, constant social and civic intercourse seems to have been the norm between blacks and mulattoes during the 1840s in Boston.[47]

Matrifocality And Downward Mobility

The probate records also touch upon the issue of the matrifocal Afro-American family, if only glancingly, by addressing its material dimension. Economic discrimination and privation, as well as disease, worked against the continuity of the black couple-headed household. It is not so much the narration of personal possessions in the inventories of the 1840s decedents, but rather the probate records taken in their entirety that illuminate the elusiveness of material stability for the black community.

The inventories do document a range of life styles, from the pitiable to the decent to the extravagant. According to their inventories, John W. Brown seems to have owned nothing but a trunk and wearing apparel valued at $7.00, although he did have $550.00 in notes and $243.00 in real estate; Edward Lawson owned a few refinements along with household fundamentals, as well as $286.00 on deposit in the Provident Institution for Savings; and John Robinson possessed stylish appointments and $944.23 worth of equity in three pieces of real estate. Of these three, only Edward Lawson died solvent--able to meet all just debts--with his estate worth $195.00 after settlement. The other two died both insolvent and with negative net worth: John W. Brown $140 and John Robinson $605 in the red after settlement (table 46). In each instance, regardless of the broad spectrum of their material conditions as encapsulated in their inventories or the dollar span of their ultimate net worth, all three decedents left much reduced estates. Death seriously sapped whatever wealth had been accumulated, because that wealth teetered on the brink of dissolution.

It is difficult to imagine that this overhanging threat was unfelt in the black community; there must have been a pervasive sense of uncertainty insofar as material circumstances were concerned when hard-won gains were so easily lost. The psychological response to the realities of a restricted opportunity structure that denied access to upward mobility was no doubt heightened by consciousness of the devastation that death wrought upon whatever material advancement had been achieved. The plummeting in value of an estate after probate represents a variety of downward mobility that must have discouraged confidence in the rewards ascribed to adhering to mainstream strategies and values for achieving social and economic success.

Moreover, widows and children bore the brunt of the slide downward when a husband and father died with more apparent than actual wealth (table 52). It was their--not his--standard of living that suffered when settlement occasioned the sale of real estate and/or personal estate to retire mortgages and satisfy creditors. When someone like Delia G.R. Brooks--as did Margaret Scarlett and Ann Hall--petitioned the court in October 1843 "to set off and assign to her, her dower, or thirds" out of the real estate owned by her recently deceased husband, John Brooks, she was calling upon a traditional and legal protection afforded a widow when faced with the loss of what she and her husband had managed together to obtain. But no matter how Delia and John Brooks may have shared the struggle to acquire "a piece of land and tenement" on Cypress Street, no matter how encumbered it may have been--and it must have been encumbered to necessitate Delia G.R. Brooks's petition--at least John Brooks died "seized and possessed" of the fruits of his labor. A woman experienced during her lifetime the downward mobility that the estate underwent only after the man's death.

Thus, the "destructive conditions of Northern urban life"[48] and their debilitating consequences on the cohesiveness of the historic black family find an echo in the probate records when they show that ascents from poverty were frequently frustrated. Afro-American women in antebellum Boston must have understood the inadvisability of being dependent upon a man financially *after* as well as before death. However, a woman did not have to accept passively total decimation of the assets that were regarded legally as solely in the man's name. A widow could use the protocol of probate to her advantage, to shelter her and her children from the claims of creditors and settlement costs, by petitioning for a widow's allowance from the husband's personal estate and a widow's dower from the husband's real estate. Clearly, during the man's life and after his death, the woman was called upon to be independent and resourceful in the struggle for economic security. The probate records therefore seem to suggest a precursor mentality for the eventual rise of the contemporary black matrifocal family as a mechanism for coping with an environment fundamentally hostile to the viability of the two-parent black family.[49]

Family And Communal Obligation

The probate records also give some slight intimations about the intermeshing of the familial with the communal in antebellum Boston, when Afro-American couple-headed households still functioned relatively successfully in tandem with a commitment to mutual aid. This balance of the private and the civic seemingly finds expression in the way estates of the 1840s decedents were probated. Because the settlement of an estate, when there was a family, had a profound effect on the economic state of the surviving members of that family, immediate kin were perforce interested parties who could only share in the probate process. To ensure the impartiality of the proceedings, disinterested parties needed to have a hand in appraising the decedent's possessions and rendering the administrative account. Public officials like Phineas Blair, N.C. Cary, Phineas Capen, and Samuel E. Sewall frequently assisted widows like Elizabeth Lawson or Margaret Scarlett who had been named executrixes, thereby fulfilling dual clerical and watchdog roles. But families did not rely primarily on these bureaucratic agents to set the deceased's estate in order.

The evidence is admittedly fragmentary, permitting only inferences, rather than conclusions, to be drawn. Nonetheless, people who carried out probate duties--posting surety, taking the inventory, acting as administrator--appear to have been both leaders of the black community and/or friends of the deceased (roster 12). Even after allowing for the fact that many of the decedents comprised a self-referential peer group as participants in a personal and public network, much of the settling of estates was handled by friends who *were* friends with the decedent by virtue of working jointly toward collective public goals.

The cases of Thomas Cole and John Robinson are the most salient. John P. Coburn and Coffin Pitts posted surety for both men upon their deaths, and Coburn and Pitts had joined with both Cole and Robinson in signing an 1844 petition to the Boston school board protesting separate black schools.[50] In the instance of Edward Lawson, however, the community leaders Robert Roberts and Jonathan Cash were reaching beyond the confines of the leadership peer group in posting surety along with Lawson's widow. Thus, again, the probate records hint at interactions that did not draw lines between the familial and the communal or between the private and the civic, even in the mere mechanics of legal formalities.

Women And Working

The probate records provide information about black women working, but primarily through the administrative accounts rather than through the inventories. The vast majority of Afro-American women worked as live-in or day-work domestics, washed or sewed at home, or took in boarders--all income-producing activities that have frequently been undercounted and underappreciated when reckoning the extent of black female employment in the past.[51] The widow Amy Jackson's inventory lists the necessary equipment for taking in wash--"2 Tubs," "2 flat irons," and "2 Buckets"; but, of course, these items could easily have been for strictly personal use rather than for wage earning (transcription 2.12). Similarly, the soapboiler Primus Hall's inventory included a "Flat iron" and a "tub," which could equally have been used by his wife Ann and daughter Isannah for tending to the family's laundry or for generating income. The fact that Amy Jackson, Mrs. Primus Hall, and Isannah Trask Hall enjoyed relative material comfort apparently ought not to be taken as a sign that they did not work for pay. Elizabeth Riley, who received compensation for nursing Thomas Cole, was married to William Riley, gentleman and clothing dealer, who died in 1849 with real estate worth $3000 as well as personal property worth $1300 (transcription 1.8). Regardless of the relationship between Cole and Mrs.Riley that prompted his legacies of a handsome amount of cash along with sentimental and valuable household goods, regardless of her advantaged economic circumstances for a black woman in 1840s Boston, Elizabeth Riley was paid; her time and effort did not fall into the category of voluntarism.

The probate records indicate that home care was oftentimes seen as employment, not charity. Chloe Russell was likely to have earned her claim against the John W. Brown estate by virtue of her cooking; Eunice Senex no doubt was named the beneficiary in Amy Jackson's second will because of her caregiving. Two more instances of paid nursing are unmistakably documented in the probate records; others more than likely escape detection because they are not so clearly spelled out. The administrative account filed on November 15, 1841, that brought the settlement of Edward Lawson's estate to a close, included a reference to "Cash paid Catherine Lines   Nurse__.__ $10.00." The executor's account filed on March 27, 1843, that ended the probate process for Chloe Russell's estate, listed "For cash for Ruby Lea nursing in last sickness--6.50." These five women--Mrs. Elizabeth Riley, Chloe Russell, Eunice Senex, Catherine Lines, and Ruby Lea--epitomize the many women who rendered healthcare and housekeeping services to the elderly and the ill, converting their gender-designated role as nurturer into their livelihood.

Beyond the circumstantial evidence about taking in wash and the straightforward notations about nursing, however, no references to black women working can be directly gleaned from the probate records. The inventories and accounts do nonetheless communicate the overriding tension of the materially meager conditions that necessitated the participation of Afro-American females in the workforce, whether inside or outside their domicile.

The probate records give no hint if Margaret Scarlett, wife of John E. Scarlett the clothesdealer, worked to supplement the family income before her husband's death. Certainly, the inventory of their household goods conjures up a pleasant home environment, the four pieces of real estate point to an effort to invest wisely, and the "Schedule of Secondhand Clothes in Shop of deceased" describes a well-stocked haberdashery. Margaret Scarlett and her two young daughters may have been cushioned by John Scarlett's prosperity during his lifetime, but after his death they faced considerable dislocation. Margaret Scarlett, through a savvy manipulation of probate protocol, managed to retain her husband's personal estate as her widow's allowance and one piece of his real estate as her widow's dower. However, just as John Scarlett's precise net worth remains unclear, the story the probate records has preserved indicates only that Margaret Scarlett, mother of two minor children, ultimately was left with between one thousand and twelve hundred dollars in real and personal property after her husband's death in 1844.

Fortunately, the Boston directories pick up the story. According to the listings in 1844 and 1845, Margaret Scarlett ran the clothing business at 38 Blackstone and lived at rear 11 South May, the piece of property assigned to her as her dower in April 1845 but also one of the pieces of real estate that was to be auctioned on June 1845. Although the subsequent four directories do not mention the shop, Margaret Scarlett, widow, continued to reside at 11 South May. Despite the June 1845 auction that included this piece of property, then, she most likely must have retired the mortgage on it with the equity realized when the other three pieces of property in her husband's name were sold on the same day. If so, her financial straits were not nearly so dire as that of a mother of two turned out of her home and divested of her personal possessions. The Boston directories show that she undertook the challenge of running the business for at least two years and that she salvaged the major investment comprising her husband's estate.[52]

Personal Possessions And Status

The probate records tangentially address black cultural values as expressed in consumption patterns. The acquisition of personal property to gain status and/or of real property to obtain security can be argued by referring to wealth-holding choices recorded in the inventories of the 1840s decedents. But there seems to be no compelling reason to interpret the actual personal possessions as evidence of the entry of blacks into a state of "artifactual literacy" reminiscent of that experienced by whites in the eighteenth-century "consumer revolution." A hundred years earlier, radically altered relations among different segments of white society resulted in "more and better" possessions as a natural expression of wealth giving way to conspicuous consumption as an artificial message about class. Middle-class whites eagerly acquired the material emblems of gentility, differentiating themselves from the less affluent.[53] With black society, there appears to have been more of an economic and social continuum.[54] At the same time, there does not seem to be strong support for believing that Boston's blacks sacrificed the immediate gratification of personal possessions for the delayed satisfaction of home ownership.[55]

Analysis of the inventoried household goods of decedents in different occupations does reveal that businessmen enjoyed the most attractive position, possessing an array of necessities, amenities, and luxuries whose accumulation did not prevent the acquisition of other forms of wealth (tables 29, 32 and 33). But for the most part the businessmen's possessions were not noticeably distinct from those of other occupation groups; the very ease of categorizing and grouping the items listed in the inventories demonstrates that diversity in commonality prevailed. The fact that when the decedents' possessions were classified as necessities, amenities, and luxuries they did not progressively and strikingly increase in variety implies that Afro-Americans chose not to buy into a system that used material possessions dramatically to establish social rank and to differentiate community members.

True, the mental image of the businessman's home environment creates a domestic setting with "more and better" than the household surroundings of semi-skilled laborers' similarly visualized. But the particulars that made up that "more and better" often show up among the possessions of non-businessmen. For instance, the laborer Edward Lawson and the widow Amy Jackson owned silver; Lawson and the two semi-skilled laborers Primus Hall and Henry Robinson owned decorative items; Jackson, Hall, and Robinson owned literacy belongings (tables 37-39). In fact, there is no grouping of luxuries that businessmen possessed exclusively. In short, John Robinson's mahogany furniture and Thomas Cole's china tea set--as much as they connote the emphasis on solid splendor and delicate beauty that are the hallmarks of status-driven consumerism--nevertheless represent the culmination of a continuum of household goods that commences with Edward Lawson's "Pine Table" and "Crockery Iron and Tin Ware" (transcription 1.5). To be sure, there were Afro-Americans in antebellum Boston with virtually nothing by way of property, but among those for whom the inventories record enough possessions in sufficient detail for analysis there does not appear to be an abrupt hiatus based on class-conscious consumption patterns.

The rather limited repertory of household goods leads to the supposition that blacks were not full participants in the consumer revolution that had transformed white society a century previously. Neither socially nor economically could they afford to focus on the individual achievement and material elaboration requisite for joining the bourgeoisie as defined by the socioeconomic mainstream. It could be argued that Afro-Americans may have remained in a state of artifactual pre-literacy while whites forged ahead as consumers precisely because a commitment to a communal ethos flowered and served the black community long after an allegiance to private enterprise evolved and suited the broader society. This social and economic solidarity, however admirable, was nonetheless imposed by mainstream racism, which depressed blacks' collective standard of living by denying equal opportunity for individual Afro-American material advancement.[56]

Real Estate And Permanence

The eschewing of consumerism cannot, moreover, be readily linked to choosing to invest in real estate rather than personal property. Ten of the twenty-one 1840s decedents were inventoried as holding real estate valued at $32,343.41 in toto; they also possessed $939.16 in household goods at death (table 9). Primus Hall, who was inventoried with the greatest amount of real estate, held considerably less in domestic goods--$72.74--than did John Robinson, who owned $237.16 worth of household furnishings compared to his $944.23 in real estate. It might be easy to conclude that Hall limited consumer spending in favor of investment expenditures while John Robinson chose the opposite tack. But it is important to keep in mind that the $939.16 that the ten real-estate-owning decedents had in household goods represents the bulk of the appraised value of all the household goods owned by all twenty-one of the 1840s decedents--$1302.31 1/2. In other words, those who died owning or in the process of trying to own real estate tended to possess more household goods than those who had not invested in real estate.

That their household goods were appraised on their inventory at a much lower value than their real estate is essentially a reflection of the nature of the assets themselves. As long as feather bedding was worth $4.00 to $16.00, a gold watch and key was valued at $15.00, and a piano forte was worth $12.00 to $20.00, blacks in antebellum Boston would have been hard-pressed to expend more on personal possessions than on real estate. Even John Robinson--the most "profligate" of the 1840s decedents with his ritzy suite of parlor furniture--did not sink more of his money into household goods than into land and houses. His balancing act stumbled after his death because he pushed "trying to have it all" too far, but the value of his real estate holdings still exceeded his assets in consumer durables. A propensity for investing in real estate, as opposed to expending financial resources on personal property, may indeed have existed in the black community, but simplistic conclusions based on dollar amounts stated in inventories fail to take into account the intrinsic value of the commodities being compared.

Of course, Afro-Americans in antebellum Boston had other options for wealth-holding--business stock or cash, notes, and savings (table 9). Five of the ten decedents with real estate owned $313.70 in business stock; three non-real-estate owners died with $455.31 1/2 in business stock. In addition, fourteen of the twenty-one 1840s decedents had cash, notes, and savings. Five were real-estate-owners, and they together had $2,390 in liquid assets, whereas the nine non-real-estate owners were inventoried with $4,349.92 in cash, notes, and savings.

Again, decedents with real estate were not shut out from other forms of wealth-holding by virtue of having to apply all available funds toward the high cost of home ownership. And sizable savings like the $2,519.33 with which Thomas Cole died were an anomaly; other decedents with substantial cash, notes, and savings but no real estate--Edward Lawson, Lucinda Smith, Joseph Sprague, and Peter Williams--may have been accumulating cash toward a "down payment" on real estate (table 16). Or perhaps they inherited the money but realized that they would not be able to complete payment on mortgage notes. It is impossible today to determine with full assurance the rationale for the various forms of assets that appear on the inventories. Moreover, options for wealth-holding that the inventories seem to record must not be seen as unhampered and deliberate decisions made by the decedents. Fate determined the cash estates of mariners; probate distorted the contents of a decedent's estate when the intent of the process was expediting legal settlement to retire mortgages or pay creditors. Pronouncements about preferences for investment and expenditure among the 1840s decedents must be framed with caution when the documentation does not do full justice to the complexity of issues. It is probably safe, however, to posit that the situation was not a matter of either/or: black Americans in pre-Civil War Boston with assets enough to choose where to put their money were likely to have both personal possessions and real estate; those who died with land and houses listed on their inventories generally also had household goods (and, if not, this absence was probably more a reflection of the procedural imperfections of probate rather than the genuine absence of the stuff of everyday life).

The movable property listed on the inventories of black homeowners also does not seem to indicate any greater consciousness of legacy than does that recorded for non-homeowners. Although somewhat speculative and possibly anachronistic, three categories of possessions can be identified as potential heirlooms in light of their capacity for maintaining and accruing monetary value, as well as for embodying sentimental meaning--feather bedding, china or silver, and jewelry or clocks. As a matter of fact, what today would be regarded as the most practical of these three potential heirlooms historically was considered a precious legacy to be passed from one generation to the next; feather bedding could represent a lifetime's painstaking effort toward comfortable sleeping accommodations.[57]

Thomas Cole's will documents this attitude when he proudly bequeaths his feather bed--"which formerly belonged to my mother"--along with his "best china tea set" to Mrs. Elizabeth Riley (transcription 1.1). Thomas Cole, however, was not a homeowner; he was one of the five among the eleven 1840s decedents whose inventories have been analyzed who did not hold real estate. As it turns out, he and the four other non-homeowners were more likely than the six homeowners to possess the three kinds of potential heirlooms (table 53). In addition, there does not appear to be any tidy correlation between dying with real estate and dying testate. Afro-Americans in Boston during the 1840s may have funneled limited resources toward acquiring real estate as a symbolic stake in society, but the pursuit of permanence did not find parallel expression in either acquiring certain personal possessions or controlling the distribution of assets after death.

In sum, then, the evidence available in this pool of probate records offers interesting shadings on themes from black social history scholarship. Diversity in commonality seems to have typified the 1840s black community in Boston, whether in material circumstances or in private and civic interaction. Women appear to have been active in seeking their own and their children's financial security. The decedents' wealth-holding patterns show only partial participation in the "consumer revolution" yet indicate no discernible rejection of consumerism in favor of longer-term investments. Pertinent findings from the analysis of these twenty-three probate records therefore can be beneficially contrasted with black social history scholarship.

Probate Records As Primary Sources

In conclusion, the modest number of probate records studied supported a microcosmic approach to learning about black Bostonians who died during the 1840s. This small-scale yet multifaceted method permitted an exploration of the usefulness of probate records as primary sources for developing a richer understanding of a previously assumed inarticulate population. The findings are mixed. Without recourse to sources other than probate records, much remains mysterious or misunderstood about the chosen constituency. Yet without turning to other sources, intimate and subtle connotations about the constituency under study abound in probate records. The shortcomings of probate records as historical conduits can be attributed to their inability to answer questions that at first seem appropriate to their billing as intact time capsules of past material life. By definition, probate records are expected to document the process of "hearing and determining questions and issues arising in matters concerning the probate of wills or the administration of decedents' estates."[58] They are supposed to provide detailed lists or real and personal property, all appraised, as well as clear accountings of every administrative action. It would seem highly plausible, then, that scholars would rely on analyses of probate records to attain accurate data about material conditions and wealth-holding patterns. But even these seemingly appropriate lines of research can be stymied by flaws internal to probate records.

Inventories simply do not fulfill the Platonic ideal of total itemization of all "real estate, goods, chattels, rights, and credits." Moreover, they neither transmit the actual appearance of the itemized artifacts nor spell out the manner and order of acquisition of the inventoried assets. When questions about literacy or other biographical considerations are put to probate records, only equivocal or circumstantial conclusions can be drawn. The owning of books or a desk and the signing of a will usually are inadequate as proof of genuine literacy; the appearance of names of contemporaries and organizations in probate records rarely suffices as knowledge about the individual decedent's life and personality.

The strengths of probate records as historical conduits can be located in their responsiveness to inquiries that are appropriate to their status as partial repositories of past material conditions and cultural values. It is imperative that the tactics scholars employ include sympathetic and close readings of the probate records. This seemingly unstructured research strategy lets the documents speak; although the flaws internal to probate records cannot be fully evaded, they need not entrap the scholar, slamming the door that probate records promise to open.

In fact, probate records do open doors--not only into the domestic environments of bygone eras, but also into domains less tangible but no less significant to the historic populations who experienced them. Reference to the probate records alone made possible the description of a well-organized community of Afro-Americans living in Boston in the 1840s. The documents reveal that this community existed on several planes--psychological, political, and physical. Evidence of the network of community members, the commitment to community organizations, and the proximity in residence all imply the merging of the personal and public, the private and civic. Reference to the probate records alone also made possible the description of a struggling community. The documents show that this community lived in differentiated circumstances--pitiable, decent, and extravagant. But evidence of continuity rather than discontinuity in the possessions of the decedents, as well as the lack of socioeconomic barriers in interaction and residential patterns, suggests the melding of diversity within commonality.

This caliber of understanding draws upon the subtext of probate records. Rather than becoming mired in the fruitless pursuit of precise calculations, an intense look at a small body of documents has shown that scholars and laymen alike can embark--through the close reading of probate records--on a fascinating engagement with the quotidian as central to learning about the living past.

Appendix A

Transcriptions

NOTE

To impart a sense of probate records as artifacts, a selection of the original documents at the center of this study have been reproduced in computer-generated, visually-inflected transcriptions. Variations in typeface and size simulate the appearance of the preprinted forms; italics indicates handscript passages.

These transcriptions represent a sample of two complete probate packets in the Suffolk County Courthouse associated with two of twenty-three black Bostonians who died in the 1840s. The documents for these two decedents are organized chronologically, in accord with their court-assigned date and in keeping with internal dating or probate protocol.

These transcriptions do not manage to convey variants in penmanship, especially the character of different signatures. However, variables in names are rendered as found in each instance -- u V Sinnix versus Eunice Senex (transcriptions 2.5 and 2.7). It is clear that officialdom's rendition of a name never overrode the individual's preference. In such small matters resides the "flavor" of what superficially reads as strictly pro forma court proceedings. And, the visually-inflected transcriptions -- showing both the repetitive and the erratic elements of the primary source -- encourage the perception of probate records as both documents and artifacts.

TRANSCRIPTION 1.1

THOMAS COLE (35173) WILL: AUGUST 9, 1847

I Thomas Cole of Boston in the County of Suffolk, Hairdresser, being feeble in body, but of sound mind and memory, do make and publish this my last will testament

1. *I direct that all my debts and funeral expenses shall be paid.*
2. *I give and bequeath to the Rev. John T. Raymond Three hundred dollars; and to Mrs. John T. Raymond his wife, fifty dollars to be paid to her personally for her sole + separate use.*
3. *I give and bequeath to Mrs. Elizabeth Riley Three hundred dollars, my feather bed which formerly belonged to my mother, all my sheets, counterpanes, pillowcases, one dozen towels, and my best china tea set.*
4. *I give and bequeath to the Bay State Lodge of the Grand United Order of the Odd Fellows, number 114, Four hundred dollars, to be employed as a fund for defraying funeral expenses of deceased members and aiding their widows + orphans. I direct this money to be placed in the Savings Bank, and no part to be drawn out except by a vote of the Lodge concurred by two thirds of the members present at the meeting. In case the said Lodge should for misconduct or any other cause be deprived of its privileges, or in any other way become extinct as a lodge, then the money or what remains of it shall go to the Ogden Lodge of New Haven, Conn., to be applied to the same objects.*
5. *I give and bequeath to Eunice R. Davis of Boston Fifty dollars.*
6. *I give and bequeath to the Deacons of the First Independent Baptist Church in Belknap Street in Boston sometimes called the African Church, Three hundred dollars, to be by them deposited in the Savings Bank, and applied for the relief of the sick, poor, and destitute members of the said Church, but no part of the money is to be drawn out and appropriated for these objects except by a vote concurred in by a majority of the brethren of the Church, at some regular or special meeting of the Church.*
7. *I give to my nephew Thomas Cole Richardson, son of Mrs. E. Richardson, Three hundred dollars to be paid him when he arrives at the age of twenty one years and no part of the principal or interest is to be paid him till that time. I direct my executors to deposit the sum of Three hundred dollars in the Savings Bank, so that the said Thomas Cole Richardson may*

receive the benefits of the accumulated interest when he comes of age. If he should die before arriving at that age, I give the same sum to my executors hereafter named in trust that they shall apply the same and the accumulated interest towards erecting a Hall for the accommodation of the colored people of Boston.
8. I give to Thomas B. Hilton, son of John T. Hilton One hundred dollars, to be placed by my said Executors in the Savings Bank till be becomes of age; and when he arrives at the age of twenty one years to pay him the principal and accumulated interest. If he should die before arriving at that age of I give the same sum and accumulated interest to said John T. Hilton and his wife, to them, therein being, executors and administrators in equal Moieties.
9. I give the said J. Hilton of Boston, Hairdresser, One hundred dollars.
10. I give and bequeath to Alfred G. Howard of said Boston, hairdresser, Seventy five dollars.
11. I give and bequeath all my books to the Adelphic Union Library Association.
12. All the rest, rendue, + remainder of my property, after paying the charges of administering my estate, I direct my executors, in their discretion, to appropriate to such charitable objects as they may see fit.

Lastly, I nominate and appoint my friends the said John T. Hilton and Alfred G. Howard, Executors of this my last will and testament.

Any sums that I have in the foregoing will directed to be placed in the Savings Bank, may be invested by the parties having the control of them either by depositing them in the Savings Bank or purchasing with them any safe Bank stock likely to yield a regular annual income.

In witness thereof I the said Thomas Cole have hereunto set my hand and seal this twenty seventh day of March in the year Eighteen hundred forty seven.

Signed, sealed
published and
declared as +   Thomas Cole
for his last will
+ testament by the
said Thomas Cole in the presence of us, who in his presence + the
presence of each other at   his request, have here unto set
our names as witnesses.

Henry P. Hollandas
George W. Searle
S. E. Seawall

A codicil to the last will + testament of Thomas Cole above written. I republish the said will, declaring that by charitable objects to which my executors may appropriate the residue of my estate as provided in the 12th clause of said will I mean such charitable religious, and benevolent objects as my said Executors may approve.
In witness whereof I have hereunto set my hand + seal this twenty ninth day of March A.D. 1847.

Signed, sealed
published and
declared as +   *Thomas Cole*
for a codicil
to his last will
+ testament by the
said Thomas Cole in the presence of us, who in his ~~this~~ *[sic] presence + the presence of each other at his request, has here unto set our names as witnesses.*
  S. E. Seawall
  Henry P. Holland
  George W. Searle

Commonwealth of Massachusetts.

SUFFOLK, ss. At a Probate Court holden at Boston, within and for the county of Suffolk, on the *Ninth* day of *August* in the year *1847. By the Hon. Judge of Probate for said County.*
    THE annexed will and codicil being presented by *John T. Hilton + Alfred G. Howard* the Executors therein named, for Probate, *and the said Executors having given public notice pursuant to my order, which is on file in said Court, to all persons interested therein to appear here this day, and shew cause if any they have either for or against the Probate thereof, and no person appearing to object thereto,* -- George W. Searle, Henry p. Holland + S. E. Sewall. appear and make oath, that *they* saw the said *Thomas Cole* sign,

seal, and heard *him* publish the instrument hereto annexed, *which is dated on the twenty ninth day of March last* as and for *his* last will and testament: and that *he* was then, to the best of their discernment, of a sound disposing mind and memory, and that *t* hey

Subscribe their names thereto, as witnesses, in the presence of said testat *or* and of each other.

S. E. Sewall, Henry P. Holland + George W. Searle

appear and make oath, that *they* saw the said *Thomas Cole* sign, seal, and heard *him* publish the *other* instrument hereto annexed, *being dated on the twenty ninth day of March last* as and for a codicil to *his* last will and testament: and that *he* was then, to the best of *their* discernment, of a sound disposing mind and memory, and that *t* hey

Subscribe their names thereto, as witnesses, in the presence of said testat or and of each other.

prove
And I do ˆ approve and allow the said instruments as the last will and testament of said testator and order them to be recorded. Given under my hand and seal of office, the day and year first above written

Willard Phillips **Judge of Probate.**

TRANSCRIPTION 1.2

THOMAS COLE (35173) PETITION FOR EXECUTION: AUGUST 9, 1847

To the Honorable Judge of the Court of Probate,
for the County of Suffolk,
in the Commonwealth of Massachusetts,

HUMBLY shews *John T. Hilton & Alfred G. Howard* of Boston, in said County,
Hair dressers

That *they* *are* named and appointed Execut*ors* of the last will and testament of *Thomas Cole* of Boston, in said County of Suffolk, *Hairdresser* deceased; who at the time of making the same, was of full age, and of sane mind, and last dwelt in said Boston, where he died. Leaving estate within this Commonwealth, whereby it appertains to your petitioners to administer said estate, according to said will, *they* having legal right to accept of *their* said trust.

Whereupon the said Executors herewith present the same to your Honor, to be approved, allowed and recorded as the law directs; and pray that administration of said estate according thereto, may be granted and committed to them agreeably to the law in such cases made and provided.

Dated at Boston, this fourteenth day of June in the year 1847

John T. Hilton
Alfred G. Howard

TRANSCRIPTION 1.3

THOMAS COLE (35173) ORDER OF NOTICE: AUGUST 9, 1847

Commonwealth of Massachusetts.

Suffolk, ss. **At a Probate Court,** held at Boston, in said County, on Monday, the fourteenth day of *June* in the year one thousand eight hundred and *forty seven.*

WHEREAS a certain instrument purporting to be the last will and testament of *Thomas Cole* late of said Boston, *Hairdresser* deceased, has been presented to Court of Probate, by *John T. Hilton & Alfred G. Howard* the Execut *ors* therein named.

ORDERED, That the said *Executors* give notice to all persons interested therein, to appear at a Probate Court, to be held at said Boston, on Monday, the *ninth* day of *August next* at nine o'clock before noon, by publishing this order *three* weeks successively in the newspaper called the *Boston Chronotype*

printed in said Boston, that they may then and there appear, and shew cause, if any they have, either for or against the allowance thereof.

Willard Phillips **Judge of Probate.**

PURSUANT to the within directions, I have caused a copy of the within order of notice to be published three weeks successively in the newspaper called the *Boston Chronotype*

Suffolk, ss. AT a Probate Court held at Boston, in said County, on Monday, the *ninth* day of *August* A. D. 1847.
  Then the said *Alfred G. Howard* make solemn oath to the truth of the above return by him made before me,

Willard Phillips **Judge of Probate.**

TRANSCRIPTION 1.4

THOMAS COLE (32173) EXECUTOR'S BOND : AUGUST 9, 1847

Know all Men by these Presents,

THAT WE *John T. Hilton, Hairdresser, & Alfred G. Howard, Hairdresser, as principals, and John P. Coburn, Trader & Coffin Pitts, Trader, as sureties, all of Boston in the County of Suffolk*

in the COMMONWEALTH OF MASSACHUSETTS, are holden and stand firmly bound and obliged unto *Willard Phillips* Esquire, Judge of the Probate of Wills, and for granting administration, within the County of Suffolk, in the sum of *Five thousand* Dollars, to be paid unto the said *Willard Phillips* and his successors in the said office, to the true payment whereof, we bind ourselves, and each of us, our and each of our heirs, executors and administrators, jointly and severally, by these presents, sealed with our seals. Dated the *Ninth* day of *August* in the year one thousand and eight hundred and *forty seven*

The CONDITION of this OBLIGATION is such, that if the above bounden *John T. Hilton & Alfred G. Howard*

Executors of the last will and testament of *Thomas Cole* late of *said Boston, Hairdresser,* deceased,

 First- shall make and return into the Probate Court, for said County of Suffolk, within three months, a true inventory of all the real estate, and all the goods, chattels, rights and credits of the said testat or which are by law to be administered, and which shall have come to *their* possession or knowledge;
 Secondly - shall administer according to law, and to the will of the testat *or* all h*is* goods, chattels, rights and credits, and the proceeds of all h*is* real estate, that may be sold for the payment of h*is* debts or legacies, which shall at any time come to the possession of the executors or to the possession of any other person for *them*; and
 Thirdly - shall render upon oath a just and true account of *their* administration, within one year, and at any other times, when required by the said Judge of Probate;

171

Then the above written obligation shall be void, otherwise shall remain in full force.

Signed, sealed and delivered
    in presence of   }   *John T. Hilton*

Rengo C. Gregory   *Alfred G. Howard*
                              John P. Coburn
                              Coffin Pitts

SUFFOLK, ss. At the Court of Probate holden at Boston, in said County, on Monday, the *Ninth* day of *August* in the year 184 7
I have examined and do approve of the foregoing bond, and order the same to be recorded in the Probate Office.

Willard Phillips   **Judge of Probate.**

TRANSCRIPTION 1.5

THOMAS COLE (35173) INVENTORY: SEPTEMBER 13, 1847

Commonwealth of Massachusetts

SUFFOLK, ss,   **THE HONORABLE**
WILLARD PHILLIPS, ESQUIRE
Judge of the Court of Probate, in and
for the County of Suffolk, aforesaid,

To Phineas Capen, Benjamin P. Bassett & Edwin F. Howard, all of the City of Boston

GREETING.

YOU are hereby appointed and empowered, as three suitable persons to appraise all the real estate, goods, and chattels, rights and credits of *Thomas Cole*
of Boston, in said County of Suffolk, *Hairdresser, dec^d*

comprised in the Inventory, according to your best skill and judgment, as soon as may be, in dollars and cents, according to the present value thereof, being first sworn to the faithful discharge of that trust.
  And when you shall have completed the said appraisement as aforesaid, you are to deliver the same, together with this Warrant with you doings thereon, sealed up to
John T. Hilton & Alfred G. Howard, Exc^r of his will

who *are* hereby accordingly directed so to return and exhibit the same on oath into the Probate Office of the said County of Suffolk, within three months from the time of taking upon *them* sel *ves* that trust.

  Witness the said WILLARD PHILLIPS, Esquire, Judge as aforesaid, under his hand and seal official, this *Ninth* day of *August* in the one thousand eight hundred and forty *seven*.

Willard Phillips **Judge of Probate**

Countersigned,

H. M. Willis Register.
August 20. in the year 1847

SUFFOLK, ss.

Then the above named *Capen, Bassett, & Edwin F. Howard* personally appeared and made oath that they would faithfully and impartially discharge the trust reposed in them by the foregoing warrent.

Before me, *H. M. Willis* Justice of the Peace

To the Honorable *Willard Phillips* **Esquire,**

Judge of the Court of Probate for the County of Suffolk

Pursuant to the warrant to us directed from your Honor, we the subscribers, the Committee therein named, having been first sworn, have made the following appraisement of the estate and effects comprised in the Inventory of the real estate, goods, chattels, rights and credits of *Thomas Cole, dec^d*
as made by the *Executors*

Amount of Real Estate   *none*
Amount of Personal Estate   *$2690.84*
The particulars of which are hereto annexed.

Phin^s. Capen
Benj. P. Bassett   } *Committee*
Edwin F. Howard

Suffolk, ss. At a Probate Court held at Boston, in said County, on Monday the *thirteenth* day of *September* in the year on thousand eight hundred and forty *seven,*

John T. Hilton, Alfred G. Howard, the said Executors

exhibits the foregoing, and makes oath, that contains a true and perfect Inventory of all the estate of said *deceased* that has come to *their* hands or knowledge, and if anything further shall hereafter appear, *they* will render a just and true account thereof into the Probate Office; it is ordered by the Judge of said court, that the same be accepted and filed, and that this decree, together with the said warrant, be recorded.

Willard Phillips **Judge of Probate**

Inventory of the estate of Thomas Cole late of Boston, Hairdresser, decease.--
   To wit

Household furniture, &c.-

Bed $15. bedding 3.50 White Tea Set $5.	23.50
2 White counterpanes $2.50 & $1. 1 Doz. Towels 1.50	5.00
98 Diaper & Clash towels 3.92 4 Hair cutting clothes, 40c	4.32
11 shaving clothes small, 44c 6 window curtains .25c	.69
2 Do chairs, cushions, &stools $5. 6 Cane seat chairs 3.	8.00
2 Do Do $10.62 Office chair, 75c Rockg Do &Cush., 25c	11.62
2 Hair seat chairs, 25c Table $1. Work table, 50c	1.75
Timepiece $3. Lot of Books $30. L. Glass $2. show case, 25c	35.25
Bedstead, 75c 2 screens, 25c Lot of framed prints &c 1.68	2.68
Thermometer, 12 1/2c Map of U.S., 25c Shop Desk, 12 1/2c	.50
Pole &sign 1.50 Lot of soap 1.87 4 hones	4.87
2 Boxes of soap 1. 3 Razors & 2 Dressing cases, 75c	1.75
2 Bottles hair Oil, 25c Lot of sundreies 50c 2 Caens .37c	1.12
Lot crockery, glassware, &c. .50c Curtain, Port Polio. & Sund., 50c	1.00
Wearing apparel of dec. 34.96 Velise & bag, 50	35.46
Gold watch & key &c $15 Flute $3. 4 Trunks & 2 chests $2.	20.00
Piano Forte $12. 2 Copper boilers $2.	14.00
	$171.51
Deposit in the Prov. Institution for Savings in Boston	1500.
Deposit in Sufflk Savings Bank in Boston	1000.
Cash in the hands of the Cxecutors	19.33
	2690.84

TRANSCRIPTION 1.6

THOMAS COLE (35173)
EVIDENCE PERPETUATED: SEPTEMBER 13, 1847

Notice is hereby given, that the subscribers have been
duly appointed *Executors of the will* of *Thomas Cole* late of
Boston in the County of Suffolk, *Hairdresser*
      deceased, and have taken upon *them* sel*ves* that trust, by giving bond as the law directs. And all persons having demands upon the estate of said deceased, are required to exhibit the same; and all persons indebted to the said estate, are called upon to make payment to

    BOSTON, *Aug 9th, 1847*   *Alfred G. Howard*
                  John T. Hilton } Executor

We the *Executors* above named, testify and declare, that in pursuance of the order of the Judge of Probate for the County of Suffolk, dated the *ninth* day of *August* last past, I did within three months from said date cause a notice of my appointment to said trust, whereof the foregoing is a copy, to be published three weeks successively in the
Boston Chronotype, printed at said Boston.

    John T. Hilton
    Alfred G. Howard

    SUFFOLK, ss. On the *thirteenth* day of September in the year 1847
    Personally appeared *John T. Hilton & Alfred G. Howard* aforenamed, and made solemn oath to the truth of the foregoing affidavit, by *them* subscribed--before me,

    Phin^s. Capen **Justice of the Peace.**

    SUFFOLK, ss. Sept. 13 1847. The above affidavit was this day filed and recorded.

    Attest,
    H. M. Willis **Register of Probate.**

TRANSCRIPTION 1.7

THOMAS COLE (35173) ORDER OF NOTICE: APRIL 2, 1849

Commonwealth of Massachusetts.

Suffolk, ss. **At a Probate Court, held at Boston, in** said County, on Monday, the *twelfth* day of *March* in the year one thousand eight hundred and forty *nine*

WHEREAS *John T. Hilton & Alfred G. Howard*

Executors of the last will and testament of *Thomas Cole* late of Boston, in said County, *Hairdresser* deceased, testate, have this day presented for allowance the *first* account of *their* Executorship,

ORDERED, That the said *Executors* give notice to all persons interested therein, to appear at a Probate Court, to be held at said Boston, on Monday, the *second* day of *April*
                ten
next at ~~nine~~ o'clock, before noon, by publishing this order three weeks successively in the newspaper called the *Boston Chrontype* printed in said Boston, that they may then and there appear, and shew cause, if any they have, either for or against the allowance thereof.

Edwd. G. Loring **Judge of Probate.**

PURSUANT to the within directions, I have caused a copy of the within order of notice to be published *three* weeks successively in the newspaper called the *Boston Chronotype*
John T. Hilton
            Alfred G. Howard

SUFFOLK, ss. At a Probate Court, held at Boston, in said County, on Monday, the *second* day of *April* in the year 1849.
Then the said *Hilton & Howard* made solemn oath to the truth of the above return by them made before me,
            Edwd. G. Loring **Judge of Probate.**

TRANSCRIPTION 1.8

THOMAS COLE (35173) FIRST ACCOUNT: APRIL 2, 1849

The *First* Account of *John T. Hilton & Alfred G. Howard,* Executors of the Will of *Thomas Cole* late of Boston, in the County of Suffolk, *Hairdresser* deceased, testate.

1847	Said Executors charge *themselves* with the following--*to wit*: September 13	DOLLS.	CTS.
	With the value of personal estate in The inventory	2690.	84
	With gain on sale of personal estate,	215.	44
	~~With sums received, so stated in schedule A,~~		
		2906.	28
1849	Said Executors prays to be allowed as follows--*to wit:* June 20	DOLLS.	CTS.
	For sundry payments made, as stated in schedule B.	2399.	75
	Allowance to Executors settling estate thus far	100.	00
Balance retained by the Executors to be appropriated agreeably to the provisions of the Will of said Testator.		406.	53
		$2906	28
	John T. Hilton *Alfred G. Howard*		
	* correct sum = $2369.75 ** correct sum = $436.53		

Suffolk, ss. At a Probate Court, held at Boston, in said County, on MONDAY, the *second* day of *April* in the year 18*49,*
   The foregoing account having been presented for allowance, and *public* notice thereof having been given to the parties interested, according to the order of the Court, *and no objection being made thereto*

Edwd. G. Loring **Judge of Probate.**

1847		
Aug. 1	John Peak	$ 41.--
Aug. 23	Elizabeth Riley for nursing	60.--
July. 20	Elizabeth Riley	13.--
Aug. 24	D. H. Stoser	50.--
Sept. 3	Norris & Co.	6.--
Sept. 8	Edward Blake, rent	25.--
Sept. 8	Moses French	25.--
Aug. 23	B. B. Mussey	.25
Oct. 1	J. B. Hilton	2.75
Oct. 5	William Riley	8.--
Oct. 28	B. Marsh	.50
Dec. 30	John Curtis Jun.	5.00
Dec. 31	Sam. E. Sewall Esq.	20.--
1848		
Jan. 3	E. T. Howard	5.00
Jan. 3	B. P. Bassett	5.00
Jan. 3	P. Capen for assistance settling estate	18.75
1849		
Jan. 29	Ann Jennett Jackson	20.00
Nov. 28	W. Meriam bal of Note	.50
	And said Exec. pray Allowance for the following legacies paic Viz	
	Elizabeth Riley Legacy of furniture & C	27.50
	John T. Hilton Do	100.00
	A. G. Howard Do	75.00
	Eunice R. Davis Do	50.00
	S. M. Raymond Do	50.00
	Elizabeth Riley Do	150.00
	J. T. Raymond Do 200	
	J. T. Raymond Do 100	300.00
	Elizabeth Riley Do	150.00
	Thomas B. Hilton Do	100.00
	Thomas C. Richardson	300.00
	1st. Baptist Church	300.00
	Bay State Lodge, Odd Fellows	400.00
	Chronotype Order of Notice on this a/c	2.50
	John T. Hilton, bill	25.00
	W. Brailly--Carriages at funeral	9.00
	Alfred G. Howard bill	25.00
		$2399.75*
	* correct sum - $2369.75	

TRANSCRIPTION 2.1

Amy Jackson (32471) Will: [March 24, 1837]

I Amy Jackson of Boston in the County of Suffolk and Commonwealth of Massachusetts widow, make this my last will & testament, in manner following, to wit,
I will & bequeath all my estate real and personal, after my decease, to Mary Clark wife of Thomas Clark of Portland in the County of Cumberland & state of Maine, Mariner, the adopted daughter of my late husband Thomas Jackson, to have and to hold the same for her own use & the use of her heirs forever.
I hereby appoint Isaac V. Osgood of Boston, Esquire, to be the executor of my last will.
And I the above named Amy Jackson, the testatrix, hereby sign, publish and declare the above instrument to be my last will & testament in presence of the witnesses who in presence of the testatrix, and of each other, have herewith signed their names.

Daniel Baxter   *her*
  John Vinton   *Amy + Jackson*
  Samuel Curtve[?] Jr.   *Mark*

TRANSCRIPTION 2.2

AMY JACKSON (32471) ORDER OF NOTICE: APRIL 13, 1840

COMMONWEALTH OF MASSACHUSETTS.

Suffolk, ss. To the next of kin, and all other per-
sons interested in the estate of Amy Jackson
late of Boston, in said county, widow deceased,
intestate, *leaving no heirs or kindred in this Commonwealth who by law can inherit her estate*
WHEREAS application has been made to me to grant a letter of administration on the estate of said deceased, to *Phineas Blair, Esquire* ~~of~~ *Public Administrator in & for said County*

You are hereby cited to appear at a Probate Court to be held at said Boston, on Monday the *thirteenth* day of April next at nine o'clock before noon, to shew cause, if any you have, against granting the same.
He the said Blair is hereby directed to give public notice thereof *two weeks successively*
in the newspaper called the
Boston Courier
printed in said Boston,

Given under my hand this *twenty third* day of *March* in the year one thousand eight hundred and ~~thirty~~ *forty*
Willard Phillips *Judge of Probate*

PURSUANT to the within directions, I have caused a copy of the within order of notice to be published two weeks successively in the newspaper called the *Boston Courier, the words "on the estate of said deceased" being omitted by inadvertance in the printing*
Phineas Blair

Suffolk, ss. AT a Probate Court held at Boston, in said county, on Monday the *13th* day of April in the year 1840
Then the said Blair made solemn oath to the truth of the above return by him made before me.
Willard Phillips **Judge of Probate**

TRANSCRIPTION 2.3

AMY JACKSON (32471) ORDER OF NOTICE: APRIL 27, 1840

COMMONWEALTH OF MASSACHUSETTS.

Suffolk, ss. **At a Probate Court, held at Boston,**
in said County, on Monday the   *Thirtieth*   day of *March*
in the year one thousand eight hundred and *forty*.

WHEREAS a certain instrument purporting to be the last will and testament of   Amy Jackson   late of said Boston, Widow   deceased, ----------------   has been presented to said Court of probate, by   Eunice Senex of said Boston Widow the Executrix   therein named.

Ordered, that the said   *Eunice*   give notice to all persons interested therein, to appear at a Probate Court to be held at said Boston, on Monday the   thirteenth   day of   April next   at nine o'clock before noon, by publishing this order two   weeks successively in the newspaper called the
Liberator
printed in said Boston,   that they may then and there appear and shew cause, if any they have, either for or against the probate thereof.
   Willard Phillips   **Judge of Probate**

PURSUANT to the within directions, I have caused a copy of the within order of notice to be published   two   weeks successively   in the newspaper called the   Liberator

S.E. Sewall

Suffolk, ss.   AT a Probate Court held at Boston, in said county, on Monday the   *27th*   day of *April*   in the year 1840   Then the said   *Sewall*   made solemn oath to the truth of the   above return by him made before me.
   Willard Phillips   **Judge of Probate.**

TRANSCRIPTION 2.4

AMY JACKSON (32471)
PETITION FOR ADMINISTRATION: JULY 20, 1840

To the Honorable Judge of the Court of Probate within the County of *Suffolk*,

HUMBLY shews *Phineas Blair of Boston Public Adm^r. in and for said County that Amy Jackson Widow died in said Boston on the sixteenth of March current intestate having no heir of kindred in the Commonwealth who by law can inherit her estate, that she*
~~in said County~~   ~~that~~

was last an inhabitant of Boston, in said County,

leaving goods and estate, of which administration *in said County*

is necessary;

that your petitioner is *entitled to administer thereon*

and is ready to give bonds with sufficient sureties for the faithful discharge of that trust:
Wherefore he prays that your honor would grant *him* administration on the estate of said deceased, agreeably to law in such cases made and provided.

Dated at Boston, this   *twenty third*   **day of** March
in the year   18 43

Phineas Blair

Suffolk, ss.   **At a Probate Court, held at Boston,**
in said County, on Monday, the   *twentieth*   day of *July* in the year one thousand eight hundred and   *forty---*
continued by adjournment from Monday the twenty second day of June last past

And the said *Blair* having given public notice, pursuant
to my order, to the next of kin and all other persons
interested in the estate of said deceased to appear ~~here~~
~~this~~ *at a Probate Court held at said Boston on Monday the
thirteenth day of April last past*

and shew cause, if any they had, against granting the
 prayer of the foregoing petition, *in consideration
 thereof and continued from Court to Court to this day,* & a
*last will & testament of said deceased having been
proved and allowed*
 it is thereupon decreed by the Court here, that
the said petition be dismissed

~~on the estate of the said deceased, as therein prayed for,~~
~~be granted to the said~~
~~he giving bonds according to law for the faithful discharge~~
~~of that trust~~.

   Willard Phillips   **Judge of Probate**

TRANSCRIPTION 2.5

AMY JACKSON (32471)
PETITION FOR EXECUTORSHIP: JULY 20, 1840

To the Honorable ~~Willard Phillips~~ ~~Esquire~~,
Judge of the Court of Probate, for the County of Suffolk,
in the Commonwealth of *Massachusetts,*

HUMBLY shews, *Eunice Senex* of

Boston in said County, Widow

That *s* he *is* named and appointed
Execu*trix* of the last will and testament of *Amy Jackson*
of Boston, in said County of Suffolk, *Widow*
deceased ; who at the time of making the
same, was of full age, and of sane mind, and last dwelt in
said Boston, where *s* he died. Leaving estate within this
Commonwealth, whereby it appertains to your petitioner, to
administer said estate according to said will, *she*
having legal right to accept *her* said trust.

Whereupon the said Execu*trix* herewith presents the
same to your Honour, to be approved, allowed and recorded
as the law directs ; and prays that administration of
said estate according thereto, may be granted and committed
to *her* agreeably to the law in such cases made and
provided.

Dated at Boston, this *thirtieth* **day of** *March*
in the year *1840*

        Eunice Senex
          by
    S.E. Sewall, her atty.

TRANSCRIPTION 2.6

AMY JACKSON (32471) WILL: JULY 20, 1840

I Amy Jackson of Boston in the County of Suffolk, & Commonwealth of Massachusetts, widow, being of feeble health, but of sound and disposing mind and memory, do make and publish this my last will and testament.

After payment of all my just debts and funeral expenses I give, devise, and bequest all the rest, residue, and remainder of my estate both real and personal, of every name and description to Eunice Senex of said Boston, widow, sometimes called Venus Senex, who is now my nurse, to have and to hold the same to her, her heirs, executor, administrator, and assigns to her and their use and behoof [sic] forever.

In witness whereof I have hereunto set my hand and seal this ninth day of October A.D. Eighteen hundred and thirty nine.

And I hereby appoint the said Eunice Senex sole executrix of this my last will and testament.

Signed, sealed
published, & declared   Amy X Jackson
as & for her last   mark
will & testament
by the said Amy Jackson, in the presence of us who in her presence and the presence of each other have hereunto set our names as witnesses, at her request.

       S.E. Sewall
       Gustavus Andrews
       Albert Bowman

SUFFOLK, SS. Commonwealth of Massachusetts.
At a Probate Court holden at Boston, within and for the county of Suffolk, on the *twentieth* day of *July* in the year 1840, *continued by adjournment from Monday the twenty-second day of June last past*
      By the honorable   *Willard Phillips*   Esquire, Judge of the Probate of Wills, &c.

The annexed Will being presented by *Eunice Senex of said Boston, ~~Single woman~~, Widow* the Executrix therein named, for Probate, *on the thirtieth day of March last past. And the said Executrix having given public notice pursuant to my order which is filed in said Court, to all persons interested therein to appear at a Probate Court held at said Boston on Monday the thirteenth day of April last past and shew cause, if any they had, either for or against the probate thereof. Mary Clark, claiming to be interested, together with her husband Thomas Clark appeared by Issac P. Osgood Esquire their attorney, and Phineas Blair, Public Administrator in and for said County also appeared, and objected to said probate. And the consideration thereof was then continued from Court to Court to this day: and the allegation and testimony of the respective parties having been fully heard and considered and Samuel E. Sewall, Gustavus Andrews and Albert Bowman having* appeard and made oath, that *they* saw the said *Amy Jackson* sign, seal, and heard *her* publish the same Instrument as *her* last will and Testament ; and that *s*he was then, to the best of *their* discernment, of a sound disposing mind and memory, and that they subscribed their names thereto, as witnesses, in the presence of said Testa*trix* and of each other ; ~~and~~ I do prove, approve and allow the same, and order it to be recorded. --Given under my hand, and seal of office, the day and year ^*first* above written.

Willard Phillips **Judge of Probate.**

TRANSCRIPTION 2.7

AMY JACKSON (32471) RESIGNATION: JULY 20, 1840

Boston July 18, 1840

To the Hon Willard Phillips
     Judge of Probate

Sir,

I hereby decline acting as executrix of the last will & testament of Amy Jackson, and request that Samuel E. Sewall of Boston may be appointed administrator on her estate with the will annexed to act in my stead

unis V Sinnex

Witness
John. St. Pierre

TRANSCRIPTION 2.8

AMY JACKSON (32471)
PETITION FOR ADMINISTRATION: AUGUST 17, 1840

To the Honorable Judge of the Court of Probate within
the county of *Suffolk*,

HUMBLY shews   *Samuel E Sewall*   of Boston

in said County, *Esquire*   that   *Amy Jackson, widow deceased*

was last an inhabitant of Boston, in said County, *and died leaving a last will & testament, and which has been duly proved and allowed, and*
leaving goods and estate, of which administration

is necessary;
and Eunice V. Senex, the executrix named ~~has~~ *in said will, has declined accepting the said trust*
that your petitioner is desirous of being appointed administrator with the will annexed upon the said estate

and is ready to give bonds with sufficient sureties for the faithful discharge of that trust: *with the will annexed*
   Wherefore he prays that your honor would grant *him* administration on the estate of said deceased, agreeably to law in such cases made and provided.
  Dated at Boston, this 20 th   day of July in the year 18 40
                    S. E. Sewall

Suffolk, ss.   **At a Probate Court, held at Boston,**
in said County, on Monday, the *seventeenth* day of *August* in the year one thousand eight hundred and *forty*

And the said   *Sewall*   having given public notice,

pursuant to my order, to the next of kin and all other persons interested in the estate of said deceased to appear here
      this day

and shew cause, if any they had, against granting the prayer of the foregoing petition,
and now no person appearing to object thereto

      it is thereupon decreed by the Court here, that administration

      with the will annexed
on the estate of the said deceased, ˄ as therein prayed for, be granted to the said *Samuel E. Sewall* he giving bonds according to law for the faithful discharge of that trust.
      Willard Phillips   **Judge of Probate.**

TRANSCRIPTION 2.9

AMY JACKSON (32471) ORDER OF NOTICE: AUGUST 8, 1840

COMMONWEALTH OF MASSACHUSETTS.

Suffolk, ss. To the next of kin, and all other per-
sons interested in the estate of *Amy Jackson*
lat of Boston, in said county, *widow* deceased,
intestate,
 WHEREAS application has been made to me to grant a letter
of administration *with the will annexed* on the estate of
said deceased, to *Samuel E. Sewall*
of *said Boston, Esquire*
You are hereby cited to appear at a Probate Court to be held
at said Boston, on Monday the *Seventeenth* day of *August*
next at nine o'clock before noon, to shew cause, if any you
have, against granting the same.
 He the said *Samuel* is hereby directed to give public notice
thereof *three weeks successively*
in the newspaper called the
 Liberator
printed in said Boston,
 Given under my hand this *twentieth* day of *July*
in the year one thousand eight hundred and ~~thirty~~ *forty*

Willard Phillips Judge of Probate

PURSUANT to the within directions, I have caused a copy of
the within order of notice to be published *three weeks successively*
in the newspaper called the
 Liberator   S.E. Sewall

Suffolk, ss. AT a Probate Court held at Boston, in said
county, on Monday the 17th day of *August* in the year
18*40*
 Then said *Sewall* made solemn oath to the truth of
the above return by him made before me.

Willard Phillips **Judge of Probate**

TRANSCRIPTION 2.10

AMY JACKSON (32471)
ADMINISTRATOR'S BOND: AUGUST 17, 1840

Know all Men by these Presents,

That We *Samuel E. Sewall Esquire, as principal, and Joseph Sewall, Gentleman, and Joseph Southwick, Merchant, as Sureties, All of Boston in the County of Suffolk*

in the Commonwealth of Massachusetts, are holden and stand firmly bound and obliged unto *Willard Phillips Esquire*, Judge of the Probate
of Wills, and for granting administration, within the County of Suffolk,
in the sum of *Four Thousand* Dollars, to be paid unto the said

Willard Phillips and his successors in the said office, to the true payment whereof, we bind ourselves, and each of us, our and each of our
heirs, executors and administrators, jointly and severally, by these presents, sealed with our seals. Dated the *seventeenth* day of *August* in the year one thousand eight hundred and ~~thirty~~ *forty*

The CONDITION of this OBLIGATION is such, that if the above bounden

Samuel E. Sewall

Administrator of the last will and testament of Amy Jackson

late of *said Boston Widow-* deceased,

First--shall make and return to the Probate court, for said County of Suffolk, within three months, a true inventory of all the real estate, and all the goods, chattels, rights and credits of the said testat rix which are by law to be administered, and which shall have come to his possession or knowledge;

Secondly--shall administer according to law, and to the will of the testat *rix* all h er goods, chattels, rights and credits, and the proceeds of all h er real estate, that may be sold for the payment of h er debts or legacies, which shall at any time come to the possession of the administrat *or* to the possession of any other person for *him* ; and

Thirdly--shall render upon oath a just and true account of *his* administration, within one year, and at any other times, when required by the said Judge of Probate;

Then the above written obligation shall be void, otherwise shall remain in full force.

Signed, sealed, and delivered,
    in presence of   S.E. Sewall

Isaac Munroe   Joseph Sewall
   witness to S. Sewall & J Sewall
John Dexter Jr   Joseph Southwick
   witness to J. Southwick

SUFFOLK, ss. At the Court of Probate holden at Boston, in said County, on Monday, the *Seventeenth* day of *August* in the year 184*0*

I have examined and do approve of the foregoing bond, and order the same to be recorded in the Probate Office.

Willard Phillips **Judge of Probate.**

TRANSCRIPTION 2.11

AMY JACKSON (32471)
EVIDENCE PERPETUATED: OCTOBER 12, 1840

Notice is hereby given, that the subscriber has been duly appointed *Administrator with the will annexed of the estate of Amy Jackson* late of Boston in the county of Suffolk, widow deceased, and has taken upon him self that trust, by giving bond as the law directs. And all persons having demands upon the estate of said deceased, are required to exhibit the same; and all persons indebted to the said estate, are called upon to make payment to

BOSTON, *August 17th* 1840   *S.E. Sewall Adm^r.*

I the *Administrator* above named, testify and declare, that in pursuance of the order of the Judge of Probate for the County fo Suffolk, dated the *Seventeenth* day of *August* last past, I did within three months from said date cause a notice of my appointment to said trust, whereof the foregoing is a copy, to be published three weeks successively in the Atlas Liberator Daily Centinel and Gazette, printed at said Boston.

S.E. Sewall

SUFFOLK, ss. On the *twelfth* day of *October* in the year 1840

Personally appeared *Samuel E. Sewall* afore-named, and made solemn oath to the truth of the foregoing affidavit, by him subscribed --before me,

Oliver WB. Peabody **Justice of the Peace.**

SUFFOLK, ss. *October 12th* 1840 The above affidavit was this day filed and recorded.

Attest,
Oliver WB. Peabody **Register of Probate.**

TRANSCRIPTION 2.12

AMY JACKSON (32741)
INVENTORY: OCTOBER 19, 1840

To The Honorable *Willard Phillips* **Esquire,**

*Judge of the Court of Probate
for the County of Suffolk.*

PURSUANT to the warrant to us directed from your Honor, we the subscribers, the Committee therein named, having been first sworn, have make the following appraisement of the estate and effects comprised in the Inventory of the real estate, goods, chattels, rights and credits of
     Amy Jackson, of Boston
Widow.
as made by the *Administrator, with the will annexed, on the Estate of the said Amy.*

  Amount of Real Estate, -- -- -- -- -- 2605.00

  Amount of Personal Estate, -- -- -- -- 23.45
              $2628.45
  The particulars of which are hereto annexed.

    Thomas R. Sewall
    Gustavus Andrews } Committee.
    Charles B. Class

1 Beauro	1.00
1 Looking Glass & frames	.25
2 Tubs & Lot of crockery	1.50
1 Lot of tin ware & 2 flat irons	.50
3 Thin Silver Spoons	.75
2 pair sheets & 1 pr of pillow cases	1.25
3 Quilts & 1 Comforter	4.00
1 Bible & 3 old books	.50
1 chest & wearing apparel	2.50
1 Feather Bed & pillows	4.00
1 pr Iron Dogs & shovel & tongs	.50
8 chairs	1.20

2 Iron pots .75
1 Bake kettle 2 spiders 1 skillet & tea kettle 1.50
1 Lot wood & bark .50
1 Bedstead & 2 tables 1.75
2 Buckets 2 Lugs & 1 axe .50
$22.95
2 Blankets & 1 p pillow cases . 50
$23.45

TRANSCRIPTION 2.13

AMY JACKSON(32471) ORDER OF NOTICE: MARCH 1, 1841

COMMONWEALTH OF MASSACHUSETTS.

Suffolk, ss. AT a Probate Court, held at Boston,
in said County, on Monday the *fifteenth* day of *February*
in the year of our Lord, one thousand eight hundred and ~~thirty~~ *forty one*

WHEREAS *Samuel E. Sewall*

with the will annexed
Administrator of the goods and estate of *Amy Jackson* late of said Boston, *widow* deceased, intestate, has this day presented for allowance the *first* account of *his* administration upon said estate, *with a list of the claims*

against the same

ORDERED, that the said *Sewall* give notice to all persons interested therein, to appear at a Probate Court to be held at said Boston, on Monday the *first* day of *March next* at nine o'clock before noon, by publishing this order *two* weeks successively in the newspaper called the *Liberator*

printed in said Boston, that they may then and there appear and shew cause, if any they have, either for or against the probate thereof.

Willard Phillips **Judge of Probate.**

PURSUANT to the within directions, I have caused a copy of the within order of notice to be published *two* weeks successively in the newspaper called the *Liberator*

W.E. Sewall

Suffolk, ss. At a Probate Court held at Boston, in said County, on Monday the *first* day of *March* A.D. 1841

Then the said *Samuel Sewall* made solemn oath to the truth of the above return by *him* made before me.

Willard Phillips **Judge of Probate**

TRANSCRIPTION 2.14

AMY JACKSON (32471) FIRST ACCOUNT: MARCH 1, 1841

The First Account of Samuel E. Sewall Administrator of the Goods and Estate of Amy Jackson, late of Boston, in the County of Suffolk, Widow deceased, intestate, with the will annexed

184*1* Said Administrator charges *himself* with the following--*to wit*:	DOLLS.	CTS.
Jan		
With the value of personal estate of said deceased, as appraised in the Inventory,	23	45
~~With the gain on sale of the personal estate,~~		
~~With the several sums collected and received, as stated in schedule A,~~		
Balance due administrator	52	85
	$76	30

184*1* Said Administra*tor* prays to be allowed as follows--*to wit*:	DOLLS.	CTS
Jan		
For sundry payments, and charges, ~~as stated in schedule B,~~ to wit		
To cash paid advertising Probate of Will	1	50
" do " advertising notice of administration	1	
" do " witnesses on trial of probate of will	6	
" do " constable for summoning witnesses	1	40
" do " appraisers--------------------	7	50
" do " S. E. Sewall, counsel fees on trial of the will	40	
" do " services of administrator	10	
" Loss in selling personal property	7	90
" ~~Cash paid advertising administration~~		
" pd Advertising presentation of account	1	
	$76	30

Suffolk, ss. At a Probate Court, held at Boston, in said County, on MONDAY, the *first* day of *March* in the year 184*1*.

to appear at a Probate Court held at said Boston, on Monday

the ninth day of June instant; the consideration thereof was thence continued to this day, and no objections being made thereto--
And the same having been verified by the oath of
        the subscriber thereto, and examined and considered by the Court, it is decreed that the same be allowed.

        Willard Phillips   **Judge of Probate.**

TRANSCRIPTION 2.15

AMY JACKSON (32471) LIST OF CLAIMS: MARCH 1, 1841

List of claims against the Estate of Amy Jackson,
which have been presented to the Administrator
Jonathan P. Hall   1856.44
*   Stone & Adams   7.*
*   1863.44*

I have heard a physician has a claim on the estate, but do not know the amount.

S.E. Sewall,
Admr. with the will annexed
Boston Feb. 15, 1841.

TRANSCRIPTION 2.16

AMY JACKSON (32471) REQUEST: MARCH 1, 1841

Sir
   I U V Senix want the property of Amy Jackson sold by the S E Sewall by the sixteenth of March which will be a year and one day since her Death if he is not disposed to do so their is another gentleman that stands ready to take it and settle it right away

   U V Senix

please not to publish it in the Liberator for it is not so public a paper as some others
   this paper is very limmeted in deed &I want it put in the morning post and the dayly advertizer

   unis V Sinnix

TRANSCRIPTION 2.17

AMY JACKSON (32471)
PETITION, SALE OF REAL ESTATE: MARCH 29, 1841

To the Honorable *Willard Phillips Esquire* **Judge of the Probate**

Court in and for the County of Suffolk, in the Commonwealth of Massachusetts.

The petition of *Samuel E. Sewall* of *Boston* in the County of *Suffolk, Administrator with the will annex* of the *estate* of *Amy Jackson* late of *Boston* in said County of Suffolk, deceased, testate, humbly shews, that the just debts which the said deceased owed at the time of his death, as nearly as the same can be ascertained,

amount to the sum of *Eighteen hundred & sixty three dollars forty four cents*

and the charges of administration

to the sum of *Seventy six dollars thirty cents*
That the value of the personal estate of said deceased, is *Twenty three dollars forty five cents*
being insufficient for the payment of

said debts and charges by the sum of *Nineteen hundred and sixteen dollars twenty nine cents*
The real estate of the said deceased has been appraised at the sum of Twenty six hundred and sixteen dollars twenty nine cents and consists of *A lot of land with two small houses or tenements on it at the corner of Southac and Bultolph Streets in said Boston, and another lot of land in May Street in said Boston with a dwelling house upon it-bounded Westerly on land now or late of John Vinton*

formerly of Peter Virginia, being the same land which was conveyed to Thomas Jackson by said Virginia's deed dated February 24, 1804 ~~seconded with Suffolk Deeds Lib~~ recorded with Suffolk Deeds

Wherefore your petitioner prays, that he may be licensed to sell the whole of the said real estate, for the payment of said debts and charges, the same being more than is necessary for the payment thereof, for by a partial sale of *either parcel* the residue will be greatly injured.

S. E. Sewall

SUFFOLK, SS. At a Probate Court holden at Boston in and for said County of Suffolk, on Monday the *first* day of March in the year 1841

UPON the Petition aforesaid, this day preferred, by the above-named
Samuel E. Sewall

Ordered, that the said Petitioner give notice to all persons interested therein, to appear at a Probate Court, to be holden at said Boston, on Monday the *twenty ninth* day of March current ~~next~~, by

publishing the foregoing Petition, with this order thereon, three weeks successively, in the newspaper called
American Traveller
printed at said Boston, the last publication to be two days at least before the said twenty ninth day of *March* When and where they may be heard concerning the same: - And make return of his doings herein unto said court

Willard Phillips **Judge of Probate.**

I have given notice to all persons interested in the foregoing Petition, by publishing the same, with the order of the Court, three weeks successively in the ~~Boston~~

American Traveller in the manner and within the time above prescribed.

S. E. Sewall

SUFFOLK, SS. At a Probate Court held at Boston, in said County, on Monday the *twenty ninth* day of *March* in the year 1841

Personally appeared the said *Samuel E. Sewall* and made oath to the truth of the above return, by him subscribed - before me,

Willard Phillips **Judge of Probate.**

TRANSCRIPTION 2.18

AMY JACKSON (33471)
BOND & OATH, SALE OF REAL ESTATE: APRIL 5, 1841

Know all Men by these Presents,
THAT WE *Samuel E. Sewall Esquire* as principal and *Joseph Sewall, Gentleman, and Joseph Southwick, Merchant, all of Boston in the County of Suffolk*

and all within the COMMONWEALTH OF MASSACHUSETTS, are holden and stand firmly bound and obliged unto *Willard Phillips* Esq., Judge of the Probate Court in and for the County of Suffolk, in the full and just sum of Five Thousand dollars, to be paid to the said *Willard Phillips* and his successors in said office; to the true payment whereof we do bind ourselves and each of us, our and each of our heirs, executors, and administrators, jointly and severally, by these presents. Sealed with our seals. Dated this *twenty ninth* day of *March* in the year one thousand eight hundred and forty one

THE CONDITION OF THIS OBLIGATION IS SUCH, THAT WHEREAS THE ABOVE BOUNDEN *Samuel E. Sewall*

in his capacity of *Administrator with this will annexed of the estate of Amy Jackson* late of *Boston* in said County of Suffolk, deceased, testate by the Court of Probate holden at Boston in and for the said County of Suffolk, on the *29th day of March A.D. 1841* was licensed to make sale of *the whole of* ~~of~~ the real estate of the said *deceased, consisting of a lot of land with two small houses or tenements on it at the corner of Southac & Bultolph Streets in said Boston, and another lot of land in May Street in said Boston with a dwelling house upon it--bounded Westerly on land now or late of John Vinton formerly of Peter Virginia, being the same land which was conveyed to Thomas Jackson by said Virginia's deed dated February 23, 1804 recorded with Suffolk deeds*

for the payment of her debts and charges of administration, being a sale of more than is necessary for that purpose, the sale thereof being licensed, because by a sale of a part, the residue would be greatly injured.

Now Therefore, if the said Samuel E. Sewall shall account for all the proceeds of the sale of said real estate, that shall remain after the payment of the said debts, and charges, and shall dispose of the same according to law, then this Obligation to be void; otherwise to remain in full force and virtue.

*Signed, sealed, and delivered
 in presence of us,*   S. E. Sewall

E.T. Osborn   Witnesses   Joseph Southwick
                to S. E. Sewall &
Alx Moseley   J. Southwick
     Charles Hayward Witness to J Sewall
                          Joseph Sewall

SUFFOLK, SS. At a Probate Court held at Boston in said County, on Monday the *twenty ninth* day of March in the year one thousand eight hundred and *forty-one*

I have examined and do approve of the foregoing bond, and order the same to be filed and recorded in the Probate Office.

Willard Phillip **Judge of Probate.**

I Samuel E. Sewall do solemnly swear, that in disposing of the estate lately belonging to Amy Jackson late of Boston widow deceased I will use my best judgement in fixing on the time and place of sale, and that I will exert my utmost endeavors to dispose of the same in such manner as will be most for the advantage fo all persons interested therein. So help me God.
              S. E. Sewall

SUFFOLK, SS. April 5, in the year 18 41 The above named Samuel E. Sewall took and subscribed the foregoing oath, this day.
          Before me,

           Rich Robins **Justice of the Peace.**

TRANSCRIPTION 2.19

AMY JACKSON (32471) ORDER OF NOTICE: OCTOBER 11, 1841
Commonwealth of Massachusetts.

Suffolk, ss. AT a Probate Court, held at Boston, in said County, on Monday the *thirteenth* day of *September* in the year of our Lord, one thousand eight hundred and ~~thirty~~ *forty one*

WHEREAS *Samuel E. Sewall*

with the will annexed
Administrator ^ of the goods and estate of *Amy Jackson* late of said Boston, *Widow* deceased, intestate, has this day presented for allowance the *second* account of his administration upon said estate,

ORDERED, that the said *Sewall* give notice to all persons interested therein, to appear at a Probate Court to be held at said Boston, on Monday the *twenty seventh* day of *September current* at nine o'clock before noon, by publishing this order *two* weeks successively in the newspaper called the *Liberator*

printed in said Boston, that they may then and there appear and shew cause, if any they have, either for or against the allowance thereof.

Willard Phillips **Judge of Probate.**

PURSUANT to the within directions, I have caused a copy of the within order of notice to be published *two* weeks successively in the newspaper called the *Liberator*

S.E. Sewall

Suffolk, ss. At a Probate Court held at Boston, in said County, on Monday the *11th* day of *October* in the year 1841
Then the said *Sewall* made solemn oath to the truth of the above return by him made before me.

Willard Phillips **Judge of Probate.**

TRANSCRIPTION 2.20

AMY JACKSON (32471)
SECOND ACCOUNT: OCTOBER 11, 1841

The Second Account of *Samuel E. Sewall* Administrator
the will annexed
with ^ of the Goods and Estate of *Amy Jackson*, late of Boston, in the County of Suffolk, Widow deceased, intestate.

		DOLLS.	CTS.
1841	Said Administrat*or* charges *himself* with the following--*to wit*:		
	~~With the value of personal estate of said deceased, as appraised in the Inventory~~		
	With the gain on sale of the personal estate,		
	With the several sums collected and received,.		
	~~as stated in schedule A,~~ to wit		
May 1	of J.P. Coburn, price of land sold him in Bultolph St.		
" 13	" John Thompson, part payment for estate 19 May St sold him	1000.	
July 16	" John Thompson part payment for same & interest	399.	
July	" John Thompson, balance of interest	792.	
			.79
1841	Said Administrat*or* prays to be allowed as follows--*to wit:*	DOLLS.	CTS.
	For sundry payments, and charges, ~~as stated in schedule B,~~ to wit		
	(For)		
Mar 1	" *balance of first account*	52.	.85
" "	*pd advertising petition for leave to sell real estate*	4.	.50
" " "	" *Whitwell, Seaver & Co auctioneers bill--*	14.	.50
May 15	" *advertising sale of real estate*-------	2.	.50
" 20	" *J. P. Hall's Executor in part*-------------	12.	.00
Aug 9	*Dr. Parker's bill*-----------------------------	54.	.85
" 16	" *Stone & Adam's acct*---------------------	7.	
Sept 6 "	" *J. P. Hall's Executor, balance of his acct*	656.	.44
" 13	" *services as administrator in selling real estate & distributing proceeds*	79.	.80
Oct 11	" *pd for advertising notice of accts*----------	1.	
" " "	*Balance to be paid according to the will---*	118.	.75
		$2192.	.19
	S. E. Sewell		

Suffolk, ss. At a Probate Court, held at Boston, in said County, on MONDAY, the *eleventh* day of October in the year 184*1*.

to appear at a Probate Court held at said Boston, on Monday the twenty seventh day of September last past, the consideration thereof was then continued to this day, and notice thereof
              having
objections   ^   *been made thereto--*

And the same having been verified by the oath of
      the subscriber thereto, and examined and considered by the Court, it is decreed that the same be allowed.

              Willard Phillips   **Judge of Probate.**

TRANSCRIPTION 2.21

AMY JACKSON
THIRD ACCOUNT: MAY 9, 1842

The *Third* Account of *Samuel E. Sewall* Administer *the will annexed* with ^ of the Goods and Estate of *Amy Jackson,* late of Boston, in the County of Suffolk, *Widow* deceased, ~~in~~testate.

	DOLLS.	CTS.
1841 Said Administra*tor* charges *himself* with the following--*to wit* ~~With the value of personal estate in the Inventory, With the gain on sale of the personal estate, With the sums received, as stated in schedule A.,~~		
Oct 11 With the Balance of his second account	118.	.75
	$118.	.75
1841 Said Administra*tor* prays to be allowed as follows--*to wit:* ~~For sundry payments made, as stated in schedule B,~~	DOLLS.	CTS.
Oct 27 For amount paid Eunice V. Senex residuary legatee under the will--	59.	.37
Nov 8 " amount paid Nathan Winslow trustee of Mrs. Mary Clark by order of siad Eunice V. Senex	59.	.37½
Boston May 9, 1842 S. E. Sewell	$118.	.74½

Suffolk, ss. At a Probate Court, held at Boston, in said County, on MONDAY, the *ninth* day of *May* in the year 1842.

The foregoing account having been presented for allowance, ~~and notice thereof having been given to the parties interested, according to the order of the Court~~

And the same having been verified by the oath of
the subscriber thereto, and examined and considered by the Court, it is decreed that the same be allowed.

Willard Phillips   **Judge of Probate.**

APPENDIX B

ROSTERS

Roster 1

Black Heads of Households in Boston
From the Fifth U.S. Census (1830)

Name	Ward	Name	Ward
George Grimes	1	Oliver Nash	6
Job Riggins	1	Coffin Pitts	6
Joseph Bantista/Battiste	2	William Rand	6
Henry Forman	2	William Riley	6
Ann (AMA) Jackson	2	John Robinson	6
Arthur Jones	2	William Robinson	6
John Thompson	2	John Smith	6
John Brooks	3	Lewis Smith	6
Emily Higgins	3	Joseph Sprague	6
Henry Johnson	3	Henry L. Thacker	6
Emiliano F.B. Mundrucu	3	Henry Tyler	6
John Scarlett	4	Charles Williams	6
Henry Benson	5	John Williams	6
William Brown	5	Peter Williams	6
Jonathan Cash	5	John W. Brown	7
Thomas Fisher	5	Thomas Brown	7
Cyrus E. Foster	5	Hamlet Earl	7
Peter Gray	5	Ceaser Fletcher	7
Peter Howard	5	James Gould	7
James H. Howe	5	John Henry	7
William Kerr	5	William Henry	7
Robert Roberts	5	William Jackson	7
John Rogers	5	John Pero	7
David Walker	5	Cuff Roberts	7
John Aiken	6	Chloe Russell	7
Reuben Bowers	6	Peter Smith	7
John Brown	6	Samuel Snowden	7
William Castell/Costle	6	Pompey Thurston	7
Jonas W. Clark	6	George Washington	7
Thomas Cole	6	Isaac Woodland	7
Thomas Dalton	6	Jane Burns (Bense)	8
Primus Hall	6	Eli Ceaser	9
James Hill	6	John Billings	10
Amy (AMA) Jackson	6	Edward Lawson	10
William Johnson	6	Jane E. Lewis	10
John Lewis	6	John Williams	10

Source: Beth Anne Bower, "Black Heads of Households from the 1830 U.S. Census with Probate in Suffolk County, Massachusetts" (Washington, DC: Smithsonian Institution, National Museum of American History, Afro-American Communities Project, n.d.), photocopied.

Roster 2

Prominent Blacks in Antebellum Boston

Name	Probate in Suffolk County, MA	Name	Probate in Suffolk County, MA
Macon R. Allen	No	John Hay	No
S.R. Alexander	No	Lewis Hayden	Yes
Jacob R. Andrews	No	John T. Hilton	No
J.B. Bailey	Yes	Peter Howard	Yes
Frederick G. Barbadoes	No	Thomas Jackson	--
James G. Barbadoes	No	Thomas Jennings	No
Benjamin P. Bassett	Yes	W.S. Jennings	Yes
Jehial C. Beman	No	George Johnson	No
Welsley Bishop	Yes	Richard Johnson	No
George Black	?	Robert Johnson	Yes
Frederick Brimley	No	Daniel Laing	No
Thomas Brown	Yes	George Latimer	No
William Wells Brown	No	Edward B. Lawton	No
Othello Berghard	No	Joel E. Lewis	No
Lemuel Burr	No	Simpson H. Lewis	Yes
C.V. Caples	No	Walker Lewis	No
Jonas W. Clark	Yes	John Lockley	No
John P. Coburn	Yes	William H. Logan	Yes
Thomas Cole	Yes	James Mars	No
William Craft	No	James Sella Martin	No
Thomas Cummings	?	Robert Morris	Yes
Thomas Dalton	Yes	William C. Nell	No
John V. DeGrasse	Yes	William G. Nell	No
George T. Downing	No	Thomas Paul	No
Hosea Easton	No	N.L. Perkins	No
Joshua Easton	No	Coffin Pitts	Yes
John J. Fatal	No	Richard Potter	No
Nestor P. Freeman	No	George Putnam	No
Charles H. Gardner	No	Peter Randolph	No
Edward Gray	No	John T. Raymond	No
Ira S. Gray	No	Charles L. Remond	No
Leonard A. Grimes	No	Benjamin Roberts	No
Henry Hatton	No	Robert Roberts	Yes
Peter Hawkins	Yes	John S. Rock	Yes

Roster 2
(continued)

Name	Ward	Name	Ward
George L. Ruffin	Yes	Enoch I. Stallard	No
Joseph Russell	No	Payton Stewart	No
Joseph Scarlett	No	Henry L.W. Thacker	Yes
John E. Scarlett	Yes	Thomas Thomas	No
P.I. Schuyler	No	George W. Thompson	No
James Scott	?	John Thompson	Yes
Charles C. Seth	No	Henry G. Tracy	No
James Simmons	No	E.G. Walker	No
William H. Simpson	No	George Washington	Yes
Elijah Smith	No	William J. Watkins	No
John B. Smith	No	Henry Watson	No
Joshua B. Smith	No	Benjamin Weeden	No
Samuel Smith	?	Henry Weeden	No
Thomas Paul Smith	No	John Wesley	No
Isaac H. Snowden	No	Isaac Woodland	No
Samuel Snowden	Yes	John Wright	Yes

Source: Beth Anne Bower, "Prominent People" (Washington, DC: Smithsonian Institution, National Museum of American History, Afro-American Communities Project, n.d.), photocopied.

Roster 3

1840s Decendents

Decendent	Docket Number	Year of Death	Age	Occupation
Charles Biner	35041	1847	--	Teamster
John Lewis Brent alias John Lewis	34132	1844	--	Laborer
John Brooks	33783	1843	67	Laborer
John Brown	35007	1847	--	Mariner
John W. Brown	32659	1840	--	Waiter
Thomas Cole	35173	1847	42	Hairdresser
Peter Gray	33133	1842	57	Clothesdealer
Primus Hall	33174	1842	84	Soapboiler
James H. Howe	34458	1845	42	Hair renovator
Calvin T. Hoyt alias Charles Williams	34900	1846	--	Mariner
Amy Jackson	32471	1840	70	Widow
William S. Jinnings	32642	1840	--	Trader
Arthur Jones	32789	1841	47	Barber
Edward Lawson	33004	1841	51	Laborer
William Riley	36235	1849	60	Gentleman
Henry Robinson	36092	1849	35	Chimneysweep
John Robinson	36470	1849	54	Clothing trader
Chloe Russell	33170	1842	64	Widow/cook
John E. Scarlett	33895	1844	58	Clothing dealer
Lucinda Smith	32591	1840	36	Singlewoman
John Smith alias Freeman Smith	34259	1845	--	Mariner
Joseph Sprague	33309	1841	40	Laborer
Peter Williams	35871	1848	--	Rigger

Sources: Probate records in Suffolk County Courthouse, Boston, MA, and Beth Anne Bower, "Black Heads of Households from the 1830 U.S. Census with Probate in Suffolk County, Massachusetts', (Washington, DC: Smithsonian Institution, National Museum of American History, Afro-American Communities Project, n.d.), photocopied.

Roster 4

Literacy Indices of Selected 1840s Decedents
(Grouped by Occupation Type)

Decedent	Books	Furniture	Other	Testacy	Signature
Laborer					
E. Lawson	--	--	--	Intestate	--
Semi-skilled laborer					
J. W. Brown	--	--	--	Intestate	--
P. Hall	Books	Broken Desk	--	Testate	Yes
H. Robinson	One case of books &c	--	--	Intestate	--
P. Williams	--	--	--	Intestate	--
Businessman					
T. Cole	Lot of books	--	Map of U.S.	Testate	Yes
J. H. Howe	--	1 desk	--	Intestate	Yes
W. S. Jinnings	--	--	--	Intestate	--
J. Robinson	--	desk	--	Intestate	Yes
J. E. Scarlett	--	Writing Desk, Bookcase	--	Intestate	Yes
A. Jackson	1 Bible & 3 Old books	--	--	Testate	"X"

Source: Probate records in Suffolk County Courthouse, Boston, MA.

Roster 5

Literacy Indices of 1840s Decedents
(Grouped by Occupation Type)

Decedent	Books	Furniture	Other	Testacy	Signature
Mariner					
J. Brown	--	--	--	Intestate	--
C. T. Hoyt	--	--	--	Intestate	--
J. Smith	--	--	--	Intestate	--
Laborer					
J. L. Brent	--	--	--	Intestate	--
J. Brooks	?	?	?	Intestate	--
E. Lawson	--	--	--	Intestate	--
J. Sprague	--	--	--	Intestate	--
Semi-skilled laborer					
C. Biner	?	?	?	Testate	Yes
J. W. Brown	--	--	--	Intestate	--
P. Hall	Books	Broken Desk	--	Testate	Yes
H. Robinson	One Case of books &c	--	--	Intestate	--
P. Williams	--	--	--	Intestate	--
Businessman					
T. Cole	Lot of Books	--	Map of U.S.	Testate	Yes
P. Gray		?	?	Testate	Yes

Roster 5
(continued)

Decedent	Books	Furniture	Other	Testacy	Signature
Businessman (continued)					
J.H. Howe	--	1 desk	--	Intestate	Yes
W. S. Jinnings	--	--	--	Intestate	--
A. Jones	?	?	?	Intestate	--
W. Riley	?	?	?	Testate	"x"
J. Robinson	--	desk	--	Intestate	Yes
J. E. Scarlett	--	Writing desk, bookcase	--	Intestate	Yes
Woman					
A. Jackson	1 Bible, 3 old books	--	--	Testate	"x"
C. Russell	--	--	--	Testate	"x"
L. Smith	--	--	--	Intestate	--

Source: Probate records in Suffolk County Courthouse, Boston, MA

Roster 6

Literacy of 1840s Decedents' Peer Group From the Seventh U. S. Census (1850)

Name		Literate		Children	
		Self	Wife	No. 6 to 16 years old	No. in School
Jonathan Cash	Handcart-man	Yes	Yes	4	2
Jonas W. Clark	Clothes-dealer	Yes	Yes	--	--
John P. Coburn	Clothes-dealer	Yes	Yes	--	--
Robert Morris	Lawyer	Yes	Yes	--	--
Emiliano Mundrucu	Clothes-dealer	Yes	Yes	2	2
Coffin Pitts	Clothes-dealer	Yes	Yes	--	--
John Rogers	Clothes-dealer	Yes	Yes	--	--
George Washington	Laborer	Yes	Yes	6	6

Source: Seventh United States Census (1850).

NOTE: The census recorded "persons over 20 years of age who cannot read and write

Roster 7

Signature Literacy Among Black Women In Antebellum Boston

Name	Signature
Decedent	
Amy Jackson	"X"
Chloe Russell	"X"
Widow	
Ruth Biner	"X"
Delia G. R. Brooks	Yes
Ann Hall	Yes
Adeline Jones	Yes
Elizabeth Lawson	"X"
Elizabeth Riley	"X"
Maryann Robinson	Yes
Margaret Scarlett	Yes
Hannah William	"X"
Daughter	
Isannah Trask Hall	Yes
Susan Robinson	Yes
Eliza [Dianna Riley] Smith	Yes
Kin	
Hannah M. Benson	Yes
Non-Kin Heir	
Elenor Hayden	"X"
Unis V. Sinnix	Yes

Source: Probate records in Suffolk County Court, Boston, MA.

Roster 8

Literacy Indices of 1840s Decedents' Peer Group

Name	Books	Furniture	Other	Testacy	Signature
Laborer					
George Washington	--	?	--	Testate	Yes
Handcartman					
Jonathan Cash	--	?	?	Testate	"X"
Clothes-dealer					
Jonas W. Clark	--	?	?	Testate	Yes
John P. Coburn	--	?	?	Testate	Yes
Emiliano Mundrucu	16 vols. + "sett of Shakes-peares works" = $39.50	--	--	Intestate	--
Coffin Pitts	--	--	--	Testate	Yes
John Rogers	?	?	?	Testate	Yes
Lawyer					
Robert Morris	books, Law Library	Desks, Bookcases	no	Testate	Yes

Source: Probate records in Suffolk County Courthouse, Boston, MA.

NOTE: A question mark indicates that the inventory was insufficiently itemized to make a determination.

Roster 9

Thomas Cole's Personal Network

Name	Occupation		Intersection
Joseph Bantista	Boarding-house keeper	1.	1831, partner and debtor of Emiliano Mundrucu
Jonas W. Clark	Clothesdealer	1.	1831, bond for David Walker
		2.	1842/3, surety, executor & debtor of Primus Hall
		3.	1842, guardian of minor children of Joseph Sprague
		4.	1845, surety for James H. Howe
		5.	1849, surety & administrator for John Robinson
		6.	1863, witness for Emiliano Mundrucu
John B. Coburn	Clothesdealer	1.	1842, surety for Primus Hall
		2.	1847, surety for Thomas Cole
		3.	1849, surety for John Robinson
		4.	1863, witness for Emiliano Mundrucu
Primus Hall	Soapboiler	1.	1831, bond for David Walker
		2.	1842, Hall's surety - John B.Coburn
		3.	1842/3, Hall's surety, executor, & creditor--Jonas B.Clark
		4.	1843, Hall's debtor--John Rogers
John T. Hilton	Hairdresser	1.	1840, inventory for William S. Jinnings
		2.	1844, inventory for John Scarlett
		3.	1847, surety & executor for Thomas Cole
		4.	1849, witness & inventory for William Riley
		5.	1851, creditor of John Robinson
Alfred G. Howard	Hairdresser	1.	son of Peter Howard
Peter Howard	Hairdresser	1.	1854, Howard's witness-Robert Morris
James H. Howe	Hairdresser	1.	1845, Howe's surety--Jonas W. Clark
		2.	1846, Howe's creditor--John Rogers

Name	Occupation		Intersection
William S. Jinnings	Clothesdealer	1.	1840, Jinnings's inventory-John T. Hilton
		2.	1840, Jinnings's executor-John Robinson
		3.	1840, Jinnings's inventory-John Rogers
		4.	1840, Jinnings's executor-John E. Scarlett
Robert Morris	Lawyer	1.	1849, surety for John Robinson
		2.	1854, witness for Peter Howard
Emiliano Mundrucu	Clothesdealer	1.	1831, partner & creditor of Joseph Bantista
		2.	1863, Mundrucu's witness-Jonas W. Clark
		3.	1863, Mundrucu's witness-John P. Coburn
Coffin Pitts	Clothesdealer	1.	1847, surety for Thomas Cole
		2.	1849, surety for William Riley
		3.	1849, surety for John Robinson
William Riley	Clothesdealer	1.	1849, Riley's witness & inventory - John T. Hilton
		2.	1849, Riley's surety--John Rogers
		3.	1849, Riley's witness-Henry L.W. Thacker
John Robinson	Clothesdealer	1.	1840, executor for William S.Jinnings
		2.	1849, Robinson's surety-Jonas W. Clark
		3.	1849, Robinson's surety-John P. Coburn
		4.	1849, Robinson's surety-Robert Morris
		5.	1849, Robinson's surety-Coffin Pitts
		6.	1851, Robinson's creditor-John T. Hilton
John Rogers	Clothesdealer	1.	1840, inventory for William S. Jinnings
		2.	1843, creditor of Primus Hall
		3.	1846, paid estate--James H. Howe
		4.	1849, surety for William Riley
John E. Scarlett	Clothesdealer	1.	1830, surety for David Walker
		2.	1840, executor for William S. Jinnings
		3.	1844, Scarlett's inventory-John T. Hilton
Joseph Sprague	Laborer	1.	1842, Sprague's childrens' guardian--Jonas W. Clark
Henry L. W. Thacker	Waiter	1.	1849, witness for William Riley

Name	Occupation		Intersection
David Walker	Clothesdealer	1.	1830, Walker's surety--John E. Scarlett
		2.	1831, Walker's bond--Jonas W. Clark
		3.	1831, Walker's bond--Primus Hall

Source: Probate records in Suffolk County Courthouse, Boston, MA

Roster 10

Thomas Cole's Public Network

Name	Occupation		Intersection
James G. Barbadoes	Hairdresser	1.	Anti-American Colonization Society (31.02.12*; 01:0030 &31.02.26; 01:0036 & 31.03.12*; 01:0039)
		2.	For establishment of a black college (31.11.12*; 01:0133)
		3.	Support for Garrison (33.03.23*; 01:0261)
		4.	Mourning Elijah P. Lovejoy (37.12.29*; 02:0346)
		5.	National Conventian of Colored Inhabitants (40.06.16; 03:0534)
		6.	Welcome back to Garrison (40.08.18; 03:0614)
Benjamin P. Bassett	Hairdresser	1.	For temperance (39.08.30*; 03:0135)
		2.	National Convention of Colored Inhabitants (40.06.16; 03:0534)
		3.	Call for national convention of free people of color (43.07.14*. 04:0609)
Jonathan Cash	Handcartman	1.	Petition to school board protesting separate school for colored children (44.00.00; 04:0723)
Jonas W. Clark	Clothesdealer	1.	Petition to school board protesting separate school for colored children (44.00.00; 04:0723)
John B. Coburn	Clothesdealer	1.	Celebration of anniversary of emancipation in British West Indies (42.07.08; 04:0451)
Thomas Dalton	Doorman, Laborer	1.	Anti-American Colonization Society (31.03.12*; 01:039 & 31.02.26; 01:0036)
		2.	For establishment of black college (31.11.05*; 01:0131)
		3.	Petition to school board protesting separate school for colored children (44.00.00; 04:0723)

Name	Occupation		Intersection
Primus Hall	Soapboiler	1.	For establishment of black college (31.11.05˚; 01:0131 & 31.11.12˚; 01:0133)
		2.	Silver cup to Garrison (33.04.04; 01:0272)
		3.	For Samaritan Orphanage (39.02.21; 03:0022)
John T. Hilton	Hairdresser	1.	Anti-American Colonization Society (31.02.12˚; 01:0030 & 31.02.26; 01:0036 & 31.03.12˚; 01:0039)
		2.	For establishment of black college (31.11.05˚; 01:0131 & 31.11.12*; 01:0133)
		3.	Silver cup to Garrison (33.04.04; 01:0272)
		4.	Mourning Elijah P. Lovejoy (37.12.29; 02:0346)
		5.	For temperance (38.08.10˚; 02:0551)
		6.	For Samaritan Orphanage 39.02.21; 03:0022)
		7.	Temperance dinner in honor of anniversary of emancipation in British West Indies (39.07.26˚; 03:0150)
		8.	National Convention of Colored Inhabitants (40.06.16; 03:0534)
		9.	Welcome back to Garrison (40.08.18; 03:0614)
		10.	Regrets to soiree in honor of David Ruggles (40.12.18; 03:1023)
		11.	Celebration of anniversary of emancipation in British West Indies (42.07.08; 04:0451)
		12.	Call for national convention of free people of color (43.07.14˚; 04:0609)
Peter Howard	Hairdresser	1.	For establishment of black college (31.11.05˚; 01:0131)
		2.	Silver cup to Garrison (33.04.04; 01:0272)

227

Name	Occupation		Intersection
William S. Jinnings	Clothes-dealer	1.	Mourning Elijah P. Lovejoy (37.12.29; 02:0346)
		2.	For Samaritan Orphanage (39.02.21; 03:0022)
		3.	Support for Colored American (40.01.06; 03:0337)
Emiliano F. B. Mundrucu	Clothes-dealer	1.	Silver cup to Garrison (33.04.04; 01:0272)
William C. Nell	Printer, Historian	1.	National Convention of Colored Inhabitants (40.06.16; 03:0534)
		2.	Regrets to soiree in honor of David Ruggles (40.12.18; 03:1023)
		3.	Call for national convention of free people of color (43.07.14*; 04:0609)
		4.	Petition to school board protesting separate school for colored children (44.00.00; 04:0723)
Coffin Pitts	Clothesdealer	1.	Anti-American Colonization Society (31.03.12*; 01:039)
		2.	Call for national convention of free people of color (43.07.14*; 04:0609)
		3.	Petition to school board protesting separate school for colored children (44.00.00; 04:0723)
George Putnam	Hairdresser	1.	For establishment of black college (31.11.05*; 01.0131 & 31.11.12*; 01:0133)
		2.	Support for Garrison (33.03.23*; 01:0261)
		3.	Silver cup to Garrison (33.04.04; 01:0272)
William Riley	Clothes-dealer	1.	Petition to school board protesting separate school for colored children (44.00.00; 04:0723)

Name	Occupation		Intersection
Robert Roberts	Stevedore	1.	Anti-American Colonization Society (31.02.12*; 01:0030 & 31.03.12*; 01:0039)
		2.	For establishment of black college (31.11.12*; 01:0133)
John Robinson	Clothes-dealer	1.	Petition to school board protesting separate school for colored children (44.00.00; 04:0723)
John Rogers	Clothes-dealer	1.	Petition to school board protesting separate school for colored children (44.00.00; 04:0723)
Samuel Snowden	Minister	1.	Anti-American Colonization Society (31.02.12*; 01:0030)
		2.	For establishment of black college (31.11.12*; 01:0133)
		3.	Support for Garrison (33.03.23*; 01:0261)
		4.	Silver cup to Garrison (33.04.04; 01:0272)
		5.	National Convention of Colored Inhabitants (40.06.16; 03:0534)
Henry L. W. Thacker	Waiter	1.	For establishment of black college (31.11.05*; 01:0131)
		2.	Silver cup to Garrison (33.04.04; 01:0272)
George Washington	Laborer	1.	Celebration of anniversary of emancipation in British West Indies (42.07.08; 04:451)
		2.	Call for a national convention of free people color (43.07.14*; 04:0609)
		3.	Petition to school board protesting separate school for colored children (44.00.00; 04:0723)

Source: George E. Carter and C. Peter Ripley, eds. Black Abolitionist Papers, 1830-1865: A Guide to the Microfil',, Edition. New York: Microfilming Corporation of America, 1981.

NOTE: The numbers in parentheses refer to the indexing system in the Black Abolitionist Papers.

Roster 11

Participation of 1840s Decedents' Peer Group, By Color,
In Thomas Cole's Networks

	Number of Intersections	
Name	Personal Network	Public Network
Black		
J. W. Clark	5	1
J. P. Coburn	4	2
R. Morris	2	--
C. Pitts	3	3
G. Washington	--	3
Mulatto		
J. Cash	--	1
E. Mundrucu	3	1
J. Rogers	4	1

Sources: Seventh United States Census (1850) and rosters 9 and 10.

Roster 12

Relationship of 1840s Decedents to People
Carrying Out Probate Duties

Decedent	Public Official	Community Leader	Friend	Kin	Unknown
C. Biner	1	--	--	1	3
J. L Brent	1	--	--	--	--
J. Brooks	--	--	--	--	--
J. Brown	1	--	--	--	--
J. W. Brown	1	--	2	--	--
T. Cole	1	[6]	[6]	--	--
P. Gray	1	--	--	--	2
P. Hall	1	[2] + 1	[2]	--	--
J. H. Howe	1	1	--	1	3
C. T. Hoyt	1	--	--	--	--
A. Jackson	4	--	1	--	--
W. S. Jinnings	1	[4]	[4]	2	--
A. Jones	--	--	--	1	1
E. Lawson	1	2	--	1	1
W. Riley	2	[3] + 1	1	1	--
H. Robinson	1	--	--	1	2
J. Robinson	[1] + 1	[1] + [4]	[1] + [4]	--	1
C. Russell	--	--	--	1	1
J. E. Scarlett	2	1 + [1]	[1]	1	1
J. Smith	1	--	--	--	--
L. Smith	1	--	--	1	2
J. Sprague	--	1	--	--	1
P. Williams	2	--	--	1	3

Source: Probate records in Suffolk County Courthouse, Boston, MA.

NOTE: A bracketed number indicates persons who fit more than one category of relationship.

Appendix C

Lists

LISTS 1.1 - 1.3

JOHN W. BROWN (32659)

LIST 1.1   NECESSITIES

Wearing apparel	$5.00
Trunk	2.00
	$7.00

LIST 1.2   AMENITIES

None   --

LIST 1.3   LUXURIES

None   --

LISTS 2.1 - 2.3

THOMAS COLE (35173)

LIST 2.1   NECESSITIES

bedding	$ 3.50
Table	1.00
Bedstead	.75
Lot crockery, glass ware &	.50
Wearing apparel of dec^d	34.96
4 Trunks & 2 chests	2.00
	$42.71

LIST 2.2   AMENITIES

Bed*	$15.00
2 White counterpanes $2.50 & $1	3.50
1 Doz. Towels	1.50
6 window curtains	.25
Rock^g chair & Cush^n	.25
Time piece	3.00
L. Glass	2.00
Curtain, Port Folio, & Sund	.50
Velise & bag	.50
	$26.50

LIST 2.3   LUXURIES

White Tea Set	$5.00
Lot of Books	30.00
Lot of framed prints &c	1.68
Map of US	.25
Gold watch & key &c	15.00
Flute	3.00
Piano Forte	12.00
	$66.93

*Cole's will indicates that this is a feather bed.

LISTS 3.1 - 3.3

PRIMUS HALL (33174)

LIST 3.1   NECESSITIES

2 Bedsteads, Bed & bed^g 7 & 5	$12.00
9 Broken Chairs	.50
Trunks 75c Table 25c	1.00
a Bed $5 6 Chairs $1	6.00
Stove Fire Place	2.50
8 Benches	1.33
Bed & Bed^g	5.00
Clothing & Chest	5.00
Table	.12
2 Tables	1.00
11 Chairs 6 @ 37 1/2 - 5 @ 25c	3.50
Stove	4.00
Shovel & Tongs $1 Crockery 4	5.00
Iron Ware $2.50 Copper Kettle 75c	3.25
Flat iron 12c Lot of Crockery $1	1.12
Tin Ware 50c Old chests, tub 50c	1.00
	$52.32

LIST 3.2   AMENITIES

1 Rock^g Chair 1.0^2 1 Look Glass .60	$1.62
3 Curtains	.25
Moveable Cupboard	.75
Bureau	2.00
6 Curtains	2.00
1 Sofa	5.00
1 Look^g Glass	1.50
1 Carpet & Rug	1.50
Sofa Bedstead	2.00
	$16.62

LIST 3.3   LUXURIES

Broken Desk & Bureau	$ 1.50
Books	2.00
5 Pictures @ 6c	.30
	$ 3.80

LISTS 4.1 - 4.3

JAMES H. HOWE (34458)

LIST 4.1 NECESSITIES

4 Chairs	$ .50
1 Stove	.25
2 Lamps	.06
	$ .81

LIST 4.2 AMENITIES

1 Bureau	$ 1.00
1 Sofa	1.00
1 Clock	.25
	$ 2.25

LIST 4.3 LUXURIES

1 Desk	$ .50
1 Large picture	.50
	$ 1.00

LISTS 5.1 - 5.3

AMY JACKSON (32471)

LIST 5.1 NECESSITIES

2 Tubs & Lot of crockery	$ 1.50
1 Lot of tin ware & 2 flat irons	.50
1 chest & wearing apparel	2.50
1 pr Iron Dogs & shovel & tongs	.50
8 chairs	1.20
2 Iron pots	.75
1 Bake kettle 2 spiders 1 skillet & tea kettle	1.50
1 Lot wood & bark	.50
1 Bedstead & 2 Tables	1.75
2 Buckets 2 Lugs & 1 axe	.50
	$11.20

LIST 5.2 AMENITIES

1 Beauro	$ 1.00
1 Looking Glass & frames	.25
2 pair sheets & 1 pr of pillow cases	1.25
2 Quilts and 1 Comforter	4.00
1 Feather Bed & pillows	4.00
2 Blankets & 1 pr linen cases	.50
	$11.00

LIST 5.3 LUXURIES

3 Thin Silver Spoons	$ .75
1 Bible & 3 old books	.50
	$ 1.25

LISTS 6.1 - 6.3

WILLIAM S. JINNINGS (32642)

LIST 6.1   NECESSITIES

Wearing apparel $20.00

LIST 6.1   AMENITIES

None   --

LIST 6.3   LUXURIES

None   --

LISTS 7.1 - 7.3

EDWARD LAWSON (33004)

LIST 7.1 NECESSITIES

7 Chairs & 1 Rocking Do	$ 2.50
Pine Table	.75
Bedstead Bed & Bedding	25.00
Fire Set Bellows and Brush	1.50
Crockery Iron and Tin Ware	6.00
Wearing Apparel	25.00
Cooking Stove	7.00
	$67.75

LIST 7.2 AMENITIES

Carpet	$ 8.00
Small L. Glass	.50
	$ 8.50

LIST 7.3 LUXURIES

6 Small Silver Tea Spoons	$ 3.00
Lot Pictures	.75
	$ 3.75

LISTS 8.1 - 8.3

HENRY ROBINSON (36092)

LIST 8.1   NECESSITIES

Three military coats	$ .75
One pr military pants & vests	.25
Two hats	1.00
Eight bonnets	.50
Three overcoats	1.50
Other old coats & vest	1.00
Ten pr light colored pants old	2.50
Eleven light colored vests old	1.50
Six dark colored vests old	1.25
Seven pr old pants	1.75
Two coats & pr of pants	6.00
Two scarfs	.50
Stove and funnel	1.00
Three chairs	.33
Thread & buttons	.37 1/2
One cloak	3.00
	$23.20 1/2

LIST 8.2   AMENITIES

One toilet table	$ .50
One dining table broken	.25
One watch	12.00
	$12.75

LIST 8.3   LUXURIES

One case of birds shells of several kinds	$ 5.50
Two boxes of shells	2.50
Eight boxes of little shells	1.50
Two coral baskets	.50
One other case of sea shells	1.50
One case of birds with silver haired fox	13.00
One box of insects &c	2.00
One other case of birds	1.50
Woodchuck & Weasel	.50
Several other birds	3.00
One duck	.25
Two vases, three carton boxes & four egg cups	1.00
One statue	.12 1/2
One toy ship	.75
Broken violins	.06

LIST 8.3--Continued

Three pr Epauletts	.37 1/2
Three swords belt & viser	2.00
Two african swords & arrow	1.00
Eleven pictures & frames	.50
One case of books &c	1.75
One box of bottles	.50
One astral lamp	.50
Playing cards	.25
Box of trinkets hone & razors	2.00
Hubble bubble, lock & bust	.50
Bird of paradise	8.00
	$51.06

LISTS 9.1 - 9.3
JOHN ROBINSON (36470)

LIST 9.1   NECESSITIES

10 Common chairs	3.66
1 " dining table	2.00
2 Bedsteads	4.00
8 Common chairs	1.00
Fender and Andirons	2.00
2 Old Stoves	1.00
1 Cooking stove	12.00
1/2 doz. Knives & forks	4.00
Crockery & Glass ware	7.50
One Common table	1.00
One trundle Bedstead	1.50
	$39.66

LIST 9.2   AMENITIES

3 Looking glasses	$7.00
1 Settle $1.50 & Rocking chair $1	2.50
3 Feather beds & boulsters	12.00
11 Coverlids	6.00
1 Common Bureau	1.00
1 Old sofa & table	3.00
1 Entry Lamp	2.00
One Old Carpet	2.00
	$35.50

LIST 9.3   LUXURIES

3 Pictures & frames	$10.00
1 Mahogany side Board	10.00
" do dining table	10.00
" do centre do	10.00
" do card do	5.00
" do work do	5.00
10 do chairs at $2	20.00
2 Astral Lamps	5.00
1 Mantle clock & case	25.00
24 yards woollen carpeting	24.00
1 Mahogany sofa	10.00
1 Piano Forte	20.00
1 Music Stool	2.00
desk	1.00
10 Silver tea Spoons	5.00
	$162.00

LISTS 10.1 - 10.3

JOHN E. SCARLETT (33895)

LIST 10.1 NECESSITIES

2 Bedsteads Bed & Bedding	$9.00
Trunk	.50
Cot Bedstead, Bed &c	3.00
Table	.50
6 Com Chairs	.50
Cook^s Stove	3.00
5 Com^n Lamps & 2 Brass Candlesticks	1.00
Crockery	3.00
Iron, Tin, and Woodware	3.00
Wearing apparel belonging to said deceased	10.00
	$33.00

LIST 10.2 AMENITIES

Carpet & Backing	$3.00
7 Flag Bot. Chairs	3.50
L. Glass	3.50
Work Table	2.50
Timepiece	5.00
Old Bureau	1.00
Sofa	3.00
Small L. Glass	1.50
Dining Table	2.50
Light Stand	.75
	$26.25

LIST 10.3 LUXURIES

Card Table & Cloth	$3.50
Writing Desk	3.00
3 Small Pictures	.50
Book case	4.00
6 Small Silver Spoons	3.00
	$14.00

LISTS 11.1 -11.3

PETER WILLIAMS ESTATE (35871)

LIST 11.1   NECESSITIES

Dishes Plates & Iron Ware	$ 2.00
One Doz. Common Chairs	1.00
Two Tables	1.50
Two Bedsteads	1.00
One Pine Table	.50
Three Bedsteads	3.00
Lot of Lamps	.50
Wearing apparel	5.00
	$14.50

LIST 11.2   AMENITIES

One Beureau	$ 2.00
One Clock	5.00
One Looking Glass	.50
Six Feather Beds	16.00
Lot of Bedcloths	6.00
One Beureau	1.00
	$30.50

LIST 11.3   LUXURIES

None   --y

APPENDIX D

GRAPHS

Graph 1

Proportion of crisscrossing decedents' household goods, by necessities, amenities, and luxuries

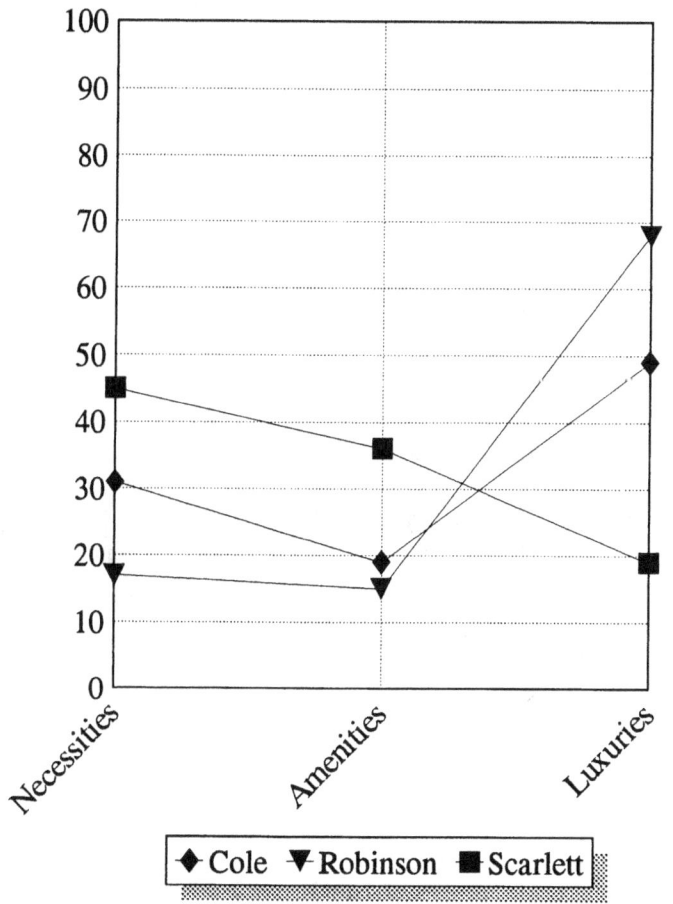

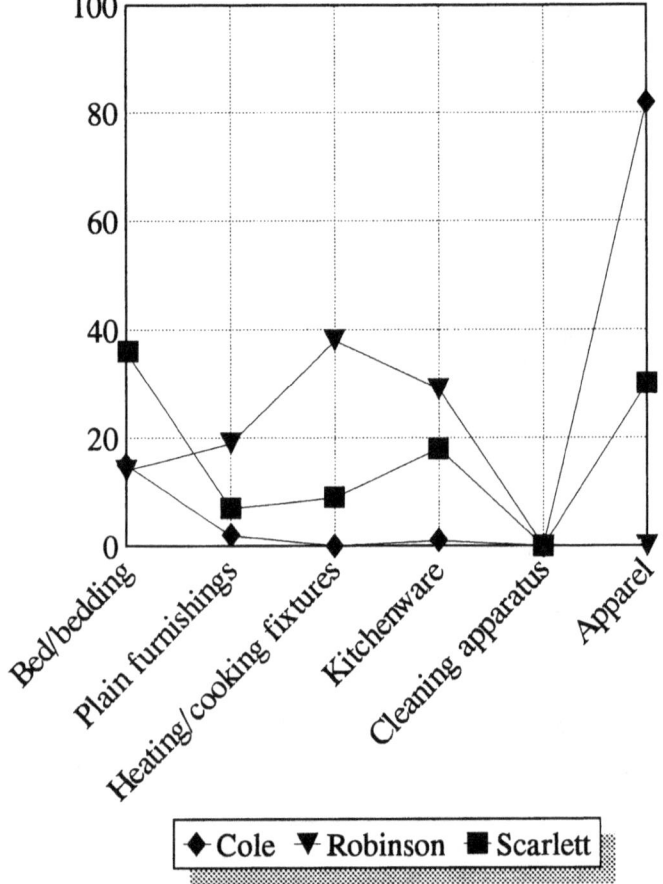

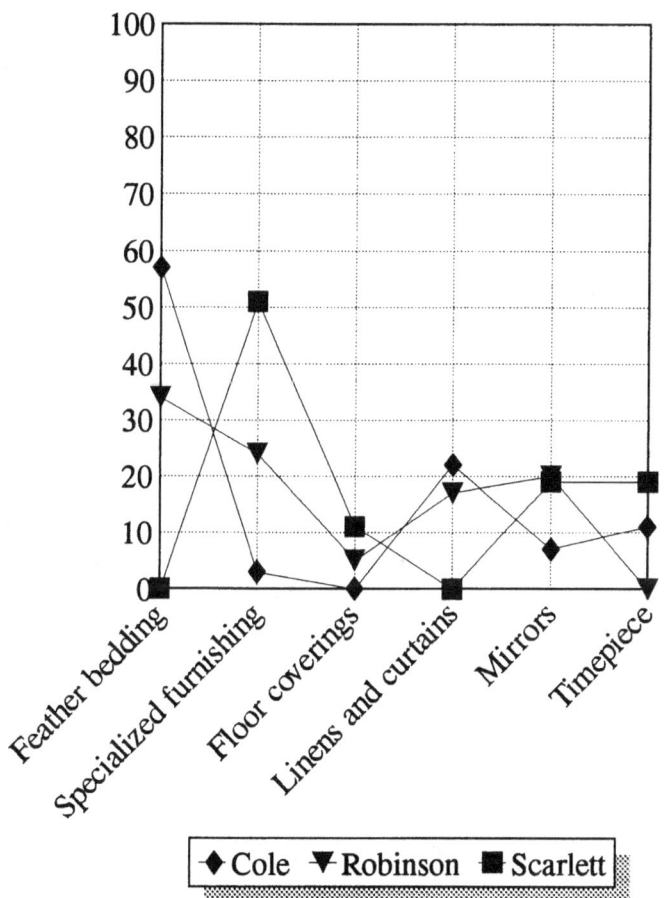

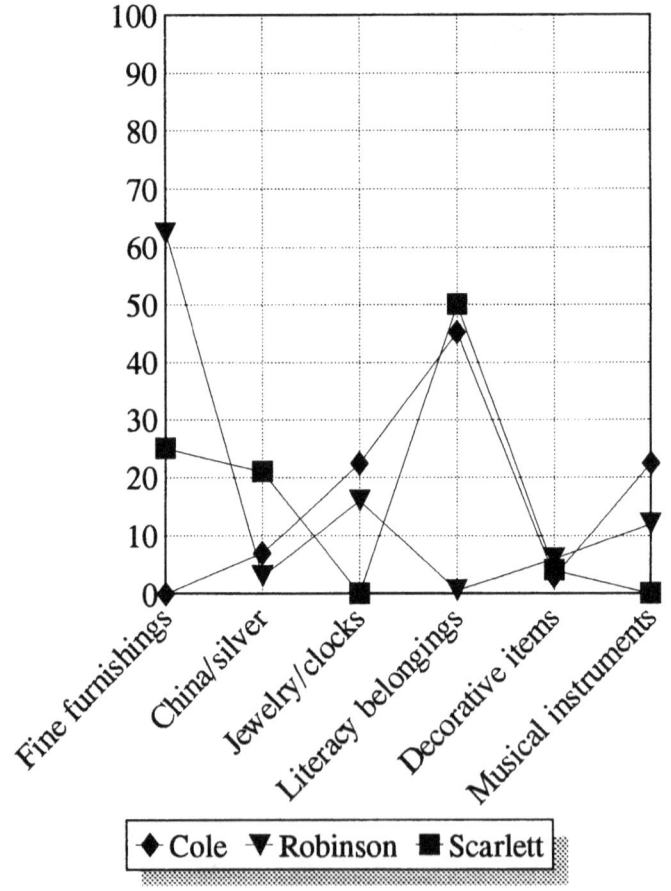

Graph 4
Proportion of crisscrossing decedents' luxuries, by generic sets

Appendix E

Charts and Figures

NOTE

The charts that follow set forth the street addresses from various primary sources for the 1840s decedents and/or their fellow black Bostonians= = "network members." These charts are in turn keyed to computer-genterated versions of two maps of Boston. Since ward boundaries were redrawn in 1838, Boston City maps in the collection of the Library of Congress from both the 1835 and 1838 editions of *Stimpson's Boston Directory* (Boston: Charles Stimpson, Jr.) were used. Symbols referring to 1840s decedents and network members appear on both the charts and the maps.

Chart 1
Home and Business Locales of Associated Decedents

Street	Number	Name	Occupation	Symbol
Brattle	14	J. Rogers	Clothes Dealer	●
	22	W. Riley	Gentleman	◆
Congress	--	T. Cole	Hairdresser	◫
Court	121	J. Robinson	Clothing trader	▬
South May	9	J. E. Scarlett	Clothing trader	▲
Southac	court	W. Riley	Gentleman	✚
West Cedar	--	J. Robinson	Clothing trader	■

Source: Probate records in the Suffolk County Courthouse, Boston, MA

NOTE: Keyed to Figure 1

Figure 1. City of Boston (1838), showing home and business Locales of associated decedents. See chart 1.

Key:

▯	=	T. Cole's home
✦	=	W. Riley's home
■	=	J. Robinson's home
⬤	=	J. E. Scarlett's home
◆	=	W. Riley's business
▭	=	J. Robinson's business
⬤	=	J. Roger's business

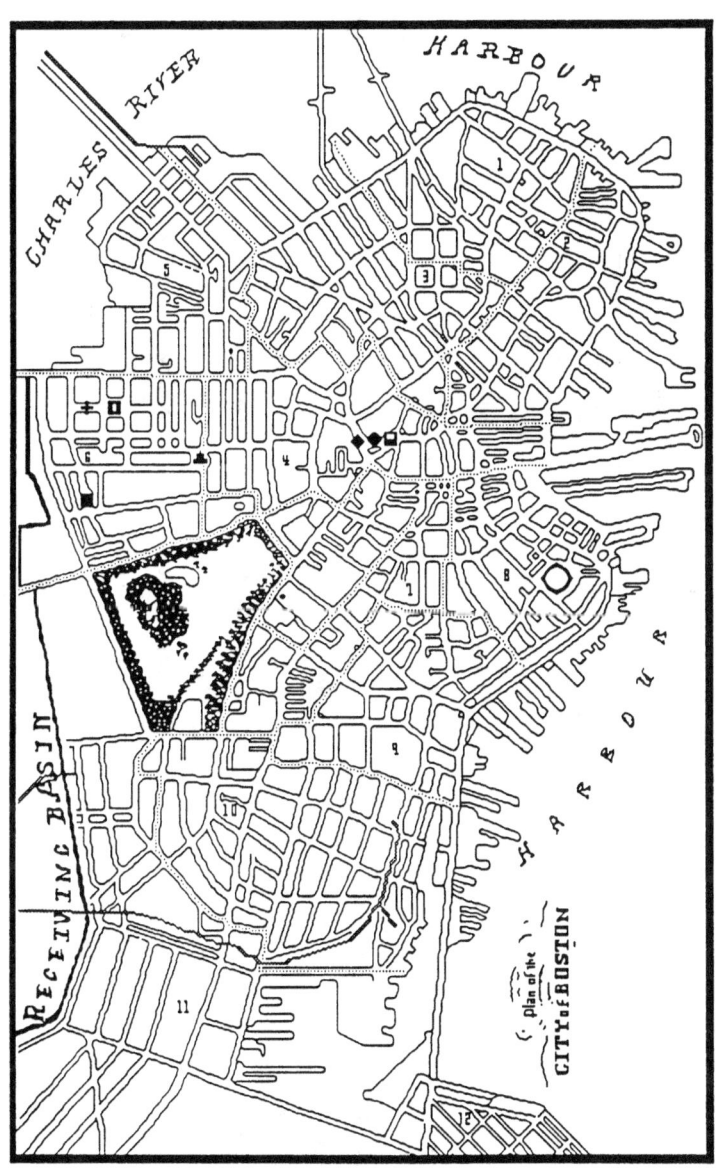

CHART 2
Real Estate Owned by 1840s Decedents

Street	Number	Name	Occupation	Symbol
Belknap	--	John W. Brown	Waiter	■
	--	Chloe Russell*	Cook/Widow	■
	17	John E. Scarlett	Clothes dealer	■
Bridge Place	--	John Robinson	Clothes dealer	■
	W. Cedar	John Robinson	Clothes dealer	■
Bultolph Street	Southac	Amy Jackson	Widow	■
Centre Street	rear	John L. Brent	Laborer	■
Cypress Street	near Vine	John Brooks	Laborer	■
Grove Street	2	John L. Brent	Laborer	■
Kennard Avenue	--	James H. Howe	Laborer	■
May Street	19	Amy Jackson	Widow	■
South May St.	9	John E. Scarlett	Clothes dealer	■
	11	John E. Scarlett	Clothes dealer	■
Southac	--	Peter Gray	Clothes dealer	■
	Cedar	Primus Hall	Soap boiler	■

Vine Street	Court	William Riley	Gentleman
Washington St.	2	Peter Gray	Clothes dealer
	S. May	Charles Biner	Teamster
	710-712	John E. Scarlett	Clothes dealer

Source: Probate records in the Suffolk County Courthouse, Boston, MA.
NOTE: Keyed to Figure 1.

* Life Interest

Figure 2 City of Boston (1838), showing real estate owned by 1840s decedents. See chart 2.

Key: ∎   = approximate location

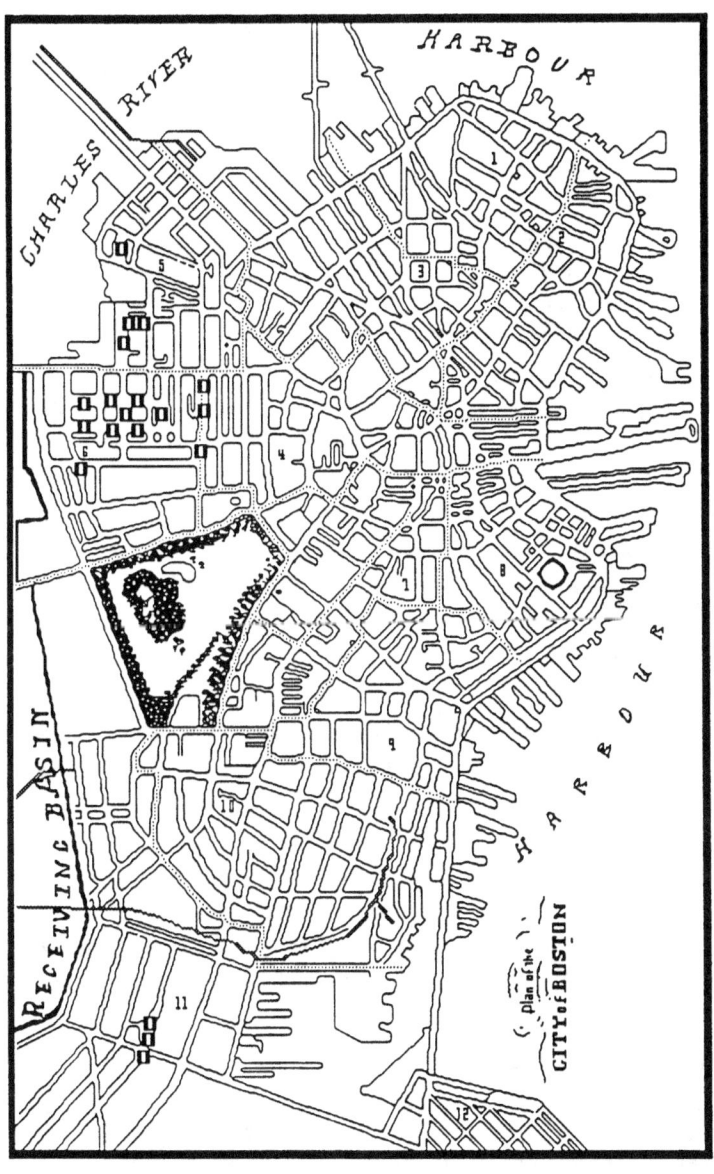

CHART 3
Residence by Wards of 1840s Decedents
and Network Members in 1830

Ward	Name	Occupation	Symbol
2	Arthur Jones	Boarding	■
3	John Brooks	Laborer	■
	Emiliano Mundrucu	Clothing	+
4	John E. Scarlett	Shop	■
5	Jonathan Cash	Handcartmen	+
	Peter Gray	Clothes	■
	Peter Howard	Hairdresser and Musician	+
	James H. Howe	Renovator of human hair	■
	Robert Roberts	[Stevedore]	+
	John Rogers	Clothes	+
	David Walker	Clothes	+
6	J. L. Brent	Laborer	■
	John Brown	[Mariner]	■
	Jonas W. Clark	[Clothes]	+
	Thomas Cole	Hairdresser	■
	Thomas Dalton	Boot black	+
	Primus Hall	Soap maker	■
	Coffin Pitts	Clothes shop	+
	William Riley	Clothes dealer	■
	John Robinson	Clothes dealer	■
	Joseph Sprague	[Laborer]	■
	Henry L. W. Thacker	Boot black	+
7	John W. Brown	Waiter	■
	Chloe Russell	Cook	■
	Samuel Snowden	Preacher	+
	George Washington	Boot black	+
10	Edward Lawson	[Laborer]	■
12	Charles Biner	[Teamster]	■

Sources: United States Census (1830) for wards and *Boston Directory* (Boston: Charles Stimpson, Jr., 1830) for occupations. When bracketed, occupation identified through probate records in Suffolk County Courthouse, Boston, MA, or an earlier or later directory listing.
NOTE: Keyed to figure 3.

Figure 3. City of Boston (1835), showing residence by wards of 1840s decedents and network members in 1830. See chart 3.

Key: ■ = 1840s decedent

✚ = network member

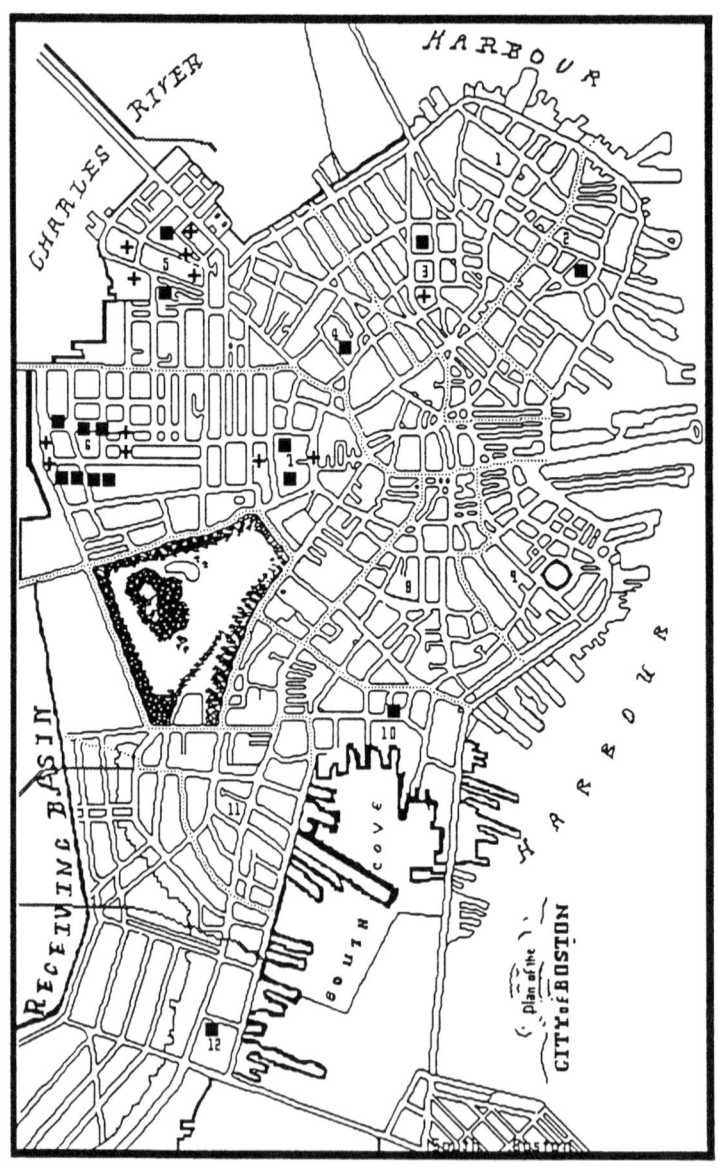

CHART 4
Residence by Wards of 1840s Decedents
and Network Members in 1840

Ward	Name	Occupation	Symbol
2	Arthur Jones	Barber	■
4	Coffin Pitts	Clothes	✚
	Henry Robinson	Chimney sweep	■
5	Jonathan Cash	Handcartman	✚
	Peter Howard	Hairdresser and Musician	✚
	Robert Roberts	[Stevedore]	✚
	John Rogers	Clothes	✚
	J. L. Brent	Laborer	■
	John Brown	[Mariner]	■
	Jonas W. Clark	[Clothing dealer]	■
	Peter Gray	Clothes	■
	Primus Hall	Soap boiler	■
	John T. Hilton	Clothes dealer	✚
	Edward Lawson	[Laborer]	■
	William Riley	Clothes dealer	■
	Chloe Russell	[Cook]	■
	Joseph Sprague	[Laborer]	■
11	John E. Scarlett	Shop	■

Source: Sixth United States Census (1840) for ward and *Stimpson's Boston Directory* (Boston: Charles Stimpson, Jr., 1840) for occupations. When bracketed, occupation identified through probate records in Suffolk County Courthouse, Boston, MA, or an earlier or later directory listing.
NOTE: Keyed to figure 4.

Figure 4. City of Boston (1838), showing residency by wards of 1840s decedents and network members in 1840. See chart 4.

Key: ■ = 1840s decedent

✚ = network member

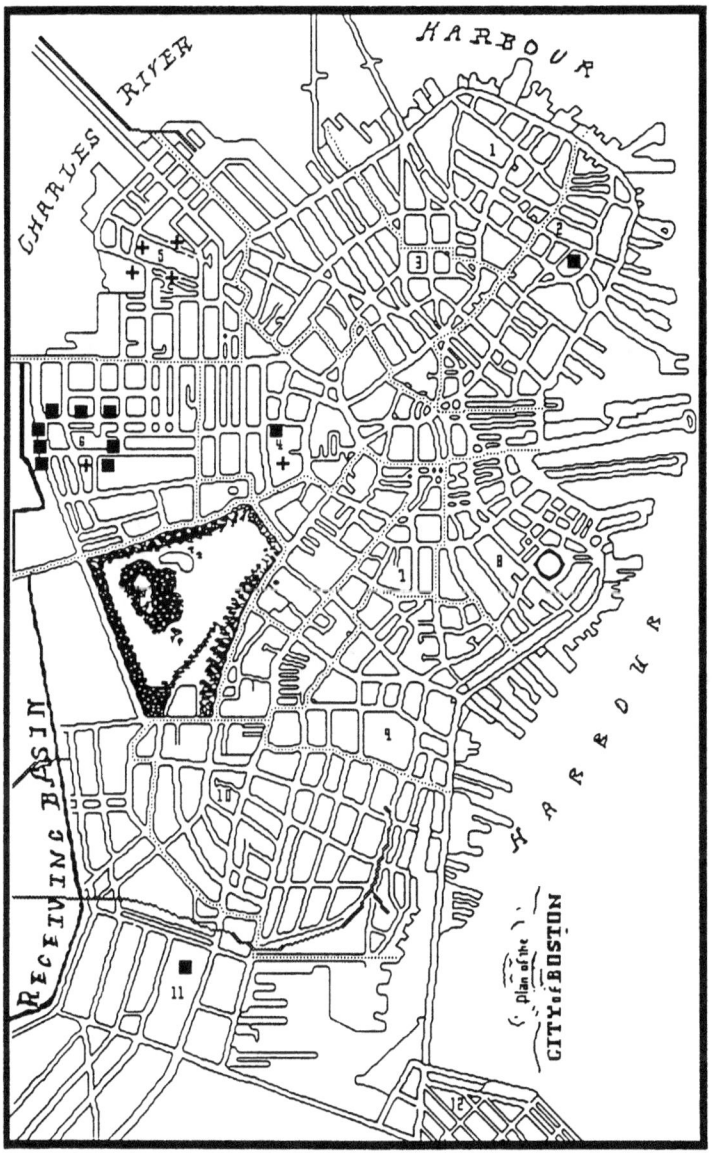

CHART 5
Home Locales of 1840s Decedents and Network Members in 1830

Street	Number	Name	Occupation	Symbol
Belknap	--	Chloe Russell	Cook	■
	5	Samuel Snowden	Preacher	+
	12	John T. Hilton	Hairdresser	+
	16	George Putnam	Hairdresser	+
	17	John W. Brown	Waiter	■
	29 rear	George Washington	Boot black	+
Bridge	--	David Walker	Clothes	+
Butolph	--	John Brooks	Laborer	■
Chambers	103	Jonathan Cash	Handcartman	+
Centre	--	Coffin Pitts	Clothes shop	+
Elm	19	John Robinson	Clothes dealer	■
Flagg Alley	--	John E. Scarlett	Shop	■
George	-- rear	Primus Hall	Soapmaker	■
Langdon Place	--	Arthur Jones	Boarding	■
May	--	Joseph Sprague	--	+

Poplar	--	Henry L. W. Thacker	Boot black	+
	18	Peter Howard	Hairdresser and Musician	+
Russell	32	John Rogers	Clothes	+
Second	--	Thomas Dalton	Boot black	+
	9	James G. Barbadoes	Hairdresser	+
Vine	--	Peter Gray	Clothes	■

Source: *The Boston Directory* (Boston: Charles Stimpson, Jr., 1830).
NOTE: Keyed to figure 5.

CHART 6
Business Locales of 1840s Decedents and Network Members in 1830

Street	Number	Name	Occupation	Symbol
Ann	50	Mundrucu and Bautista	Clothing	■
	139	Coffin Pitts	Clothes shop	■
Brattle	12	Peter Gray	Clothes	⊣
	14	John Rogers	Clothes	■
	20	John P. Coburn	Clothes dealer	■
	22	William Riley	Clothes dealer	⊣
	24	John E. Scarlett	Shop	⊣
	42	David Walker	Clothes	■
	56	James G. Barbadoes	Hairdresser	■
Cambridge	8	Peter M. Howard	Hairdresser and Musician	■
Congress	—	Henry L. W. Thacker	Boot black	■
	—	Thomas Cole	Hairdresser	⊣

Street	No.	Name	Occupation	Symbol
Court	106	James H. Howe	Renovator of human hair	⊥
Flagg Alley	121	John Robinson	Clothes dealer	⊥
Howard	--	Thomas Dalton	Boot black	■
Howard	--	John T. Hilton	Hairdresser	■
Washington	211	George Putnam	Hairdresser	■
Water	--	George Washington	Boot black	■

Source: *The Boston Directory* (Boston: Charles Stimpson, Jr., 1830).
NOTE: Keyed to figure 5

268

Figure 5. City of Boston (1835), showing home and business locales of 1840s decedents and network members in 1830. See charts 5 and 6.

Key: ▯   = 1840s decedent's home
      ✚   = network member's home
      ▲   = 1840s decedent's business
      ■   = network member's business

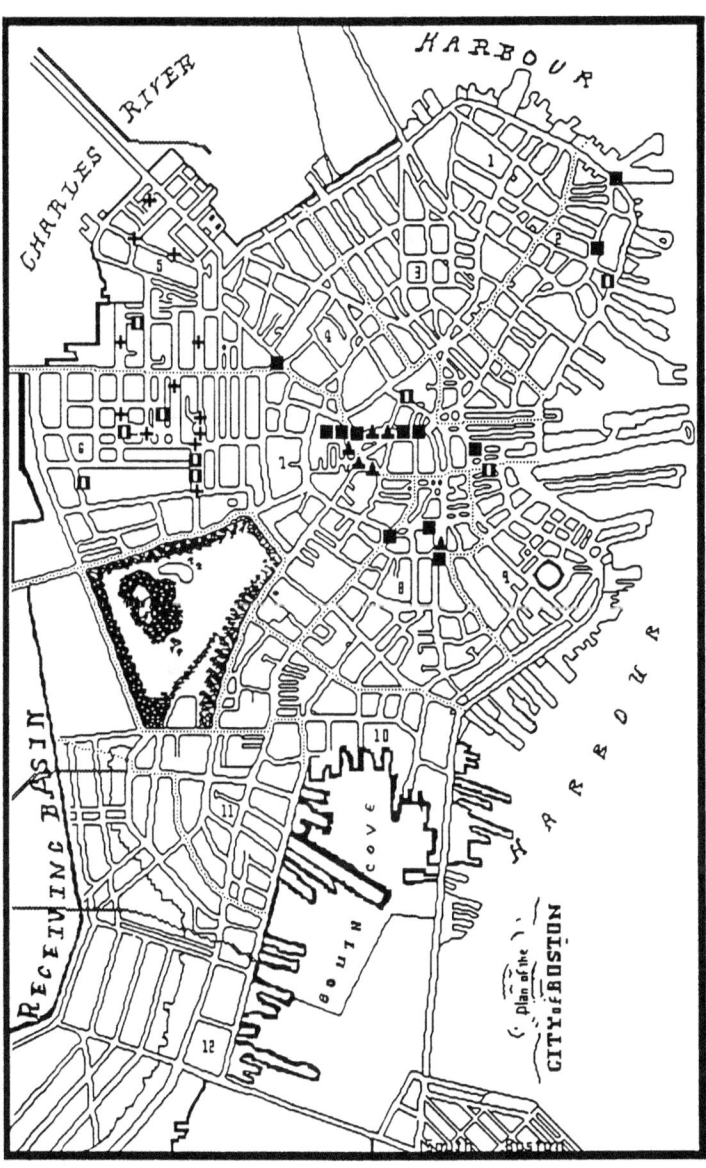

CHART 7
Home Locales of 1840s Decedents and Network Members in 1835

Street	Number	Name	Occupation	Symbol
Belknap	5	Samuel Snowden	Preacher	✚
	16	George Putnam	Hairdresser	✚
	17	John W. Brown	--	■
	29 rear	George Washington	Boot black	✚
Bultolph	--	James G. Barbadoes	--	✚
Chambers	103	Jonathan Cash	Handcartman	✚
George	--	John Robinson	Clothes	■
Langdon Place	--	Arthur Jones	Barber	■
May	--	Jonas W. Clark	Clothes dealer	✚
	--	Joseph Sprague	--	■
Peck Lane	--	Edward Lawson	Laborer	■
Poplar	18	Peter Howard	Hairdresser and Musician	✚
Russell	29 rear	John Rogers	Clothes	✚
	29 S.	Thomas Dalton	Boot black	✚
Second	9	Robert Roberts	--	✚

Street	No.	Name	Occupation	Symbol
South May	9	John Scarlett	Shop	■
Southac	--	John P. Coburn	Clothes dealer	+
	--	Thomas Cole	Hairdresser	■
	--	William Riley	Clothes dealer	■
	--	Henry L. W. Thacker	Boot black	+
	--	Charles Williams	Mariner	■
Vine	2	Peter Gray	Clothes	+
	3	Coffin Pitts	Clothes	+
Washington	706	Charles Biner	Teamster	■

Source: *Stimpson's Boston Directory* (Boston: Charles Stimpson, Jr., 1835)
NOTE: Keyed to Figure 6

CHART 8
Business Locales of 1840s Decedents and Network Members in 1835

Street	Number	Name	Occupation	Symbol
Ann	154 1-2	Arthur Jones	Barber	┥■
Brattle	5	John T. Hilton	Clothes	┥■
	8	John Coburn	Clothes dealer	┥■
	12	Peter Gray	Clothes	┥■
	14	John Rogers	Clothes	┥■
	18	Jonas W. Clark	Clothes dealer	┥■
	22	William Riley	Clothes dealer	┥■
	28	Coffin Pitts	Clothes	┥
	40	John E. Scarlett	Shop	┥
	42	John Robinson	Clothes	┥■
Bromfield	2	George Putnam	Hairdresser	┥■
Cambridge	82	Peter Howard	Hairdresser and Musician	
Congress	--	Thomas Cole	Hairdresser	┥
Exchange	31	James G. Barbadoes	--	■
Franklin Avenue	--	William S. Jinnings	Clothes dealer	┥

Pond	68	Benjamin P. Bassett	Hairdresser
Spring Lane	3	Henry L. W. Thacker	Boot black
Water	—	George Washington	Boot Black

Source: *Stimpson's Boston Directory* (Boston: Charles Stimpson, Jr., 1835).
NOTE: Keyed to Figure 6.

274

Figure 6. City of Boston (1835), showing home and business locales of 1840s decedents and network members in 1835. See charts 7 and 8.

Key: ▯ = 1840s decedent's home
 ✚ = network member's home
 ▲ = 1840s decedent's business
 ■ = network member's business

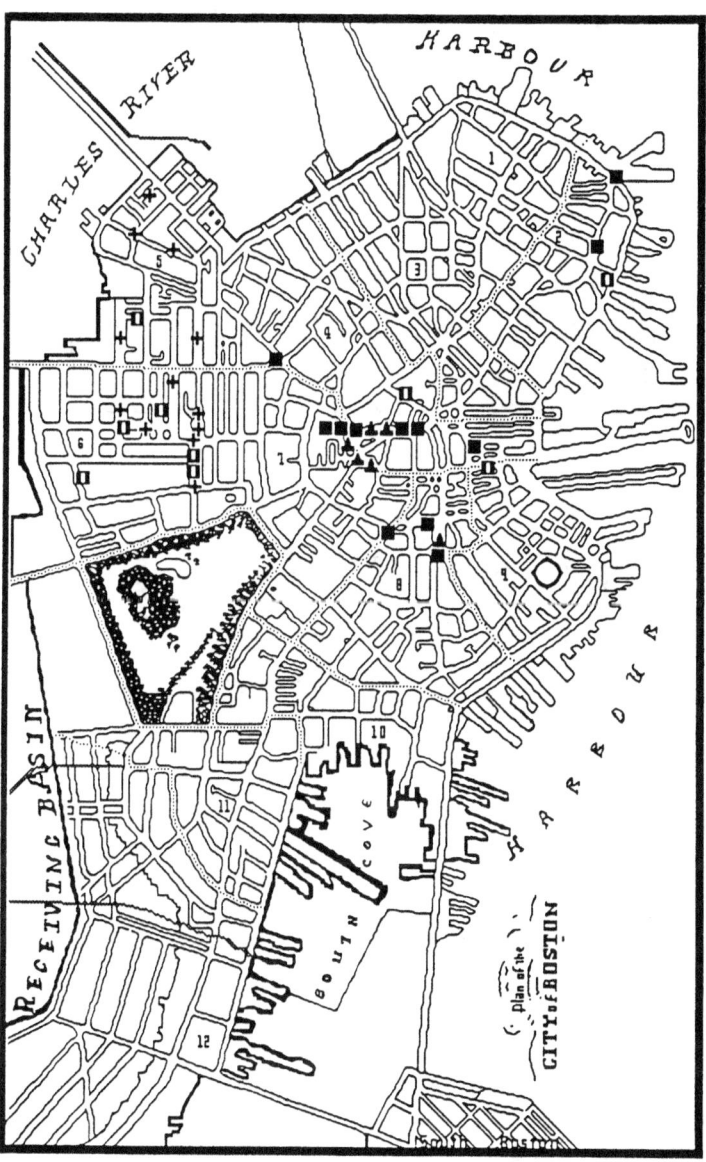

CHART 9
Home Locales of 1840s Decedents and Network Members in 1840

Street	Number	Name	Occupation	Symbol
Belknap	--	John Smith	Mariner	■
	15	Samuel Snowden	Preacher	+
	16	George Putnam	Hairdresser	+
	18	Coffin Pitts	Clothes	+
	29 rear	George Washington	Boot black	+
Centre	-- W.	Benjamin P. Bassett	Hairdresser	+
Chambers	103	Jonathan Cash	Handcartman	+
Fruit	12	James B. Barbadoes	--	■
Grove	-- rear	Joseph Sprague	--	+
May	--	Jonas W. Clark	--	+
Myrtle	18	John T. Hilton	Clothes dealer	■
Peck Lane	--	John Brooks	--	+
Poplar	18	Peter Howard	Hairdresser and Musician	+
Second	29 rear	John Rogers	Clothes	+
	9	Robert Roberts	--	+

Street	No.	Name	Occupation	Symbol
South May	--	Charles Biner	Teamster	■
	9	John E. Scarlett	Shop	■
Southac	--	John L. Brent	Laborer	■
	--	John P. Coburn	Clothes dealer	+
	--	Thomas Cole	Hairdresser	■
	--	Peter Gray	Clothes	■
	--	Primus Hall	Soap Boiler	■
	-- court	William Riley	Clothes dealer	■
	--	Henry L. W. Thacker	Boot black	+
West Cedar	--	John Robinson	Clothes	■

Source: *Stimpson's Boston Directory* (Boston: Charles Stimpson, Jr., 1840).
NOTE: Keyed to Figure 7.

CHART 10
Business Locales of 1840s Decedents and Network Members in 1840

Street	Number	Name	Occupation	Symbol
Atkinson	near Milk	Thomas Cole	Hairdresser	⊣
Blackstone	--	Jonas W. Clark	--	■
Brattle	8	John P. Coburn	Clothes dealer	■
	12	Peter Gray	Clothes	⊣
	14	John Rogers	Clothes	■
	22	William Riley	Clothes dealer	⊣
	28	Coffin Pitts	Clothes	■
	36	John T. Hilton	Clothes dealer	■
	40	John E. Scarlett	Shop	⊣
	42	John Robinson	Clothes	⊣
Cambridge	82	Peter Howard	Hairdresser and Musician	■
Court	62	James G. Barbadoes	--	■

	100	William S. Jinnings	Clothes dealer	⊥
	123	Henry Robinson	Chimney sweep	⊥
Devonshire	--	Henry L. W. Thacker	Boot black	■
Endicott	33	Benjamin P. Bassett	Hairdresser	■
North Square	--	Arthur Jones	Barber	■
School	14	Putnam G. and Clark	Hairdresser	■
Water	--	George Washington	Boot black	■

Source: *Stimpson's Boston Directory* (Boston: Charles Stimpson, Jr., 1840).
NOTE: Keyed to Figure 7.

Figure 7. City of Boston (1838), showing home and business locales of 1840s decedents and network members in 1840. See charts 9 and 10.

Key: ▯ = 1840s decedent's home
       ✚ = network member's home
       ▲ = 1840s decedent's business
       ■ = network member's business

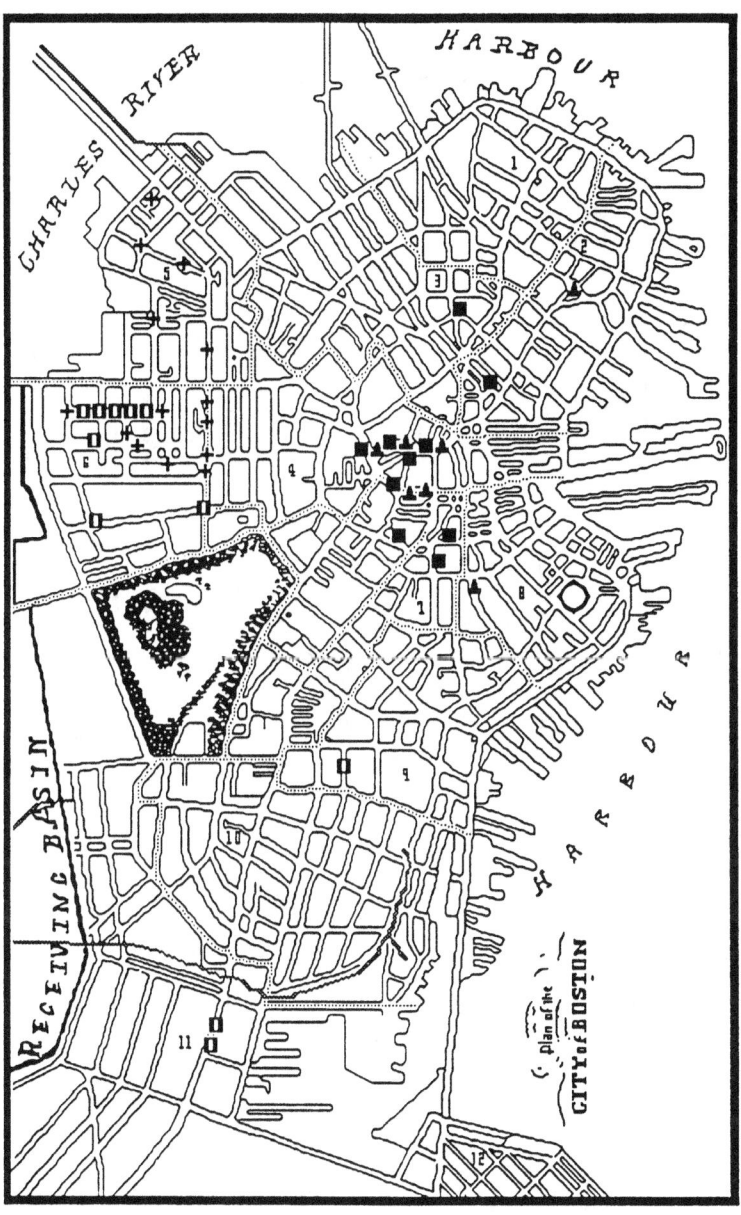

CHART 11
Home Locales of 1840s Decedents and Network Members in 1845

Street	Number	Name	Occupation	Symbol
Belknap	16	George Putnam	Hairdresser	✦
	18	Benjamin P. Bassett	Hairdresser	✦
	18	Coffin Pitts	Clothes	✦
	25 rear	George Washington	Waiter	✦
	27 rear	John Brown	Mariner	■
Chambers	103	Jonathan Cash	--	✦
	103	William C. Nell	--	✦
Kennard Ave	--	James H. Howe	Hair Renovator	■
May	--	Jonas W. Clark	Clothes dealer	✦
Poplar	--	Peter Howard	Hairdresser	✦
	29 rear	John Rogers	Clothes	✦
Russell	29. S.	Thomas Dalton	Waiter	✦
Second	9	Robert Roberts	Stevedore	✦
South May	--	Charles Biner	Teamster	■
Southac	--	John P. Coburn	Clothes dealer	✦

	court	Thomas Cole	Hairdresser	■
	near Grove	Samuel Snowden	Preacher	+
West Cedar	--	Henry L. W. Thacker	Boot black	+
Winter	1	John Robinson	Clothes	■
	19	Robert Morris Jr.	Clerk	+

Source: *Stimpson's Boston Directory* (Boston: Charles Stimpson, Jr., 1845).
NOTE: Keyed to **Figure 8.**

CHART 12
Business Locales of 1840s Decedents and Network Members in 1845

Street	Number	Name	Occupation	Symbol
Atkinson	--	Thomas Cole	Hairdresser	⊥
Blackstone	82	James H. Howe	Hair renovator	⊥
Brattle	20	John Rogers	Clothes	■
	28	Coffin Pitts	Clothes	■
	36	John T. Hilton	Hairdresser	■
	42	John Robinson	Clothes	■
	52	Jonas W. Clark	Clothes dealer	■
Cambridge	82	Peter Howard	Hairdresser	⊥
Cornhill	51	John P. Coburn	Clothes dealer	■
Devonshire	17	Henry L. W. Thacker	Boot black	■
Endicott	33	Benjamin P. Bassett	Hairdresser	■
School	14	Putnam G. and Clark A. F.	Hairdresser	■
State	27	Robert Morris Jr.	Clerk	■
Water	2	George Washington	Waiter	■

Source: *Stimpson's Boston Directory* (Boston: Charles Stimpson, Jr., 1845).
NOTE: **Keyed to Figure 8.**

285

Figure 8. City of Boston (1838), showing home and business locales of 1840s decedents and network members in 1845. See charts 11 and 12

Key: ▯ = 1840s decedent's home

✚ = network member's home

⊥ = 1840s decedent's business

■ = network member's business

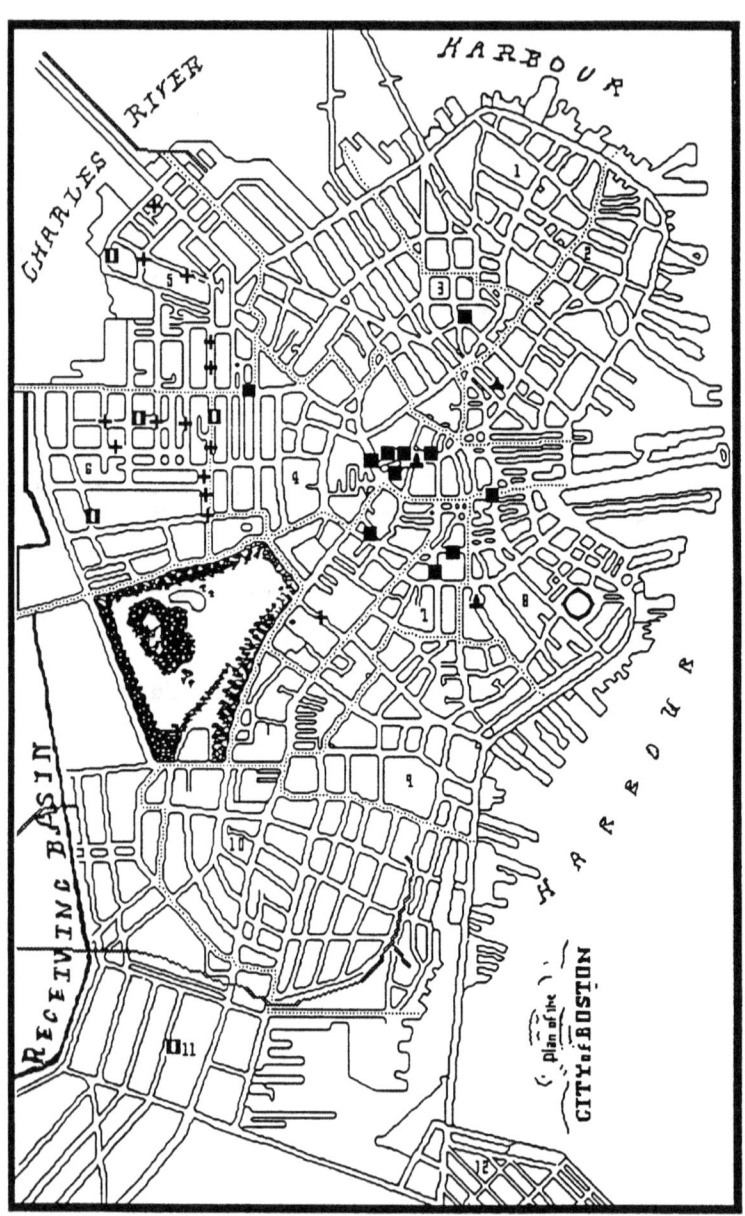

NOTES

Chapter 1

1.. *Webster's Third New International Dictionary of the English Language, Unabridged* (1981), s. v. "probate."

2.. The following description of the probate process is based loosely on Alice Hanson Jones, *Wealth of a Nation to Be: The American Colonies on the Eve of the Revolution* (New York: Columbia University Press, 1980), 2-6, and Bernard L. Herman, "Delaware's Orphan Court Valuations and the Reconstitution of Historic Landscapes, 1785-1830," Paper presented at the Dublin Seminar for New England Folklife on Early American Inventories, Deerfield, Massachusetts, July 11-12, 1987, photocopied, 1.

3.. Although technically classed as property, "according to Edgar J. McManus in *Black Bondage in the North* (Syracuse, NY: Syracuse University Press, 1973), 61-3, "slaves also had some of the attributes of legal personality. They could own and transfer property, receive and bequeath legacies, and work for their own benefit during their free time. The master's property in the slave did not automatically entitle him to the property of the slave . . . . The numerous legacies that [slaves] received made it clear that their right to own property was taken for granted . . . . Sometimes the slaves themselves made wills leaving their possessions to relatives and friends." In fact, the inheritance of slave property in accord with "rules governing lines of descent" has been documented by Philip D. Morgan, "Work and Culture: The Task System and the World of Lowcountry Blacks, 1700-1880," in *Material Life in America, 1600-1860*, ed. Robert Blair St. George (Boston: Northeastern Press, 1988), 220-1.

4.. The A-ACP is pursuing an ambitious research agenda that is based on the premise that members of a community structure it to meet their particular requirements. Assembling the most extensive data base on free blacks in the antebellum North will permit the A-ACP to explore the local social, political, and economic environment that shaped the ten communities under investigation. Information from many sources has been computerized—censuses, military description books of the Veteran's Administration for the Civil War, newspaper accounts of abolitionist activities, and organizational records.

5.. James Oliver Horton, *Eye of the Storm: Blacks in the Colonial North* (N.p., n.d, photocopied), chap. 2, pp. 25-77, chap. 3, p 16.

6.. Ibid., chap. 2, p.3, chap. 3, p. 19. In *Black Bostonians: Family Life and Community Struggle in the Antebellum North* (New York: Holmes & Meier, 1979), vii, James Oliver Horton and Lois E. Horton assert that New England slaves "generally possessed more rights and legal protections than southern plantation slaves. They were more than 'inventory.'"

7.. Horton, *Eye of the Storm*, chap. 2, pp. 27-28, chap, 3. pp. 20-21. McManus, 164-6, outlines the "Quork Walker Case" that led to the extinction of slavery in Massachusetts.

8.. "The key predictor in the treatment of blacks and the tolerance displayed by colonial whites was the extent to which Afro-Americans were seen as a threat. . . . in the South, when the number of blacks increased substantially or at a rapid rate, whites fearing for their lives, property, or perhaps only the resulting social instability, reacted strongly. Thus, in the northern colonies, laws were passed and enforced to varying degrees depending upon the perceived security of colonial society." The underlying fear grew from whites' judgment that blacks were unable to internalize the values and exercise the restraints conducive to orderly progress in a democracy. Horton, *Eye of the Storm*, chap. 2, p. 4, chap. 4, p. 5.

9.. Horton and Horton, 2-7.

10.. James Oliver Horton, "Shades of Color: The Mulatto in Three Antebellum Northern Communities," *Afro-Americans in N.Y. Life & History*, 8, no. 2 (July 1984), 44; and Horton, Eye of the Storm, chap. 9, p. 8.

11.. Ibid., chap. 8, p. 7, chap. 10, pp. 2, 9-15.

12.. "The rhetoric of freedom and equality changed if not the reality of America, at least the perceptions of significant numbers of its non-elite whites who were, in theory, raised to the level of citizen, removing the common ground on which interracial alliance made sense." Moreover, "a racial consciousness which linked white ownership and labor in a racial alliance against blacks at various economic levels . . . almost always operated to the long range disadvantage of blacks and laboring whites as well as reinforced the status differential between black and white workers." Ibid., chap. 2, p. 2, chap. 4, p. 18.

Chapter 2

1.. "Implied here," states Thomas C. Holt, "Introduction: Whither Now and Why?," in *The State of Afro-American History: Past, Present, and Future*, ed. Darlene Clark Hine (Baton Rouge, LA: Louisiana State University Press, 1986), 10, "is the notion that the future is somehow imprinted in the past, not because of any mystical determinism, but because minds are shaped for action by their understanding of the past."

2.. Theodore Hershberg, ed., *Philadelphia: Work, Space, Family, and Group Experience in the Nineteenth Century. Essays Toward an Interdisciplinary History of the City.* (New York: Oxford University Press, 1981), vi; Theodore Hershberg and others, "A Tale of Three Cities: Blacks, Immigrants, and Opportunity in Philadelphia, 1850-1880, 1930, 1979," in *Philadelphia: Work, Space, Family, and Group Experience in the Nineteenth Century. Essays Toward an Interdisciplinary History of the City*, ed. Theodore Hershberg (New York: Oxford University Press, 1981), 485; Hershberg, ed., *Philadelphia*, 457-8.

3.. James Oliver Horton, "The Historian and Social Policy: Moynihan and Black Families in Pre-Civil War Boston," Paper presented at the National Urban League Conference on Black Families, Chicago, Illinois, November 1977, photocopied, 1-2, 12-3.

4.. A sample of the progression of scholarship concerning mobility: Clyde Griffen, "Occupational Mobility in Nineteenth-Century America: Problems and Possibilities," *Journal of Social History* 5 (Spring 1972), 326; Roberta Balstad Miller, "The Historical Study of Social Mobility: A New Perspective," *Historical Methods Newsletter*, 8,no. 3 (June 1975), 95; Theodore Hershberg and Robert Dockhorn, "Occupational Classification," *Historical Methods Newsletter* 9,no. 2 & 3 (March/June 1976), 61-62; Michael B. Katz, "Social Class in North American Urban History," *Journal of Interdisciplinary History* 11 (Spring 1981), 599; and Howard P. Chudacoff, "Success and Security: The Meaning of Social Mobility in American," *Reviews in American History* 10, no.4 (December 1982), 106-109.

5.. The second study deliberately picks up where the first left off. James A. Henretta, "Economic Development and Social Structure in Colonial Boston," *William and Mary Quarterly*, 3d ser., 22 (January 1965), 75-95; Allan Kulikoff, "The Progress of Inequality in Revolutionary Boston," *William and Mary Quarterly*, 3d ser., 28 (July 1971), 375-412. Hershberg comments upon the intellectual milieu that spawned an interest "in answering questions about inequality. . . . It is clear from the questions that lay at the center of the mobility studies—How open was American society? How fluid was its population movement and its class structure? How true was its 'rags to riches' dream?—that the analytic focus was not on the city *per se*" but on the veracity of the ideology of American culture. Theodore Hershberg, "The New Urban History: Toward an Interdisciplinary History of the City," in *Philadelphia*, 13-4.

6.. James Oliver Horton, "Shades of Color: The Mulatto in Three Antebellum Northern Communities," *Afro-Americans in N.Y. Life & History* 8, no. 2 (July 1984), 41-2.

7.. Henretta, 402-3; Miller, 92; Kathleen Neils Conzen, "The New Urban History: Defining the Field," in *Ordinary People and Everyday Life: Perspectives on the New Social History*, ed. James B. Gardner and George R. Adams, (Nashville TN: American Association for State and Local History, 1983), 75-6; Hershberg, "The New Urban History," 14; The Rhode Island Black Heritage Society, *Creative Survival: The Providence Black Community in the 19th Century*, Catalog of the exhibition at the Rhode Island Black Heritage Society, (Providence, RI: The Rhode Island Black Heritage Society, [1984]), 33, 38.

8.. Chudacoff, 108.

9.. James Oliver Horton, "The Migrant and the Community: An Analysis of Adaptation," n.p., n.d., photocopied, 4-5, 7-8. See also James Oliver Horton, "Links to Bondage: Northern Free Blacks and the Problem of Slavery," n.p., 1984, photocopied, 10-2, and idem, *Eye of the Storm: Blacks in the Colonial North* (N.p., n.d., photocopied), chap. 4, p. 8. Howard N. Rabinowitz points to chain migration and group settlement as mechanisms for reducing alienation from the new environment in "Race, Ethnicity, and Cultural Pluralism in American History," in *Ordinary People*, 30-1.

10.. Herbert G. Gutman, *The Black Family in Slavery and Freedom, 1750-1925* (New York: Vintage Books, 1977), 209; Leslie Howard Owens, *This Species of Property: Slave Life and Culture in the Old South* (New York: Oxford University Press, 1976), 86.

11.. Claudia Goldin, "Family Strategies and the Family Economy in the Late Nineteenth Century: The Role of Secondary Workers," in *Philadelphia*, 277-8.

12.. Rabinowitz, 20, characterizes migrants as "highly self-selective, . . . more aggressive and ambitious individuals seeking to better their economic situation"; Hershberg connects geographical mobility leading to property mobility with assertiveness in "Free Blacks in Antebellum Philadelphia: A Study of Ex-Slaves, Freeborn, and Socioeconomic Decline," in *Philadelphia*, 381.

13.. Henretta, 86; Kulikoff, 411.

14.. Ibid., 392. Scholarly distance appears difficult to maintain when historical behavior seems to run counter to the best interests of the groups studied. Horton in *Eye of the Storm*, chap. 3, pp. 19, 26, chap. 4, pp. 2-3, finds that blacks were anything but quiescent in the colonial North. He similarly details activism in "Weevils in the Wheat: Northern Free Blacks and the Constitution, 1787-1860," n.p., n.d., photocopied, 17, and in "Black Education at Oberlin College: A Controversial Commitment," *Journal of Negro Education* 54 (Fall 1985), 499.

15.. Katz, "Social Class," 590.

16.. Michael B. Katz, Michael J. Doucet, and Mark J. Stern, *The Social Organization of Early Industrial Capitalism* (Cambridge: Harvard University Press, 1982), 135. Robert J. Cottrol remarks upon a similar mentality in *The Afro-Yankees: Providence's Black Community in the Antebellum Era*, Foreword by Stanley L. Engerman. Contributions in Afro-American and African Studies no. 68 (Westport, CT: Greenwood Press, 1982), 123.

17.. Katz, Doucet, and Stern, 158, 160-91. Olivier Zunz in *The Changing Face of Inequality: Urbanization, Industrial Development, and Immigrants in Detroit, 1880-1920* (Chicago: University of Chicago Press, 1982), 153, identifies home ownership as more of "an ethnocultural phenomenon than one of class." Hershberg, "Free Blacks in Antebellum Philadelphia," 381, notes a dramatic correlation between home ownership and males who purchased their own freedom: "To these ex-slaves, owning their own home or a piece of land must have provided something (perhaps a stake in society) of peculiarly personal significance."

18.. Chudacoff, 108; Cottrol, 106; Rabinowitz, 34; Conzen, "New Urban History," 80; Griffen, 326.
19.. Katz, Doucet, and Stern, 157; Zunz, 161.
20.. Horton, *Eye of the Storm*, chap. 2, p. 1, citing Gary Nash, *The Urban Crucible: Social Change, Political Consciousness, and the Origins of the American Revolution* (Cambridge: Harvard University Press, 1979), 13. See also James Oliver Horton, "The Life and Times of Edward Ambush: An Illustration of Social History Methodology," in *History and Tradition in Afro-American Culture*, ed. Guenter Lenz (Frankfurt am Main: Campus Verlag, 1984), 10. Owens, 136-7 gives some inkling of what constituted "the bottom" domestically for slaves: "There was not much furniture. Just beds and a table and some stools, and dishes made of wood, and an iron pot, and some other cooking utensils." Slave housing was crudely constructed, small, with holes for windows. Ira Berlin in *Slaves without Masters: The Free Negro in the Antebellum South* (New York: Oxford University Press, 1974), 246, points to the "immense symbolic importance" of property mobility that superceded the measure of comfort it afforded, "a means of compensating for the barriers to the traditional routes of occupational mobility."
21.. Katz, Doucet, and Stern, 160. The concept of "loser" carries severe opprobrium by today's standards. Lawrence W. Levine in *Black Culture and Black Consciousness: Afro-American Folk Thought from Slavery to Freedom* (New York: Oxford University Press, 1977), 54, warns against making ahistorical judgments of behaviors in the past.
22.. Horton, *Eye of the Storm*, chap. 2, p. 2, chap. 3, p. 27. "Only gender rivaled [race] as the major determining factor in the life experience of an American."
23.. Hershberg, ed., *Philadelphia*, 41.
24.. Ibid., 125.
25.. Ibid., 237.
26.. Ibid., 346.
27.. "Having on the one hand been denied full participation in American society and on the other having resisted complete acculturation, Negroes had not succumbed to many of the society's central projections and dreams. This pattern of denial and resistance increased black separateness and autonomy." Levine, 282-3.
28.. Melvin Wade, "'Shining in Borrowed Plumage': Affirmation of Community in the Black Coronation Festivals of New England, ca. 1750-1850," in *Material Life in America, 1600-1860*, ed. Robert Blair St. George (Boston: Northeastern Press, 1988), 174-6, 180. See also *Creative Survival*, 56, and James Oliver Horton, "Double Consciousness: Afro-American Identity in the Nineteenth Century," in *Sharing Traditions: Five Black Artists in Nineteenth-Century America*, ed. Lynda Roscoe Hartigan (Washington, DC: Smithsonian Institution Press for the National Museum of American Art, 1985), 19, for a discussion of the dual identity blacks eventually evolved.
29.. According to Gutman, 154, 223, 219-20, "supporting institutions developed within slave communities to sustain persons in the grief of separation and to perpetuate the cultural affinity among them for distinctive slave domestic and kin arrangements." Over several generations, cumulative adaptive beliefs and behaviors transformed kin obligations into non-kin social obligations, so that unrelated blacks were bound together by "conceptions of obligation that had flowed initially from kin obligations rooted in blood and marriage."
30.. James Oliver Horton in "Black Urbanites: An Interpretation of Afro-American Life in the Antebellum City," Book review essay on *The Free Black in Urban America, 1800-1850* by Leonard P. Curry, *Afro-Americans in N.Y. Life & History* 7, no. 4 (January 1983), 5-6, highlights the essential communality of nineteenth-century black life, an outgrowth of both racial restrictions and Afro-American cultural values. In James Oliver Horton and Lois E. Horton, *Black Bostonians: Family Life and Community Struggle in the Antebellum North* (New York: Holmes & Meier, 1979), xi, the argument is made that the "necessities of individual survival spurred communal action." See also Cottrol, 163.
31.. "The Negro bourgeoisie, however, although often contemptuous of the less successful, could not dissociate itself from the lower classes. In the segregated community, it depended on Negro patronage. Moreover, racial pride and the fact that legislation applied to all colored classes insured the existence of a Negro community with common grievances, interests, and goals." Leon Litwack, *North of Slavery: The Negro in the Free States, 1790-1860* (Chicago: University of Chicago Press, 1961), 186. See Zunz, 194, for cohesiveness in the Polish community based on the upper stratum's dependence on the community for its attainment of upward mobility. "Success was achieved within the community; consequently, [Poles] did not leave their area of initial settlement to join native white Americans. Instead, social mobility was reinvested in the community and used as a means to reinforce ethnic identity."
32.. "Blacks, understanding that they could not depend on white institutions, set about providing for their communities as best they could," Horton reports in *Eye of the Storm*, chap. 4, p. 20. They organized themselves, in particular, to protest slavery and aid fugitives. See also James Oliver Horton, "Class and Occupation in Antebellum Boston," Paper presented at the Annual Meeting of the American Historical Association, New York, December 1979, photocopied, 22, and Horton, "Double Consciousness," 13.
33.. John Modell, "Changing Risks, Changing Adaptations: American Families in the Nineteenth and Twentieth Centuries," in *Kin and Communities: Families in America*, ed. Allan Lichtman and Joan Challinor; Preface by S. Dillon Ripley; Foreward by Wilton S. Dillon. Smithsonian International Symposia Series (Washington DC; Smithsonian Institution Press, 1979), 128.
34.. Horton in "The Migrant and the Community," 25, underscores the viability of the organizational structure of the poor black community regardless of its departure from sociological preconceptions of what constitutes "order." See also James Borchert, *Alley Life in Washington: Family, Community, Religion, and Folklife in the City, 1850-1970* (Urbana, IL: University of Illinois Press, 1980), 101, 195, 223; George W. McDaniel, *Hearth and Home: Preserving*

a People's Culture (Philadelphia: Temple University Press, 1982), 145; and Carol B. Stack, *All Our Kin: Strategies for Survival in a Black Community* (New York: Harper and Row Publishers, 1974), 124-5.

35.. Horton and Horton, xi. "The remarkable cohesiveness of ethnic communities suggests, however, that the forces behind their autonomy effectively compensated them for the persistent social inequality they faced outside their own neighborhood," according to Zunz, 81. Hershberg, ed., *Philadelphia*, 122-3, draws attention to the effect of geographic as well as numerical size when looking at urban communities in the past.

36.. Ibid., 347.

37.. Horton and Horton, 10. For instance, "traditional class divisions" do not take into account critical factors for understanding the occupational structure of black society. Two jobs that would be categorized as unskilled differed significantly for the black laborer if one were seasonal and the other steady.

38.. Ibid., 8, 10; Hershberg, "Free Blacks in Antebellum Philadelphia," 382; and Horton, "Class and Occupation," 11, 13; Cottrol, 132.

39.. Berlin, 234-6. See also Cottrol, 119, 121; and *Creative Survival*, 40-3, 47-51.

40.. Herbert J. Foster, "Occupational Class in the Black Community of Atlantic City and in Other Northern Cities: 1850-1915," n.p., n.d., photocopied, 20-1. See also Horton and Horton, 8, 11; Borchert, 9, n. 27; Litwack, 179; Cottrol, 132; Berlin, 244; and Paul J. Lammermeier, "The Urban Black Family of the Nineteenth Century: A Study of Black Family Structure in the Ohio Valley, 1850-1880," *Journal of Marriage and the Family* 35 (August 1973), 445.

41.. Horton, "Class and Occupation," 11; Horton and Horton, 60; and Litwack, 236, 241.

42.. Horton, "Class and Occupation," 11. See also Cottrol, 121.

43.. Hershberg, "Free Blacks in Antebellum Philadelphia," 372; Horton, "Class and Occupation," 11, 13; and Cottrol, 121, 127-130.

44.. Hershberg, "Free Blacks in Antebellum Philadelphia," 372, Hershberg, ed., *Philadelphia*, 346, 388, n. 12. Theodore Hershberg and Henry Williams, "Mulattoes and Blacks: Intra-group Color Differences and Social Stratification in Nineteenth-Century Philadelphia," in *Philadelphia*, 395, 426. See also Horton, "Shades of Color," 39, 57.

45.. Levine, ix (author's emphasis).

46.. Owens, 221, 5, 175-7. See also Gutman, 85.

47.. Gutman, 95, 99, 143.

48.. Levine, 24, argues that a people need not "originate or invent all or even most of the elements of their culture. It is necessary only that these components become their own, embedded in their traditions, expressive of their world view and life style." See also Gutman, 316.

49.. McDaniel, 26. See also Horton, "The Migrant and the Community," 25; Borchert, 101, 195, 223; McDaniel, *Hearth and Home*, 145; and Stack, 124-5.

50.. "If mid-twentieth-century historians have difficulty perceiving the sacred universe created by slaves as a serious alternative to the societal system created by southern slaveholders, the problem may be the historians' and not the slaves'," according to Levine, 54. Rhys Isaac, "Ethnographic Method in History: An Action Approach," in *Material Life in America*, 41, stresses that "the importance of the distinction between observers' perspectives (for example, our own as twentieth-century social scientists) and participants' categories (for example, those of the past peoples we study) should be borne in mind throughout the reading of this essay."

51.. Hershberg, "Free Blacks in Antebellum Philadelphia," 372, 388, n. 12; Hershberg, ed., *Philadelphia*, 346; and Hershberg and Williams, 395, 426. See also Horton, "Shades of Color," 57, who admits that "until recently the volatility of this issue made it almost impossible to analyze dispassionately."

52.. "Some may want to argue that the central problem of Black women is related to their race and not their sex. Such an argument then presumes that the problem cannot be resolved apart from the Black struggle. I contend that as long as the Black struggle refuses to recognize and deal with its sexism, the idea that women will receive justice from that struggle alone will never work," declares Jacquelyn Grant, "Black Women and the Church" in *But Some of Us Were Brave: Black Womens' Studies*, ed. Gloria T. Hull, Patricia Bell Scott, and Barbara Smith (Old Westbury, NY: The Feminist Press, 1982), 144. See also James Oliver Horton, "Freedom's Yoke: Gender Conventions among Antebellum Free Blacks," *Feminist Studies* 12, no. 1 (Spring 1986), 73-4: "Investigating the history of this contemporary situation is painful; it threatens to lay bare the rough inner sores of a world long protected by a facade of racial unity."

53.. Hershberg in "Free Blacks in Antebellum Boston," 370, chastises the Abolitionists and Quakers who in their zeal "to document that free Negroes were not worthless, that they could indeed survive outside of the structured environment of slavery and even that they could create a community with their own churches, schools, and beneficial societies" overstated the case by arguing "that the people and the institutions they created actually *prospered* in the face of overwhelming odds" (author's emphasis). See also Zunz, 257, who has formed a relatively jaundiced opinion of the absence of consistent family strategies among blacks in Detroit in the late nineteenth and early twentieth century, "a diversity which did not reflect an adaptability to different pressures but rather an inability to establish one type of household or another." Elizabeth Higginbotham in "Two Representative Issues in Contemporary Sociological Work on Black Women," in *Some Are Brave*, 96, speaks out on developing a perspective for revealing "the complex lives of Black women. Any framework which attempts to do this must be equipped to handle positive and negative findings." Thus, "focusing on resourcefulness and adaptability" has the potential of obscuring the poverty, racism, sexism, and other barriers with which black women have had to cope.

54.. Gutman, 113, 118-123, 128. See also Hershberg and Williams, 423.

55.. Gutman, chap. 3, v, between 130-1, ii between 134-5, xix-xx between 114-5. Hershberg and Williams, 421-3, 433, n, 33.
56.. Gutman, 128, table 17.
57.. Horton and Horton, 53-4, 60.
58.. Not that this is a forbidden practice, but Katz, Doucet, and Stern, 171, caution against the individual focus: "Despite a considerable amount of individual movement between jobs and even between ranks, the occupational structure and the relationships between work and ethnicity remained relatively fixed." Their concern is to counteract the "illusion of a society more open than it actually was." Yes, there were "limited ladders of mobility" and "reasonable chances for home ownership," but both of these "distracted people from the larger structural consequences of mobility patterns and property transactions—namely, the perpetuation of the structure of inequality." While the nineteenth-century denizens of Hamilton, Ontario, may be forgiven for not discerning these larger structural consequences, today's social historians have to keep an eye on both the individual's and the group's experience.
59.. "Social historians launched a full-scale search for the American experience of the ordinary people of the nation. That search led scholars away from the theme of individualism," Horton explains. "Most often the scholar must reconstruct the lives of community people and their relations with one another one piece at a time from a number of public documents." "Life and Times of Edward Ambush," 4-5.
60.. Ibid., 3-4.
61.. Ibid., 5-10, facsimile of Ambush's will between 11 and 12. The issue of the inheritance of property and privilege seems not to have been fully addressed or resolved in social history literature. Here, Horton presents Ambush's legacy in a positive light, giving his grandchild access to the privilege of education. But Katz, Doucet, and Stern, 199, note the inequity of prospects between the great majority of laborers' sons who were somewhat upwardly mobile and "the young men who inherited the accumulation of privileges available to the fortunate." At what point does "inherited privilege" slide from the positive to the negative, signifying a just or an unjust society?
62.. Horton, "The Life and Times of Edward Ambush," 10.
63.. Hershberg, ed., *Philadelphia*, xii-xiii.
64.. Horton, "Class and Occupation," 1-2. Hershberg and Williams, 393, state in "Mulattoes and Blacks," "The recent literature has begun to dispel the myth that the black experience was monolithic and to make clear the complexities of the variant forms of black internal differentiation and social structure."
65.. Horton and Horton, xi, 6-11.
66.. Hershberg and Williams, 395-6, 425-7. See also Cottrol, 139, and Litwack, 182-3. In Norval D. Glenn, "Negro Prestige Criteria: A Case Study in the Bases of Prestige," *American Journal of Sociology* 68 (May 1963), 645, the focus is on distinguishing between "primary and secondary class characteristics, that is between the bases of prestige and its correlates and consequences." Glenn continues, "For instance, if most high-prestige Negroes are found to be light-skinned, it is important to know whether their prestige is based to a large extent upon their skin color or whether it is based largely upon other attributes, which, for historical reasons, mulattoes are more like[ly] to possess than other Negroes."
67.. Horton, "Shades of Color," 51, 47-8, 52-3; Hershberg and Williams, 404-5.
68.. Hershberg and Williams, 406.
69.. Gutman, 134, establishes that even when "detached from their late-eighteenth and early-nineteenth-century Afro-American immediate families," slaves "reconstituted themselves in a community characterized by conventional Afro-American families and kin networks." He goes on, 153, to argue that *all* slave marriages were insecure (author's emphasis). . . . slave parents everywhere had good reasons to socialize their children to prepare for either the possible breakup of their marriages or sale from an immediate family."
70.. Ibid., 16, 9, 433. See also *Creative Survival*, 16-7, and Lammermeier, 441.
71.. Horton, "The Historian and Social Policy," 6.
72.. Frank F. Furstenberg, Jr., Theodore Hershberg, and John Modell, "The Origins of the Female-Headed Black Family: The Impact of the Urban Experience," in *Philadelphia*, 440-1. See also Lammermeier, 444, "The average proportion of female-headed families was greater in Cincinnati than in any other city," foreshadowing "future trends for blacks in the urban context." Compare with Lammermeier, 451, "Three quarters of the black children 15 years of age and younger lived in two-parent families in the urban Ohio Valley in the latter half of the nineteenth century."
73.. Furstenberg, Hershberg, and Modell, 443, 447, 449, 451-2.
74.. Stack, in collaboration with John R. Lombardi, 124. This seven-part pattern characteristic of today's poor black family is stated with scholarly neutrality, but clearly divides between the four strategies ("co-residence, kinship-based exchange network . . . , elastic household boundaries, [and] lifelong bonds to three-generational households") and their three consequences ("social controls against the formation of marriage . . . , the domestic authority of women, and limitations on the role of the husband or male friend.").
75.. Horton, "The Migrant and the Community," 24.
76.. Higginbotham, 95-6. See also Patricia Bell Scott, "Debunking Sapphire: Toward a Non-Racist and Non-Sexist Social Science," in *Some Are Brave*, 86-7; and Horton, "Freedom's Yoke," 56, 60, 73-4.
77.. Ibid., 58. See also Horton, *Eye of the Storm*, chap. 4, pp. 16-7; Cottrol, 135; *Creative Survival*, 40; and Furstenberg, Hershberg, and Modell, 449. Goldin, 298-9, identifies "differential relative discrimination" as "the primary factor in encouraging black families to send their children to school and their mothers to work." It seems that industries did not hire black children but black women could find jobs, and, "having had a longer history of labor force

participation [by 1880]," they "may have been less prejudiced against working outside the home than were white women."
78.. Lammermeier, 445-6, n. 17.
79.. Cottrol, 135-6, 133.
80.. Horton and Horton, 20. See also Suzanne Lebsock, *The Free Women of Petersburg: Status and Culture in a Southern Town, 1784-1860* (New York: W.W. Norton & Company, 1984), 187-9, 166-9.
81.. Cottrol, 121.
82.. Hershberg, "Free Blacks in Antebellum Philadelphia," 370, 372.
83.. Hershberg and Williams, 416, table 14.
84.. Horton and Horton, 10, 12.
85.. Berlin, 97.
86.. Litwack, 278.
87.. Horton and Horton, vii. Philip D. Morgan, "Work and Culture: The Task System and the World of Lowcountry Blacks, 1700-1880," in *Material Life*, 219-20, shows that "the scale and range of property owning by slaves . . . asssumed significant dimensions by the middle of the nineteenth century" on the rice plantations of lowcountry South Carolina and Georgia.
88.. Stack, in collaboration with Lombardi, 124 and 95-6, finds "biculturalism"–simultaneous enculturation and socialization into one's own culture and mainstream culture–as a useful model for explicating the "value-mosaic" of the poor. The most telling example of this dual value system can be seen in the story of Lydia, who when succeeding economically in the wider society, had distanced herself from the kinship network, but when matters took a turn for the worse, reobligated the kinship network to her by sharing her material success.
89.. Cottrol, 123-6.
90.. Leonard P. Curry, *The Free Black in Urban America, 1800-1850: The Shadow of the Dream* (Chicago: University of Chicago Press, 1981), 39-41.
91.. Berlin, 245-6. See also Katz, Doucet, and Stern, 135, 158, 160-91; Zunz, 153; Hershberg, "Free Blacks in Antebellum Philadelphia," 381; and Cottrol, 123.
92.. McDaniel, *Health and Home*, 248-9, speaks eloquently of the potential for learning from previously untapped sources. See also Jack Larkin, "The View from New England: Notes on Everyday Life in Rural America to 1850," *American Quarterly* 34, no. 3 (1982), 250: "In the 'infinite' details of past everyday life we can find both some of the surest traces of social transformation and a sense of personal encounter."
93.. Levine, xi.

Chapter 3

1.. Robert J. Cottrol, *The Afro-Yankees: Providence's Black Community in the Antebellum Era*, Foreword by Stanley L. Engerman, Contributions in Afro-American and African Studies no. 68 (Westport, CT: Greenwood Press, 1982) 126-7, 172.
2.. Vernon G. Baker, "Archaeological Visibility of Afro-American Culture from Black Lucy's Garden, Andover, Massachusetts," *Archaeological Perspectives on Ethnicity in America: Afro-American and Asian American Culture History*, ed. Robert L. Schuyler, (Farmingdale, NY: Baywood Publishing Company, Inc, 1980) 30-1. Baker traces Black Lucy's life through the probate records of her owners and employers, from around 1783 to 1812. Other examples of innovative and aggressive scholarship give the lie to claims that certain populations are "inarticulate." For instance, a transgenerational study of probate inventories has identified five types of property transfers to wives and to daughters, thereby disclosing female values and rights in the past. Barbara McLean Ward, "Women's Property and Family Continuity in Eighteenth-Century Connecticut," Paper presented at the Dublin Seminar for New England Folklife on Early American Inventories, Deerfield, Massachusetts, July 11-12, 1987, photocopied, shows that understanding women's property (what they owned, received, and/or controlled) thus requires more than simply examining the relatively scarce probate records of singlewomen and widows. Similarly, Randolph B. Campbell, "Slave Hiring in Texas," *American Historical Review* 93, no. 1 (February 1988), 108, looked at probate administrative accounts to gain insight into the effect of estate settlement on blacks–their status as property to be deployed in the support of the decedent's minor children or in the payment of the decedent's debts.
3.. Joan H. Geismar, "Skunk Hollow: A Preliminary Statement on Archaeological Investigations at a 19th Century Black Community," in *Archaeological Perspectives*, 63; and Lorena S. Walsh, "Urban Amenities and Rural Sufficiency: Living Standards and Consumer Behavior in the Colonial Chesapeake, 1643-1777," *Journal of Economic History* 43, no. 1 (March 1983), 111.
4.. Alice Hanson Jones, *Wealth of a Nation to Be: The American Colonies on the Eve of the Revolution* (New York: Columbia University Press, 1980) xxiii-xxvi, devotes several instructive and persuasive introductory pages to describing "the key to [her] entire study . . . the use of a small, rigorously selected, statistical sample" of probate inventories.
5.. For example, Gloria L. Main, "The Correction of Biases in Colonial American Probate Records," *Historical Methods Newsletter* 8, no. 6 (December 1974), 11, does not mention a precise number but claims to have used "a complete set of inventories in microfilmed records for Suffolk and Hampshire Counties, Mass., for 1650-1719." Most intriguing are the on-going massive accumulation (and computerization) of inventories by the Colonial Williamsburg Foundation, by Old Sturbridge Village, and by St. Mary's City Commission.

6.. Jones, *Wealth of a Nation to Be*, xxiii-xxvi, serves as the prime example of the identification of the specific site(s) from which the inventories are to be gathered; Carole Shammas, "The Domestic Environment in Early Modern England and America," *Journal of Social History* 18 (1980), 5, for the example of the selection of the inventories from a certain locale.

7.. Alice Hanson Jones exemplifies this model in "Wealth Estimates for the American Middle Colonies, 1774," *Economic Development and Cultural Change* 18, no. 4: pt.2 (July 1970); "Wealth Estimates for the New England Colonies about 1770," *Journal of Economic History* 32 (1972), 99; and *Wealth of a Nation to Be*, xxiii-xxv.

8.. Gloria L. Main, *Tobacco Colony: Life in Early Maryland, 1650-1720*, (Princeton, NJ: Princeton University Press, 1982), is the key piece in the literature, but these tactics are also to be found in Russell R. Menard. P.M.G. Harris, and Lois Green Carr, "Opportunity and Inequality: Distribution of Wealth on the Lower Western Shore of Maryland, 1638-1705," *Maryland Historical Magazine* 69, no. 2 (Summer 1974), 170; Daniel Scott Smith, "Underregistration and Bias in Probate Records: An Analysis of Data from Eighteenth Century Hingham, Massachusetts," *William and Mary Quarterly* 3d ser., 32 (January 1975), 104; and Kathryn S. Smith, "Household Inventories as Sources for the Study of Nineteenth-Century Non-Elites," n.p., 1982, photocopied, 2.

9.. Shammas, "Domestic Environment" 5, provides the most far-flung analysis, echoed a bit by Walsh, 111.

10.. Main, *Tobacco Colony*, 289.

11.. Jones, *Wealth of a Nation to Be*, 3-4.

12.. Gloria L. Main, "Probate Records as a Source for Early American History," *William and Mary Quarterly* 3d ser., 32 (January 1975), 89, 95.

13.. Main, "Correction of Biases," 10; idem, *Tobacco Colony*, 49; Jones, "Wealth Estimates for the American Middle Colonies, 1774," 110; idem, *Wealth of a Nation*, 10.

14.. Ibid., 3-6, gives a thorough (almost docu-dramatic) account of the history and circumstances of the genesis and production of "sworn wealth appraisals" that speaks convincingly to their reliability. "The appraisers personally visited the deceased's dwelling place and listed, usually in great detail, although sometimes with regrettable lumping, the portable wealth, and gave each listed item an appraised value. . . . That the appraised values in the probate inventories were neither perfunctory nor conventional is shown by their meticulous variation from inventory to inventory. That they were not greatly understated, as might be suspected if tax avoidance were involved, is apparent from the closeness with which they approximate actual sales values in those cases where the goods were subsequently auctioned at an advertised 'public vendue' and an account of the sales survives as an additional probate document presented in court. . . . No reason appears for suspecting that values were overstated." See also Peter H. Lindert, "An Algorithm for Probate Sampling," *Journal of Interdisciplinary History* 11 (Spring 1981), 657-8.

15.. "Quantifiable information about the determinants of wealth and the general standard of living of individuals prior to the mid-nineteenth century is difficult to come by. . . . estate inventories are probably one of the best sources we have," according to Carole Shammas, "The Determinants of Personal Wealth in Seventeenth-Century England and America," *Journal of Economic History* 37 (September 1977), 676.

16.. Main, *Tobacco Colony*, 49.

17.. Main, "Probate Records as a Source," 92-3.

18.. Lois Green Carr and Lorena S. Walsh, "Inventories and the Analysis of Wealth and Consumption Patterns in St. Mary's County, Maryland, 1658-1777," *Historical Methods* 13, no. 2 (Spring 1980), 81. Carr and Walsh summarize the two great advantages of inventories: "their great detail" and "the broad range of people inventoried." Much the same data and conclusions are to be found in idem, "Changing Life Styles in Colonial St. Mary's County," *Working Papers from the Regional Economic History Research Center* 1, no. 3 (1978), photocopied.

19.. Lindert, 649. My emphasis.

20.. Ibid., 660.

21.. D. S. Smith, 105-6; Shammas, "Determinants of Personal Wealth," 688.

22.. Main, "Probate Records as a Source," 96, 98.

23.. Jones, "Wealth Estimates for the New England Colonies," 116.

24.. Jones, *Wealth of a Nation to Be*, xxii.

25.. "Biases in the data . . . prevent inventories from accurately reflecting the wealth patterns of the living population. Every wealthholder who died was not inventoried, and if one wealth group is less well represented than another in proportion to its size, wealth patterns will be distorted. In addition, inventories would be biased towards the rich even if every dead man's estate were appraised. This is because wealth tends to increase with age, and more old men than young men die in proportion to the numbers." Carr and Walsh, "Wealth and Consumption Patterns," 83.

26.. "Not only are a cross-section of the dying found too heavily in the older age brackets, as compared with an age distribution of the living, but older persons accumulate more wealth," Jones, "Wealth Estimates for the New England Colonies," 113; "strong possibility that the wealth of unprobated persons differed from that of persons whose probate inventories survive. . . . Even among persons of the same occupation, age, and so forth, those who avoided probate probably had lower wealth," Lindert, 662, 664; "probate records are biased towards older adults, and age is an important determinant of both total wealth and patterns of investment," Menard, Harris, Carr, 170; "Inventoried decedents are not necessarily representative of the living population. They are older of course, and most scholars assume richer, of higher status, and possibly better educated than the population as a whole," Shammas "Determinants of Personal Wealth" 676-7.

27.. Main, *Tobacco Colony*, 49; idem, "Correction of Biases," 10; idem, "Probate Records as a Source," 96. Menard, Harris, and Carr, 177, caution that the advanced elderly would not fit this profile of "older therefore wealthier," since wealth decreases after late middle age.
28.. Main, "Correction of Biases," 10, 16.
29.. Jones, *Wealth of a Nation to Be*, 141-2, 153.
30.. Lindert, 657-8.
31.. Carr and Walsh, "Wealth and Consumption Patterns," 82.
32.. Anna L. Hawley, "Items Missing from Inventories in Surry County, Virginia, 1690-1715," Paper presented at the Dublin Seminar.
33.. Main, *Tobacco Colony*, 171-4.
34.. Jones, *Wealth of a Nation to Be*, xxviii.
35.. Menard, Harris, and Carr, 176, n. 14.
36.. Ross W. Beales, Jr. "Literacy and Reading in Eighteenth-Century Westborough, Massachusetts," Paper presented at the Dublin Seminar, 2; Gail Fowler Mohanty, "Adding Flesh to the Dry Bones of Industrial Research: Rhode Island Handloom Weavers Revealed in Probate Records, 1810-1821," Paper presented at the Dublin Seminar, 3. See also Barbara Nachtigall, "Inventory Analysis for the Refurnishing Plan of the Moses Pierce/Nathaniel Hichborn House," Paper presented at the Dublin Seminar, 18.
37.. Menard, Harris, and Carr, 170; K. S. Smith, 6. Main also points out that a "perplexing confusion of money values" may obtain in "Probate Records as a Source," 95.
38.. Jones, *Wealth of a Nation to Be*, xxii; K.S. Smith, 6; and Shammas, "Determinants of Personal Wealth," 676.
39.. Main, "Correction of Biases," 10.
40.. Menard, Harris, and Carr, 170; K.S. Smith, 6.
41.. Main, *Tobacco Colony*, 175; idem, "Correction of Biases," 10.
42.. Jones, *Wealth of a Nation to Be*, xxii.
43.. Ibid., xxiii.
44.. Lindert, 655.
45.. Jones, *Wealth of a Nation to Be*, xxv-vii.
46.. Lindert, 668.
47.. D. S. Smith, 106.
48.. Main, *Tobacco Colony*, 266.
49.. Jones, *Wealth of a Nation to Be*, 33-7, conscientiously details the included (all free adult males; a small proportion of free adult females; all free black men; a small proportion of free black women in New England and the Middle Colonies, but none in the South) and the excluded (children and youths twenty and under, married women, non-free adults—slaves and indentured servants, free black women in the South, Indians) among her category of wealth holder, "only those who could, legally or by social convention hold wealth," even though most produced wealth and all used wealth. Main, *Tobacco Colony*, 285, speaks of the "complete collection of all records" but then limits this universe to "all adult males so encountered."
50.. K. S. Smith, 11.
51.. Main, "Correction of Biases," 10, 16. She warns that "statements regarding trends in the level, distribution and composition of wealth, whether based on tax lists or probate records, must . . . be couched in highly tentative language subject to demographic and cultural context."
52.. Ibid., 11. Carole Shammas, "Mammy and Miss Ellen in Colonial Virginia?," Paper presented at the Conference of Women in Early America, The Colonial Williamsburg Foundation and the Institute of Early American History and Culture, Williamsburg, Virginia, November 5-7, 1981, photocopied, 6, also asserts that "evidence from tax lists supports the findings from probate records." D. S. Smith, 110, supposes that tax lists "probably provide a better basis than probate inventories for determining the extent of wealth inequality."
53.. Jones, "Wealth Estimates for the American Middle Colonies," 118; idem, *Wealth of a Nation to Be*, xxvii.
54.. Lindert, 657; Jones, *Wealth of a Nation to Be*, xxviii.
55.. Main, "Correction of Biases," 11, 13, 15-6, 19, 22, proffers guidance in identifying and adjusting for the "peculiar characteristics of colonial probate records." See also D.S. Smith, 107-8.
56.. Lindert, 667-8. "In the case of studies of American wealth across the nineteenth century, the natural testing ground is the set of census returns of real and personal estate in 1850, 1860, and 1870. The easier kind of test is the aggregate one: does probate sampling plus reweighting for group bias and differences in death rates yield an aggregate wealth distribution for the living that resembles the census results? Alternately, at much more expense, one can test the conformity of the census and probate results for individuals, *e.g.* for individuals caught in the 1870 census and again in probates during the 1870s."
57.. D. S. Smith, 102.
58.. Suzanne Lebsock, *The Free Women of Petersburg: Status and Culture in a Southern Town, 1784-1860* (New York: W.W. Norton & Company, 1984), 187-9, 166-9. In the introduction, Lebsock gives notice that "this study is based on a reading of almost every extant document written in or about Petersburg, Virginia, from 1784, when the town record books were begun, to 1860" in order to recover the female past. She holds no brook with scholars who exclude women from community studies on the grounds of source limitations. "Women surface in every kind of source," 'traditional'" ("letters, diaries, institutional records, and newspapers") as well as progressive ("wills, deeds,

court minutes, census schedules, city directories and tax lists"). Accumulating evidence about ordinary women requires particularly patient methods.

59.. John S. Otto, "Race and Class on Antebellum Plantations" in *Archaeological Perspectives*, 11, similarly argues for the integration of evidence from several sources—archaeological and documentary—for determining status in complex societies. For a tour-de-force example of dogged scholarship, see Billy G. Smith, "The Material Lives of Laboring Philadelphians, 1750-1800," in *Material Life in America*, 233-60, who ferrets out impressively detailed information about household budgets through masterful exploration of a multitude of sources.

60.. Shammas, "Determinants of Personal Wealth," 677, suggests avoiding problematic correction of biases through a declared selective focus that seeks to determine the relationship among various socioeconomic characteristics evident in probate records, rather than to account for the distribution of each in society.

61.. K. S. Smith, 11.

62.. Shammas, "Determinants of Personal Wealth," 677-82, 687-8.

63.. Menard, Harris, and Carr, "Opportunity and Inequality," 170, 173-4, 179-80, 184. Since Maryland probate records do not systematically include real property, the listing and valuing of all movable property found in estate inventories is supplemented by information in wills, deeds, patents and quit-rent rolls, as well as administrative accounts. The authors note that measuring change over time using standard divisions like decades or thirty-year generations interferes with the emergence of real turning points and relevant patterns from the data. They further elucidate the significance of the relationship between the mean and the median of total estate value: "The greater the distance between the mean [the *average* value of all the estates at a given time] and the median [the *typical* value of all the estates at that same time], the greater the inequality." If the mean and the median neither increase nor decrease substantially over time, they point out, the distribution of wealth remains stable—in this study, stable and unequal. The association of stability with inequality arouses mixed emotions—the "good" of stability is undermined by the "bad" of inequality. Yet instability could be associated with decreasing inequality just as easily as with increasing inequality.

64.. Jones, *Wealth of a Nation to Be*, 87; Main, *Tobacco Colony*, 52, 267.

65.. Jones, *Wealth of a Nation to Be*, 87-94; Main, *Tobacco Colony*, 50-1. Note that Main lists "bound labor, including servants and slaves" in Capital, whereas Jones separates human capital from nonhuman capital before further breakdowns of the latter into portability and purpose. Given that land and its improvements are not readily available in Maryland probate records, Jones's item g. Portable nonhuman physical wealth broken down by purpose is closest to Main's Consumption Goods and Capital, minus "bound labor, including servants and slaves." Both Jones, and Main own up to the difficulties of decision-making when assigning items of "portable physical nonhuman wealth" to various categories. Main balances her acknowledgement of arbitrary decision-making with claims of consistency of application. Jones cites careful consideration of meaning and use in the assignment of items to appropriate classes and subcategories.

66.. Jones, *Wealth of a Nation to Be*, Chapter 3. Aggregate and Per Capita Private Physical Wealth for Thirteen Colonies and Three Regions and Chapter 6. Distribution of Wealth: The Rich and the Poor, p. 240-1.

67.. Main, *Tobacco Colony*, 54, Table II.1 Mean Personal Wealth of Ranked Strata of Maryland Probated Estates; 60, Table II.5 Distribution of Maryland Planter Estates by Physical Personal Wealth; 93, Table II.18 Estimating Wealth Per Capita in Maryland circa 1700; 268, Table A.1 Determining the Wealth of Age Groups: Stages of Life Cycle and Allocating Unknowns, Six Counties, Maryland; 287, Table C.1 Numbers of Inventoried Estates in Six Counties, Maryland, by Wealth and Income; 292, Table C.11 Average £ GPW of Estates in Each Stage of the Life Cycle; 7-8.

68.. Carr and Walsh, "Wealth and Consumption Patterns," 83-4; 96.

69.. K. S. Smith, 13-23.

70.. Walsh, 109-13, 117.

71.. Shammas, "Domestic Environment," 5, 7-14, 17-8.

72.. Jones, "Wealth Estimates for the New England Colonies," 120-2, 124, 126. The wealth cited to support the contention of inequality is expressed in 1969 dollars.

73.. Gloria L. Main, "Inequality in Early America: The Evidence from Probate Records of Massachusetts and Maryland," *Journal of Interdisciplinary History* 7 (1977), 572-3.

74.. Jones, *Wealth of a Nation to Be*, 169, 177, 192.

75.. Ibid., 225-7, tables 7.6, 7.7, 7.8.

76.. Ibid., 214-8.

77.. Ibid., 269, 273, 317.

78.. Main, *Tobacco Colony*, 52-3, 79, 92, 104, 263. By 1730 the growth or wealth held by the planter elite increased inequality even further, but less than it might have without the exiting of the very poorest people and the settling on still abundant cheap land by the slightly less poor. The source of this accumulation of financial advantage by the very rich in Maryland, according to Main, rested upon investment in slaves, "a long-lived capital resource" that was geometrically parlayed into further aggrandizement of wealth. Despite undeniable differences, a study of probate records from virtually the same locale over virtually the same time span reveals a fluctuating wealth pattern that nonetheless can comfortably coexist with Main's analysis. Menard, Harris, and Carr, "Opportunity and Inequality," 179-84, compare the number of estates by four wealth categories at three points in time, roughly 1640, 1660, and 1685. They, too, document Maryland's initial hierarchic, unequal social structure, which gave way twenty years later in 1660 to the predominance of middling folk and greater equity, but then by 1685 shifted to a higher proportion of the wealthy and therefore greater inequity in the distribution of wealth in the colony.

79.. Main, "Inequality in Early America," 559, 580-1.

80.. Jones, *Wealth of a Nation to Be*, 86, 45-8, 204, 326-32, 340. B. G. Smith, 255, n. 5, disputes Jones's upbeat view of economic conditions on the eve of the Revolution.

81.. Main, *Tobacco Colony*, 7-8, 79, 135-6, 151, n. 41, 153, 166, 206, 240, 249-54. The direct association of wealth level with interior architectural space in family dwellings is supported by Ronald D. Clifton, "Forms and Patterns: Room Specialization in Maryland, Massachusetts, and Pennsylvania, Family Dwellings 1725-1834" (Ph.D. diss., University of Pennsylvania, 1971). Peter Benes, "Sleeping Arrangements in the Household of Henry Lunt, Hatter, of Seventeenth-Century Newburg, Massachusetts," Paper presented at the Dublin Seminar, documents the preference for better—rather than more—bedding as a reflection of cultural norms that accepted the multiple sharing of sleeping units and economic circumstances that recognized the lifetime's labor of accumulating feathers for this most-prized-of-all-bedding. Moreover, the presence of feather bedding among the holdings of only six of twenty decedents involved in the shipbuilding trades in Boston from 1780-1810 underlines the relative scarcity of comfortable bedding. Nachtigall, Appendix I.

82.. Jones, "Wealth Estimates for the New England Colonies about 1770," 107-10. "The 1774 content reflects an economy which ranged from substantial segments of subsistence production to commercial agriculture and fishing, artisans' production, services of taverns and inns, teachers, doctors, lawyers, and some rather sophisticated commercial operations by merchants who engaged in a variety of local buying, selling and financing services and overseas shipping. The 1966 content reflects the highly intertwined industrial, agricultural and commercial economy which undergirds our 'affluent society.'"

83.. Main, *Tobacco Colony*, 239, 190, 259, 206, 240-2. Note particularly Table VII.1 Maryland Priorities Among Consumption Goods, "Young Fathers," 249-54. Nachtigall, 5-20 passim, in analyzing twenty inventories of decedents involved in the maritime trades in Boston from 1780 to 1810, finds enough similarities to identify appropriate furnishings for the Hichborn House's best chamber and parlor. For instance, she learns that every household in her sample had at least one mirror while thirteen of the twenty had at least one mirror in both the parlor and the best chamber. She concludes that the refurnishing plan for the Hichborn House should call for mirrors in both rooms. Among this particular segment of the population, the ownership and placement of mirrors appear to be uniform.

84.. Walsh, 109-13, 117. Shammas in "Domestic Environment," 8, 14, 18, compares sixteenth and seventeenth century England with eighteenth century America to uncover that bedding was consistently "the most heavily invested in consumer item" among all three wealth groups (poor, average, and above average and affluent) at all three times. Nonetheless, the eighteenth century shows a distinct move toward greater sociability as evidenced in the marked diffusion of eating and drinking goods in ordinary households. "Over the three century period, the same wealth groups progressively invested a higher proportion of their wealth in consumer goods."

85.. Carr and Walsh, "Changing Life Styles," 82, attribute the phrase "state of artifactual pre-literacy" to "some scholars." Cary Carson, "Doing History with Material Culture," in *Material Culture and the Study of American Life*, ed. Ian M.G. Quimby (New York: W.W. Norton & Co, Inc., for the Henry Francis du Pont Winterthur Museum, 1978), 62, emphatically enquotes the term "consumer revolution" without any reference to its originating source.

86.. Carr and Walsh, "Wealth and Consumption Patterns," 83.

87.. Carr and Walsh, "Changing Life Styles," 87, 89, 110; idem, "Wealth and Consumption Patterns," 96.

88.. Cary Carson and Lorena S. Walsh, "The Material Life of the Early American Housewife," Paper presented at the Conference on Women in Early America, 52.

89.. Carson, "Doing History," 62. He argues intelligently for the efficacy of material culture—artifacts—for elucidating family matters and the affairs of communities.

90.. Carr and Walsh, "Changing Life Styles," 81.

91.. Carson and Walsh, 31, 36, 39; Carr and Walsh, "Changing Life Styles," 82, 87.

92.. Carr and Walsh, "Wealth and Consumption Patterns," 96. Jones concurs, "Wealth Estimates for the New England Colonies about 1770," 106, that "per capita figures of wealth represent the accumulated savings from past production." In other words, over time, portable wealth, buildings, and developed land come into existence and serve as the baseline for the next generation's acquisition of more possessions—the transgenerational accumulation of wealth. B. G. Smith, 254, however, takes issue with such conclusions about across-the-board economic improvement after 1750: "The late colonial period was not one during which Philadelphia's laboring people enjoyed steadily increasing prosperity. Indeed, they lived so near subsistence before the Revolutionary War that there appears to have been no lower level from which they could have risen. The increasing wealth usually thought to have characterized the colonies in general and Philadelphia in particular during this period did not trickle down to the lower sort."

93.. Carr and Walsh, "Wealth and Consumption Patterns," 83; idem, "Changing Life Styles," 74-5.

94.. Carr and Walsh, "Wealth and Consumption Patterns," 102, n. 10, 83; idem, "Changing Life Styles," 112, n. 4, 74.

95.. Jones, *Wealth of a Nation to Be*, xxiii-xxv, 402-3, n. 7-9, 37, 323.

96.. Main, "Correction of Biases," 11.

97.. Most tellingly the entry besides "blacks" in the index instructs the reader to "*see* slaves" (author's emphasis). Main, *Tobacco Colony*, 205, 128-36.

98.. Menard, Harris, and Carr, 170.

99.. Shammas, "Determinants of Personal Wealth," 677-9.

100.. Shammas, "Domestic Environment" 5, 20-21, n. 10.

101.. Shammas, "Mammy and Miss Ellen," 4, 5.

102.. Ibid., 10-1.

103.. D. S. Smith, 101-6.
104.. Walsh, "Urban Amenities and Rural Sufficiency," 111.
105.. Main, *Tobacco Colony*, 128-36. Bedding was the most prized asset and the first to be improved. See Shammas, "Domestic Environment," 8, and Main, *Tobacco Colony*, 251-2.
106.. Shammas, "Mammy and Miss Ellen," 13, 9, 14, 15. There was an inverse relation between the number of female slaves and poultry, thereby substantiating the popular notion of "free enterprising" black women as the 'chicken merchants.'
107.. Jones, *Wealth of a Nation to Be*, 36, 323. One must be wary of assuming adoption of "mainstream" values when interpreting data like a free black's owning slaves. Lebsock, 96, documents the purchase of relatives and friends by free black emancipators. However, Morgan, 209, describes a slave who purchased another slave and then exchanged him for his own freedom.
108.. Baker, 34-5. Probate records spanning 1783(?) to 1812 were useful documentary sources.
109.. K. S. Smith, 8, 23.
110.. Carr and Walsh, "Changing Life Styles," 81.
111.. Carr and Walsh, "Wealth and Consumption Patterns," 96.
112.. Carr and Walsh, "Changing Life Styles," 81.
113.. Main, *Tobacco Colony*, 135.
114.. Shammas, "Mammy and Miss Ellen," 27-29; Philip D. Morgan, "Work and Culture: The Task System and the World of Lowcountry Blacks, 1700-1880," in *Material Life in America, 1600-1860*, ed. Robert Blair St. George (Boston: Northeastern Press, 1988), 220.
115.. K. S. Smith, 23.

Chapter 4

1.. Lois Green Carr and Lorena S. Walsh, "Inventories and the Analysis of Wealth and Consumption Patterns in St. Mary's County Maryland, 1658-1777," *Historical Methods*, 13, no. 2 (Spring 1980), 84. The terms "necessities," "amenities," and "luxuries" were adopted from Carr and Walsh but modified in definition for the present study.
2.. Ross W. Beales, Jr., "Literacy and Reading in Eighteenth-Century Westborough, Massachusetts," Paper presented at the Dublin Seminar for New Endland Folklife on Early American Inventories, Deerfield, Massachusetts, July 11-12, 1987, photocopied, 6-7, distinguishes between the "quantitative picture of literacy" and the "qualitative aspects of literacy." He stresses that "the ability to sign one's name may not have extended to the ability to write anything more. The ability to read a book may not have carried with it the ability to read handwriting. And the appearance of a mark, in place of a signature, may reflect only feebleness or forgetfulness and certainly tells us nothing about an individual's ability to read." See also Gloria L. Main, *Tobacco Colony: Life in Early Maryland, 1650-1720* (Princeton, NJ: Princeton University Press, 1982), 243-4; Carole Shammas, "Determinants of Personal Wealth in Seventeenth-Century England and America," *Journal of Economic History* 37 (September 1977), 681.
3.. Henry Benson (29572); James H. Howe (34458).
4.. Alice Hanson Jones, *Wealth of a Nation to Be: The American Colonies on the Eve of the Revolution* (New York: Columbia University Press, 1980), 142, states that "'debtor' and 'poor' were not synonymous .... Rather, as today, the holding of significant assets in physical forms and cash made one credit-worthy .... The richer owed more debts than the poorer and also had more financial assets."
5.. Isaac, 44, proposes the "depiction of life experience (and by extension, ongoing social life) as dramatic-encounter knots suspended in webs of continuing relationships."
6.. Emily Higgins (30775); John E. Scarlett (33895); Thomas Cole (35173).
7.. John W. Brown (32659); Chloe Russell (33170); John Lewis Brent, alias John Lewis (34132); Calvin T. Hoyt, alias Charles Williams (35871).
8.. David Walker (29332); James Gould (29625); Cesar Fletcher (29595); William S. Jinnings (32642).
9.. Bernard L. Herman, "Delaware's Orphan Court Valuations and the Reconstitution of Historic Landscapes," Paper presented at the Dublin Seminar, 1, describes the team of appraisers of the Jesse Saunders estate as "a three-man neighborhood delegation led by William Vaughan, the local justice of the peace."
10.. *The Boston Directory* (Boston: Charles Stimpson, Jr., 1830); *Stimpson's Boston Directory* (Boston: Charles Stimpson, Jr., 1835, 1840, 1845).
11.. Alice Hanson Jones, "Wealth Estimates for the New England Colonies about 1770," *Journal of Economic History* 32, no. 1 (March 1972), 110, n. 13; idem, *Wealth of a Nation to Be*, 91, 93; Main, *Tobacco Colony*, 50, 169. Schemes of categorization of assets abound in the scholarship on probate inventories; each scheme has its virtues and vices for ease and accuracy of assigning a specific asset to a particular category.
12.. Lois Green Carr and Lorena S. Walsh, "Changing Life Styles in Colonial St. Mary's County," *Working Papers from the Regional Economic History Research Center*, 1, no. 3 (1978), photocopied, 93, 110; idem, "Wealth and Consumption Patterns," 96; Cary Carson and Lorena S. Walsh, "The Material Life of an Early American Housewife," Paper presented at the Conference on Women in Early America, The Colonial Williamsburg Foundation and the Institute of Early American History and Culture, Williamsburg, Virginia, November 5-7, 1981, photocopied, 50.
13.. The topic of "absence" in probate inventories is explored in chap. 3, under "Inventories as Primary Sources: Disadvantages," in this study.

14.. Peter Benes, "Sleeping Arrangements in the Household of Henry Lunt, Hatter, of Seventeenth-Century Newbury, Massachusetts," Paper presented at the Dublin Seminar, [5], calculates "that it took a lifetime to accumulate enough feathers for a feather bed. Shammas, "Domestic Environment," 10, and Main, *Tobacco Colony*, 215, 251, also remark upon the value placed on the quality of bedding. That this propensity to prize a comfortable night's sleep–and to elevate the bed as a status symbol–did not fade out in the eighteenth-century is documented in Lizabeth A. Cohen, "Embellishing a Life of Labor: An Interpretation of the Material Culture of American Working-Class Homes, 1885-1915," in *Material Culture Studies in America*, ed. Thomas J. Schlereth (Nashville, TN: American Association for State and Local History, 1982), 302-3.

15.. Jones, *Wealth of a Nation to Be*, 142.

Chapter 5

1.. James Oliver Horton, *Eye of the Storm: Blacks in the Colonial North* (N.p., n.d., photocopied), chap. 4, pp. 14-6, touches upon the life experience of black seamen.

2.. Alice Hanson Jones, *Wealth of a Nation to Be: The American Colonies on the Eve of the Revolution* (New York: Columbia University Press, 1980), 116.

3.. This study summarizes discussions of missing items in chap. 3 under "Inventories as Primary Sources: Disadvantages."

4.. Lois Green Carr and Lorena S. Walsh, "Inventories and the Analysis of Wealth and Consumption Patterns in St. Mary's County, Maryland, 1658-1777," *Historical Methods* 13, no. 2 (Spring 1980), 82, mention specifically that "in some areas, . . . legacies mentioned in wills were not inventoried." This contrasts with the careful inventorying of, and accounting for, Thomas Cole's bequests (transcriptions 6.1, 6.5, and 6.8).

5.. Henry Benson (29572).

6.. James Gould (29625).

7.. Rhys Isaac, "Ethnographic Method in History: An Action Approach," in *Material Life in America, 1600-1860*, ed. Robert Blair St. George (Boston: Northeastern Press, 1988), 40, states that "everywhere in the documents available to the social historian there can be discovered

traces–occasionally vivid glimpses–of *people doing things* (his emphasis). The searching out of the meanings such actions contained and conveyed for the participants lies at the heart of the enterprise of enthnograpic history." Henry Glassie, "Meaningful Things and Appropriate Myths: The Artifact's Place in American Studies," in *Material Life in America*, 65, advocates a fresh appreciation for biography as "history's real substance. The truism that history is about people, that history is a patchy composition of innumeralbe unique lives, carries important implications."

Chapter 6

1.. Various scholarly explanations for missing items are detailed under "Inventories as Primary Sources: Disadvantages," in chap. 3 of this study.

2.. Henry Benson (29592).

3.. James Oliver Horton and Lois E. Horton, *Black Bostonians: Family Life and Community Struggle in the Antebellum North* (New York: Holmes & Meier Publishers, Inc., 1979), 13. See also James Oliver Horton, "Shades of Color: The Mulatto in Three Antebellum Northern Communities," *Afro-Americans in N.Y. Life & History* 8, no. 2 (July 1984), 52.

4.. George E. Carter and C. Peter Ripley, eds., *Black Abolitionist Papers, 1830-1865: A Guide to the Microfilm Edition* (New York: Microfilming Corporation of America, a New York Times Company, 1981).

5.. Ibid., 50.12.20; 05:0121. This is misdated in the *Black Abolitionist Papers*–it should be 45.12.20; 05:0121.

6.. Ibid., 37.09.00; 02:0309.

7.. Ibid., 40.12.26*; 03:0759.

8.. Ibid., 31.02.12*; 01:0030 & 31.02.26; 01:0036 & 31.03.12*; 01:0039.

9.. Ibid., 31.1105*; 01:0131 & 31.11.12*; 01:0133.

10.. Ibid., 33.03.23*; 01:0261.

11.. Ibid., 33.04.04; 01:0272.

12.. Ibid., 37.12.29*; 02.0346.

13.. Ibid., 38.08.10*; 02:0551.

14.. Ibid., 39.02.21; 03:0022.

15.. Ibid., 39.07.26*; 03.0150.

16.. Ibid., 39.08.30*; 03:0185.

17.. Ibid., 40.01.06; 03:0337.

18.. Ibid., 40.06.16; 03:0534.

19.. Ibid., 40.08.18; 03:0614.

20.. Ibid., 40.12.18; 03:1023.

21.. Ibid., 42.07.08; 04:0451.

22.. Ibid., 43.07.14*; 04:0609.

23.. Ibid., 44.00.00; 04:0723.
24.. Philip S. Foner, *The History of Black Americans*, vol. 1, *From Africa to the Emergence of the Cotton Kingdom*, Contributions to American History, ed. Jon L. Wakelyn, no. 4 (Westport, CT: Greenwood Press, 1975), 478. See also Horton and Horton, 70.
25.. *Black Abolitionist Papers*, 39.12.11; 03:0343.
26.. Horton and Horton, 120.
27.. Ibid., 37.
28.. Ibid., 101, 71, 76; John Daniels, *In Freedom's Birthplace*, The American Negro: His History and Literature (New York: Arno Press and The New York Times, 1969), 448.
29.. Horton and Horton, 40-1, 60, 71, 101; Daniels, 449; Benjamin Quarles, *Black Abolitionists* (New York: Oxford University Press, 1969), 142, 172; Jane H. Pease and William H. Pease, *They Who Would Be Free: Blacks' Search for Freedom, 1830-1861*. Studies in American Negro Life, ed., August Meier (New York: Athenaeum, 1974), 154, 290; and Foner, vol. 2, *From the Emergence of the Cotton Kingdom to the Eve of the Compromise of 1850*, Contributions to American History, ed. Jon L. Wakelyn, no. 102 (Westport, CT: Greenwood Press, 1983), 390, 399, 477.
30.. Ibid., 505.
31.. *Black Abolitionist Papers*, 42.10.27; 04:0485.
32.. Ibid., 44.08.09*; 04:0894.
33.. Ibid., 46.12.01; 05.0321.
34.. Ibid., 38.12.07; 02:0667.
35.. Ibid., 48.08.03; 05:0724.
36.. Ibid., 48.08.10; 05:0740.
37.. Sam Bass Warner, Jr., *Streetcar Suburbs: The Process of Growth in Boston, 1870-1900* (Cambridge: Harvard University Press, 1962), 15-21.
38.. Horton and Horton, 4-6, concur.
39.. When he interprets the actions of twenty-one people of different race, rank, and gender in relationship to the runaway slave Simon, Rhys Isaac in "Ethnographic Method in History: An Action Approach," in *Material Life in America, 1600-1860*, ed. Robert Blair St. George (Boston: Northeastern Press, 1988) 46, detects a loyalty to members of one's home turf that transcended customary socioeconomic divisions.
40.. Julie Winch, *Philadelphia's Black Elite: Activism, Accomodation, and the Struggle for Autonomy, 1787-1848* (Philadelphia: Temple University Press, 1988), 2, states that "throughout the antebellum era, leadership was rooted in a complex network of autonomous black organizations, which offered able and articulate men and women within the community a basis for asserting their authority and developing the skills they would require to oversee citywide and, in some cases, national organizations." She asserts that "men and women who hardly qualified as members of the upper class were also accorded the status of leaders. Though lacking in wealth and social position, they were eloquent, skilled organizers and devoted to social reform; ability rather then class status propelled them into the ranks of the leadership."
41.. *Black Abolitionist Papers*, 33.03.23*; 01:0261.
42.. Ibid., 43.07.14*; 04:0609.
43.. James Gould (29625).
44.. Emily Higgins (30775)
45.. Ross W. Beales, Jr., in "Literacy and Reading in Eighteenth-Century Westborough, Massachusetts," Paper presented at the Dublin Seminar for New England Folklife on Early American Inventories, Deerfield, Massachusetts, July 11-12, 1987, photocopied, 7, follows Lawrence Cremin's distinction between passive and active—or liberating—literacy. "Passive literacy is essentially the ability to receive, through printed media, the basic values of a culture . . . . Liberating literacy, by contrast, involved choice, curiosity, and an implicit assumption that the bounds of learning are not entirely prescribed."
46.. Horton and Horton, 7, 138, n. 14.
47.. Horton, "Shades of Color," 48, 50, 56.
48.. Frank F. Furstenberg, Jr., Theodore Hershberg, and John Modell, "The Origins of the Female-Headed Black Family: The Impact of the Urban Experience," in *Philadelphia: Work, Space, Family and Group Experience in the Nineteenth Century, Essays Toward an Interdisciplinary History of the City*, ed. Theodore Hershberg (New York: Oxford University Press, 1981), 451.
49.. Carol B. Stack, *All Our Kin: Strategies for Survival in a Black Community* (New York: Harper and Row Publishers, 1974) 122, 127. See also Bell Hooks, *Ain't I a Woman: Black Women and Feminism* (Boston: South End Press, 1981), 76-83, who examines "the matriarchy myth as popular social theory."
50.. *Black Abolitionist Papers*, 44.00.00; 04:0723.
51.. Paul J. Lammermeier, "The Urban Black Family of the Nineteenth Century: A Study of Black Family Structure in the Ohio Valley, 1850-1880," *Journal of Marriage and the Family* 35 (August 1973) 445-6, Robert J. Cottrol, *The Afro-Yankees: Providence's Black Community in the Antebellum Era*, Foreword by Stanley L. Engerman, Contributions in Afro-American and African Studies no. 68 (Westport, CT: Greenwood Press, 1982) 133, 135-6; Horton and Horton, 20; and Lebsock, 166-9, 187-9.

52.. Barbara McLean Ward, "Women's Property and Family Continuity in Eighteenth-Century Connecticut," Paper presented at the Dublin Seminar, and Marylynn Salmon, "Women and Property in South Carolina: The Evidence from Marriage Settlements," in *Material Life in America*, both emphasize the acumen with which women operated within an inequitable legal system.

53.. Cary Carson, "Chesapeake Themes in the History of Early American Material Life," Paper presented at Maryland: A Product of Two Worlds, the Third Hall of Records Conference on Maryland History, St. Mary's City, Maryland, May 17-20, 1984, photocopied, 15-6. See also Cary Carson and Lorena S. Walsh, "The Material Life of the Early American Housewife," Paper presented at the Conference on Women in Early America, the Colonial Williamsburg Foundation and the Institute for Early American History and Culture, Williamsburg, Virginia, November 5-7, 1981, photocopied, 31, 50, 53-4. "The good life rested on a complex material culture."

54.. The Balch Institute for Ethnic Studies, *Philadelphia African Americans: Color, Class and Style, 1840-1940*, Catalog of the exhibition in the Museum of the Balch Institute for Ethnic Studies, April 4 - July 9, 1988, Preface by M. Mark Stolarik (Philadelphia: The Balch Institute for Ethnic Studies, 1988), 1. See also Winch, 2-3.

55.. Michal B. Katz, Michael J. Doucet, and Mark J. Stern, *The Social Organization of Early Industrial Capitalism* (Cambridge: Harvard University Press, 1982) 135, 158, 160-91; Cottrol, 123; Olivier Zunz, *The Changing Face of Inequality: Urbanization, Industrial Development, and Immigrants in Detroit, 1880-1920*, (Chicago: University of Chicago Press, 1982) 153; and Theodore Hershberg, "Free Blacks in Antebellum Philadelphia: A Study of Ex-Slaves, Freeborn, and Socioeconomic Decline," in *Philadelphia*, 381.

56.. Jacqueline Jones, "Comment on 'The African in the Garden: Reflections about New World Slavery and Its Lifelines' by Leslie H. Owens," in *The State of Afro-American History: Past, Present, and Future*, ed. Darlene Clarke Hine, Introduction by Thomas C. Holt (Baton Rouge, LA: Louisiana State University Press, 1986), 47, rejects romanticizing blacks' plight. "Perhaps in their superior understanding of—or confrontation with—orginal sin American-style, Afro-Americans gained 'insights' of a particular kind. But, over the years, as the whites around them came to enjoy more fully the blessings of material prosperity and democratic citizenship, these insights brought cold comfort indeed. Whatever the spiritual benefits of 'soul' blacks may have gained came at the expense of justice; simply put, their 'liberation' from a slavish devotion to capitalism and its attendant myths exacted a price that was just too high for any people ever to have to pay."

57.. Peter Benes, "Sleeping Arrangements in the Household of Henry Lunt, Hatter, of Seventeenth-Century Newbury, Massachusetts," Paper presented at the Dublin Seminar, [5]; Gloria L. Main, *Tobacco Colony: Life in Early Maryland, 1650-1720* (Princeton, N.J.: Princeotn University Press, 1982) 251. That the black community put stock in the power of "potential heirlooms" can be seen in the presentaiton of a silver cup to Garrison in 1833, as documented in the *Black Abolitionist Papers* (33.04.04; 01:0272) and a gold watch to William C. Nell, as described in Horton and Horton, 76.

58.. *Webster's Third International, Unabridged*, s.v. "probate."

SELECTED BIBLIOGRAPHY

Primary Sources

The Boston Directory. Boston: Charles Stimpson, Jr., 1830.
Probate Records. Suffolk County Courthouse, Boston, Massachusetts, 1806-1895.
Stimpson's Boston Directory. Boston: Charles Stimpson, Jr., 1835, 1840, and 1844-9.
United States Census, 1830-1850.

Secondary Sources

Ames, Kenneth L. "Meaning in Artifacts: Hall Furnishings in Victorian America." In *Material Culture Studies in America*, ed. Thomas J. Schlereth, 206-221. Nashville, TN: American Association for State and Local History, 1982.
Baker, Vernon G. "Archaeological Visibility of Afro-American Culture: An Example from Lucy's Garden, Andover, Massachusetts." In *Archaeological Perspective on Ethnicity in America: Afro-American and Asian American Culture History*, ed. Robert L. Schuyler, 29-37. Farmingdale, NY: Baywood Publishing Co., Inc., 1980.
The Balch Institute for Ethnic Studies. *Philadelphia African Americans: Color, Class and Style, 1840-1940.* Catalog of the exhibition in the Museum of The Balch Institute for Ethnic Studies, April 4-July 9, 1988. Preface by M. Mark Stolarik. Philadelphia: The Balch Institute for Ethnic Studies, 1988.
Battle, Thomas C. "Research Centers Document the Black Experience." *History News* 36, no. 2 (February 1981): 8-11.
Beales, Ross W., Jr. "Literacy and Reading in Eighteenth-Century Westborough, Massachusetts." Paper presented at the Dublin Seminar for New England Folklife on Early American Inventories. Deerfield, Massachusetts, July 11-12, 1987. Photocopied.
Beckow, Steven M. "Culture, History, and Artifact." In *Material Culture Studies in America*, ed. Thomas J. Schlereth, 114-23. Nashville, TN: American Association for State and Local History, 1982.
Bell, Howard Holman, ed. *Minutes of the Proceedings of the National Negro Conventions, 1830-1864.* The American Negro: His History and Literature. New York: Arno Press and The New York Times, 1969.
Benes, Peter. "Sleeping Arrangements in the Household of Henry Lunt, Hatter, of Seventeenth-Century Newbury, Massachusetts." Paper presented at the Dublin Seminar for New England Folklife on Early American Inventories. Deerfield, Massachusetts, July 11-12, 1987. Photocopied.
Berlin, Ira. *Slaves without Masters: The Free Negro in the Antebellum South.* New York: Oxford University Press, 1985.
Blackmar, Betsy. "Rewalking the 'Walking City'": Housing and Property Relations in New York City, 1780-1840." In *Material Life in America, 1600-1860*, ed. Robert Blair St. George, 371-84. Boston: Northeastern University Press, 1987.
Borchert, James. *Alley Life in Washington: Family, Community, Religion, and Folklife in the City, 1850-1970.* Urbana, IL: University of Illinois Press, 1980.
Bower, Beth Anne, and Byron Rushing. "The African Meeting House: The Center for the 19th Century Afro-American Community in Boston." In *Archaeological Perspective on Ethnicity in America: Afro-American and Asian American Culture History*, ed. Robert L. Schuyler, 69-75. Farmingdale, NY: Baywood Publishing Co., Inc., 1980.
Bridges, Sarah T., and Bert Salwen. "Weeksville: The Archaeology of a Black Urban Community." In *Archaeological Perspective on Ethnicity in America: Afro-American and Asian American Culture History*, ed. Robert L. Schuyler, 38-47. Farmingdale, NY: Baywood Publishing Co., Inc., 1980.
Campbell, Randolph B. "Slave Hiring in Texas." *American Historical Review* 93, no. 1 (February 1988): 107-114.
Carr, Lois Green, and Lorena S. Walsh. "Changing Life Styles in Colonial St. Mary's County." *Working Papers from the Regional Economic History Research Center* 1, no.3 (1978): 73-118. Photocopied.
———. "Inventories and the Analysis of Wealth and Consumption Patterns in St. Mary's County, Maryland, 1658-1777." *Historical Methods* 13, no. 2 (Spring 1980): 81-104.
———. "Woman's Role in the Eighteenth Century Chesapeake." Paper presented at the Conference on Women in Early America, the Colonial Williamsburg Foundation and the Institute of Early American History and Culture. Williamsburg, Virginia, November 5-7, 1981. Photocopied.
Carson, Barbara G. "Living Habits in 17th Century Maryland." Paper presented at Maryland: A Product of Two Worlds, the Third Hall of Records Conference on Maryland History. St. Mary's City, Maryland, May 17-20, 1984. Photocopied.
Carson, Barbara G., and Cary Carson. "Things Unspoken: Learning Social History from Artifacts." In *Ordinary People and Everyday Life: Perspectives on the New Social History*, ed. James B. Gardner and George Rollie Adams, 181-203. Nashville, TN: American Association for State and Local History, 1983.

Carson, Cary. "Chesapeake Themes in the History of Early American Material Life." Paper presented at Maryland: A Product of Two Worlds, the Third Hall of Records Conference on Maryland History. St. Mary's City, Maryland, May 17-20, 1984. Photocopied.

———. "Doing History with Material Culture." In *Material Culture and the Study of American Life*, ed. Ian M. G. Quimby, 41-64. New York: W. W. Norton & Company, Inc., for the Henry Francis du Pont Winterthur Museum, 1978.

———. "An Embarrassment of Riches," *Early American Enterprises: Colonial Williamsburg Foundation Sales Catalogue* (Fall/Winter 1987).

Carson, Cary, and Lorena S. Walsh. "The Material Life of the Early American Housewife." Paper presented at the Conference on Women in Early America, the Colonial Williamsburg Foundation and the Institutue of Early American History and Culture. Williamsburg, Virginia, November 5-7, 1981. Photocopied.

Carter, George E., and C. Peter Ripley, eds. *Black Abolitionist Papers, 1830-1865: A Guide to the Microfilm Edition*. New York: Microfilming Corporation of America, a New York Times Company, 1981.

Chudacoff, Howard P. "Success and Security: Meaning of Social Mobility in America." *Reviews in American History* 10, no. 4 (December 1982): 101-12.

Clifton, Ronald D. "Forms and Patterns: Room Specialization in Maryland, Massachusetts, and Pennsylvania, Family Dwellings, 1725-1834." Ph.D. diss., University of Pennsylvania, 1971.

Cohen, Lizabeth A. "Embellishing a Life of Labor: An Interpretation of the Material Culture of American Working-Class Homes, 1885-1915." In *Material Culture Studies in America*, ed. Thomas J. Schlereth, 289-305. Nashville, TN: American Association for State and Local History, 1982.

Conzen, Kathleen Neils. *Immigrant Milwaukee, 1836-1860: Accommodation and Community in a Frontier City*. Cambridge: Harvard University Press, 1976.

———. "The New Urban History: Defining the Field." In *Ordinary People and Everyday Life: Perspectives on the New Social History*, ed. James B. Gardner and George Rollie Adams, 76-89. Nashville, TN: American Association for State and Local History, 1983.

Cottrol, Robert J. *The Afro-Yankees: Providence's Black Community in the Antebellum Era*. Foreword by Stanley L. Engerman. Contributions in Afro-American and African Studies no. 68. Westport, CT: Greenwood Press, 1982.

Cummings, Abbott Lowell, ed. *Rural Household Inventories: Establishing the Names, Uses, and Furnishings of Rooms in the Colonial New England Home, 1675-1775*. Boston: The Society for the Preservation of New England Antiquities, 1964.

Curry, Leonard P. *The Free Black in Urban America, 1800-1850: The Shadow of the Dream*. Chicago: University of Chicago Press, 1981.

Daniels, John. *In Freedom's Birthplace*. The American Negro: His History and Literature. New York: Arno Press and The New York Times, 1969.

Deetz, James. *In Small Things Forgotten: The Archeology of Early American Life*. Garden City, NY: Anchor Books, 1977.

Degler, Carl N. *At Odds: Women and the Family in America from the Revolution to the Present*. New York: Oxford University Press, 1980; paperback, 1981.

Demos, John. *A Little Commonwealth: Family Life in Plymouth Colony*. New York: Oxford University Press, 1970; paperback reprint, 1979.

Drobis, Susan Morganroth. "Occupation and Residential Differentiation: A Historical Application of Cluster Analysis." *Historical Methods Newsletter* 9, nos. 2 and 3 (March/June 1976): 114-34.

Dyos, H. J., and Michael Wolff, eds. *The Victorian City: Images and Realities*. 2 vols. London: Routledge and Kegen Paul, 1973.

Egan, Peggy. "Free Blacks in Antebellum Baltimore." N.p., 1987. Photocopied.

Fishel, Leslie H., Jr., and Benjamin Quarles. *The Black American: A Documentary History*. 3d ed. Glenview, IL: Scott, Foresman and Company, 1976.

Fleming, E. McClung. "Artifact Study: A Proposed Model." In *Material Culture Studies in America*, ed. Thomas J. Schlereth, 162-173. Nashville, TN: American Association for State and Local History, 1982.

Foner, Philip S. *The History of Black Americans*. Vol. 1, *From Africa to the Emergence of the Cotton Kingdom*. Vol. 2, *From the Emergence of the Cotton Kingdom to the Eve of the Compromise of 1850*. Vol. 3, *From the Compromise of 1850 to the End of the Civil War*. Contributions to American History, ed. Jon L. Wakelyn, nos. 40, 102, and 103. Westport, CT: Greenwood Press, 1975 and 1983.

Foster, Herbert J. "Occupational Class in the Black Community of Atlantic City and in Other Northern Cities, 1880-1915." N.p., n.d. Photocopied.

Franklin, John Hope. *From Slavery to Freedom: A History of Negro Americans*. 5th ed. New York: Alfred A. Knopff, 1980.

Furstenberg, Frank F., Jr., Theodore Hershberg, and John Modell. "The Origins of the Female-Headed Black Family: The Impact of the Urban Experience." In *Philadelphia: Work, Space, Family and Group Experience in the Nineteenth Century. Essays Toward an Interdisciplinary History of the City*, ed. Theodore Hershberg, 435-54. New York: Oxford University Press, 1981.

Geismar, Joan H. "Skunk Hollow: A Preliminary Statement on Archaeological Investigations at a 19th Century Black Community." In *Archaeological Perspective on Ethnicity in America: Afro-American and Asian American Culture History*, ed. Robert L. Schuyler, 60-68. Farmingdale, NY: Baywood Publishing Co., Inc., 1980.

Gillette, Howard, Jr. "The City in American Culture." In *American Urbanism: A Historiographical Review*, ed. Howard Gillette, Jr., and Zane L. Miller, 27-47. Contributions in American History, No. 125. Westport, CT: Greenwood Press, 1987.

Glassie, Henry. "Meaningful Things and Appropriate Myths: The Artifact's Place in American Studies." In *Material Life in America, 1600-1860*, ed. Robert Blair St. George, 63-92. Boston: Northeastern University Press, 1987.

──────. *Pattern in the Material Folk Culture of the Eastern United States*. University of Pennsylvania Publications in Folklore and Folklife. Philadelphia: University of Pennsylvania Press, 1968; paperback 1979.

Glenn, Norval D. "Negro Prestige Criteria: A Case Study in the Bases of Prestige." *American Journal of Sociology* 68 (May 1963): 645-57.

Goldin, Claudia. "Family Strategies and the Family Economy in the Late Nineteenth Century: The Role of Secondary Workers." In *Philadelphia: Work, Space, Family and Group Experience in the Nineteenth Century. Essays Toward an Interdisciplinary History of the City*, ed. Theodore Hershberg, 277-310. New York: Oxford University Press, 1981.

Grant, Jacquelyn. "Black Women and the Church." In *But Some of Us Are Brave: Black Women's Studies*, ed. Gloria T. Hull, Patricia Bell Scott, and Barbara Smith, 141-52. Old Westbury, NY: The Feminist Press, 1982.

Greene, Lorenzo Johnston. *The Negro in Colonial New England*. With a new preface by Benjamin Quarles. Studies in American Negro Life, ed. August Meier. New York: Athenaeum, 1968.

Griffen, Clyde. "Occupational Mobility in Nineteenth-Century American: Problems and Possibilities." *Journal of Social History* 5 (Spring 1972): 310-30.

Gutman, Herbert G. *The Black Family in Slavery and Freedom, 1750-1925*. New York: Vintage Books, 1976.

Handlin, David P. *The American Home: Architecture and Society, 1815-1915*. Boston; Little, Brown and Company, 1979.

Handlin, Oscar. *Boston's Immigrants: A Study in Acculturation*. Rev. and enl. ed. Cambridge: Harvard University Press, 1959.

Hawley, Anna L. "Items Missing from Inventories in Surry County, Virginia, 1690-1715." Paper presented at the Dublin Seminar for New England Folklife on Early American Inventories. Deerfield, Massachusetts, July 11-12, 1987. Photocopied.

Henretta, James A. "Economic Development and Social Structure in Colonial Boston." *William and Mary Quarterly*, 3d ser., 22 (January 1965): 75-92.

Herman, Bernard L. "Delaware's Orphan Court Valuations and the Reconstitution of Historic Landscapes, 1785-1830." Paper presented at the Dublin Seminar for New England Folklife on Early American Inventories. Deerfield, Massachusetts, July 11-12, 1987. Photocopied.

Hershberg, Theodore. "Free Blacks in Antebellum Philadelphia: A Study of Ex-Slaves, Freeborn, and Socioeconomic Decline." In *Philadelphia: Work, Space, Family and Group Experience in the Nineteenth Century. Essays Toward an Interdisciplinary History of the City*, ed. Theodore Hershberg, 368-91. New York: Oxford University Press, 1981.

──────. "The New Urban History: Toward an Interdisciplinary History of the City." In *Philadelphia: Work, Space, Family and Group Experience in the Nineteenth Century. Essays Toward an Interdisciplinary History of the City*, ed. Theodore Hershberg, 3-13. New York: Oxford University Press, 1981.

──────, ed. *Philadelphia: Work, Space, Family and Group Experience in the Nineteenth Century. Essays Toward an Interdisciplinary History of the City*. New York: Oxford University Press, 1981.

Hershberg, Theodore, Alan N. Burstein, Eugene P. Ericksen, Stephanie W. Greenberg, and William L. Yancey. "A Tale of Three Cities: Blacks, Immigrants, and Opportunity in Philadelphia, 1850-1880, 1930, 1970." In *Philadelphia: Work, Space, Family and Group Experience in the Nineteenth Century. Essays Toward an Interdisciplinary History of the City*, ed. Theodore Hershberg, 461-91. New York: Oxford University Press, 1981.

Hershberg, Theodore, and Robert Dockhorn. "Occupational Classification." *Historical Methods Newsletter* 9, nos. 2 & 3 (March/June 1976): 59-98.

Hershberg, Theodore, and Henry Williams. "Mulattoes and Blacks: Intra-group Color Differences and Social Stratification in Nineteenth-Century Philadelphia." In *Philadelphia: Work, Space, Family and Group Experience in the Nineteenth Century. Essays Toward an Interdisciplinary History of the City*, ed. Theodore Hershberg, 392-434. New York: Oxford University Press, 1981.

Hesseltine, William B., "The Challenge of the Artifact." In *Material Culture Studies in America*, ed. Thomas J. Schlereth, 93-100. Nashville, TN: American Association for State and Local History, 1982.

Higginbotham, Elizabeth. "Two Representative Issues in Contemporary Sociological Work on Black Women." In *But Some of Us Are Brave: Black Women's Studies*, ed. Gloria T. Hull, Patricia Bell Scott, and Barbara Smith, 93-8. Old Westbury, NY: The Feminist Press, 1982.

Hindle, Brooke. "How Much Is a Piece of the True Cross Worth?" In *Material Culture and the Study of American Life*, ed. Ian M. G. Quimby, 5-20. New York: W. W. Norton & Company, Inc., for the Henry Francis du Pont Winterthur Museum, 1978.

Hine, Darlene Clarke, ed. *The State of Afro-American History: Past, Present, and Future*. Introduciton by Thomas C. Holt. Baton Rouge, LA: Louisiana State University Press, 1986.

Holt, Thomas C. "Introduction: Whither Now and Why?" In *The State of Afro-American History: Past, Present, and Future*, ed. Darlene Clarke Hine, 1-10. Introduction by Thomas C. Holt. Baton Rouge, LA: Louisiana State University Press, 1986.

Hooks, Bell. *Ain't I a Woman: Black Women and Feminism*. Boston: South End Press, 1981.

Horton, James Oliver. "Black Education at Oberlin College: A Controversial Commitment." *Journal of Negro Education* 54 (Fall 1985): 477-99.
———. "Black Urbanites: An Interpretation of Afro-American Life in the Antebellum City." Book review essay on *The Free Black in Urban America, 1800-1850* by Leonard P. Curry. *Afro-Americans in N.Y. Life & History* 7, no. 4 (January 1983): 63-70.
———. "Class and Occupation in Antebellum Boston." Paper presented at the Annual Meeting of the American Historical Association. New York, December 1979. Photocopied.
———. "Double Consciousness: Afro-American Identity in the Nineteenth Century." In *Sharing Traditions: Five Black Artists in Nineteenth-Century America*, ed. Lynda Roscoe Hartigan, 11-23. Washington, DC: Smithsonian Institution Press for the National Museum of American Art, 1985.
———. *Eye of the Storm: Blacks in the Colonial North*. Chaps. 1-12. N.p., n.d. Photocopied.
———. "Freedom's Yoke: Gender Conventions among Antebellum Free Blacks." *Feminist Studies* 12 (Spring 1986): 51-76.
———. "The Historian and Social Policy: Moynihan and Black Families of Pre-Civil War Boston." Paper presented at the National Urban League Conference on Black Families. Chicago, Illinois, November 1977. Photocopied.
———. "The Life and Times of Edward Ambush: An Illustration of Social History Methodology." In *History and Tradition in Afro-American Culture*, ed. Guenter H. Lenz, 3-16. Frankfurt am Main: Campus Verlag, 1984.
———. "Links to Bondage: Northern Free Blacks and the Problem of Slavery." Washington, DC: Smithsonian Institution, National Museum of American History, Afro-American Communities Project, 1984. Photocopied.
———. "The Migrant and the Community: An Analysis of Adaptation." N.p., n.d. Photocopied.
———. "Shades of Color: The Mulatto in Three Antebellum Northern Communities." *Afro-Americans in N.Y. Life & History* 8, no. 2. (July 1984): 37-58.
———. "Weevils in the Wheat: Free Blacks and the Constitution, 1787-1860." *this Constitution: A Bicentennial Chronicle*, no. 8 (Fall 1985): 4-11.
Horton, James Oliver, and Lois E. Horton. *Black Bostonians: Family Life and Community Struggle in the Antebellum North*. New York: Holmes & Meier Publishers, Inc., 1979.
Hull, Gloria T., and Barbara Smith. "Introduction: The Politics of Black Women's Studies." In *But Some of Us Are Brave: Black Women's Studies*, ed. Gloria T. Hull, Patricia Bell Scott, and Barbara Smith, xvii-xxxi. Old Westbury, NY: The Feminist Press, 1982.
Isaac, Rhys. "Ethnographic Method in History: An Action Approach." In *Material Life in America, 1600-1860*, ed. Robert Blair St. George, 39-61. Boston: Northeastern University Press, 1987.
Jones, Alice Hanson. "Wealth Estimates for the Middle Colonies, 1774." *Economic Development and Cultural Change* 18, no. 4: pt. 2 (July 1970).
———. "Wealth Estimates for the New England Colonies about 1770." *Journal of Economic History* 32, no. 1 (March 1972): 98-127.
———. *Wealth of a Nation to Be: The American Colonies on the Eve of the Revolution*. New York: Columbia University Press, 1980.
Jones, Jacqueline. "Comment on 'The African in the Garden: Reflections about New World Slavery and Its Lifelines' by Leslie H. Owens." In *The State of Afro-American History: Past, Present, and Future*, ed. Darlene Clarke Hine, 42-9. Introduction by Thomas C. Holt. Baton Rouge, LA: Louisiana State University Press, 1986.
Katz, Michael B. "Occupational Classification in History." *Journal of Interdisciplinary History* 3 (Summer 1972): 63-88.
———. *The People of Hamilton, Canada West: Family and Class in a Mid-Nineteenth-Century City*. Cambridge: Harvard University Press, 1975.
———. "Social Class in North American Urban History." *Journal of Interdisciplinary History* 11 (Spring 1981): 579-605.
Katz, Michael B., Michael J. Doucet, and Mark J. Stern. *The Social Organization of Early Industrial Capitalism*. Cambridge: Harvard University Press, 1982.
Katzman, Daniel M. *Before the Ghetto: Black Detroit in the Nineteenth Century*. Blacks in the New World, ed., August Meier. Urbana, IL: University of Illinois Press, 1973.
Knights, Peter. *The Plain People of Boston, 1830-1860: A Study in Urban Growth*. New York: Oxford University Press, 1971.
Kornbluh, Andrea Tuttle. "From Culture to Cuisine: Twentieth-Century Views of Race and Ethnicity in the City." In *American Urbanism: A Historigraphical Review*, ed. Howard Gillette, Jr., and Zane L. Miller, 49-71. Contributions in American History, no. 125. Westport, CT: Greenwood Press, 1987.
Kouwenhoven, John A. "American Studies: Words or Things?" In *Material Culture Studies in America*, ed. Thomas J. Schlereth, 79-92. Nashville, TN: American Association for State and Local History, 1982.
Kulikoff, Allan. "The Progress of Inequality in Revolutionary Boston." *William and Mary Quarterly*, 3d ser., 28 (July 1971): 375-412.
Kusmer, Kenneth L. *A Ghetto Takes Shape: Black Cleveland, 1870-1930*. Urbana, IL: University of Illinois Press, 1976.
Lammermeier, Paul J. "The Urban Black Family of the Nineteenth Century: A Study of Black Family Structure in the Ohio Valley, 1850-1880." *Journal of Marriage and the Family* 35 (August 1973): 440-56.
Larkin, Jack. "The View from New England: Notes on Everyday Life in Rural America to 1850." *American Quarterly* 34, no. 3 (Bibliography 1982): 244-61.

Lebsock, Suzanne. *The Free Women of Petersburg: Status and Culture in a Southern Town, 1784-1860.* New York: W. W. Norton & Company, 1984.
Levine, Lawrence W. *Black Culture and Black Consciousness: Afro-American Folk Thought from Slavery to Freedom.* New York: Oxford University Press, 1977.
Lindert, Peter H. "An Algorithm for Probate Sampling." *Journal of Interdisciplinary History* 11 (Spring 1981): 649-68.
Litwack, Leon F. *North of Slavery: The Negro in the Free States, 1790-1860.* Chicago: University of Chicago Press, 1961.
Main, Gloria L. "The Correction of Biases in Colonial American Probate Records." *Historical Methods Newsletter* 8, no. 6 (December 1974): 10-28.
_____. "Inequality in Early America: The Evidence from Probate Records of Massachusetts and Maryland." *Journal of Interdisciplinary History* 7 (1977): 559-81.
_____. "Probate Records as a Source for Early American History." *William and Mary Quarterly*, 3d. ser. 32 (January 1975): 89-99.
_____. "The Standard of Living in Maryland and Massachusetts, 1656-1719." Paper presented at Maryland: A Product of Two Worlds, the Third Hall of Records Conference on Maryland History. St. Mary's City, Maryland, May 17-20, 1984. Photocopied.
_____. *Tobacco Colony: Life in Early Maryland, 1650-1720.* Princeton, NJ: Princeton University Press, 1982.
Marcus, Alan I. "Back to the Present: Historians' Treatment of the City as a Social System During the Reign of the Idea of Community." In *American Urbanism: A Historiographical Review*, ed. Howard Gillette, Jr., and Zane L. Miller, 7-25. Contributions in American History, no. 125. Westport, CT: Greenwood Press, 1987.
McDaniel, George W. *Black Historical Resources in Upper Western Montgomery County.* Rockville, MD: Montgomery County Office of Community Development, 1979.
_____. *Hearth and Home: Preserving a People's Culture.* Philadelphia: Temple University Press, 1982.
_____. "Preserving Family History: Black Family Life on the Bennehan-Cameron Plantation, A Case Study." Paper presented at the Annual Convention of the American Anthropological Association. Cinnacinate, Ohio, December 1, 1979.
McManus, Edgar J. *Black Bondage in the North.* Syracuse, NY: Syracuse University Press, 1973.
Meier, August, and Elliott Rudwick. *From Plantation to Ghetto.* 3d. ed. New York: Hill and Wang, 1976.
Melvin, Patricia Mooney. "The Neighborhood-City Relationship." In *American Urbanism: A Historiographical Review*, ed. Howard Gillette, Jr., and Zane L. Miller, 257-270. Contributions in American History, no. 125. Westport, CT: Greenwood Press, 1987.
Menard, Russell R., P.M.G. Harris, and Lois Green Carr. "Opportunity and Inequality: The Distribution of Wealth on the Lower Western Shore of Maryland, 1638-1705." *Maryland Historical Magazine* 69, no. 2 (1974): 169-84.
Miller, Roberta Balstad. "The Historical Study of Social Mobility: A New Perspective." Review of *The Other Bostonians: Poverty and Progress in the American Metropolis, 1880-1970*, by Stephan Thernstrom. *Historical Methods Newsletter* 8, no. 3 (June 1975): 92-7.
Modell, John. "Changing Risks, Changing Adaptations: American Families in the Nineteenth and Twentieth Centuries." In *Kin and Communities: Families in America*, ed. Allan Lichtman and Joan P. Challinor, 119-44. Preface by S. Dillon Ripley; Foreword by Wilton S. Dillon. Smithsonian International Symposia series. Washington, DC: Smithsonian Institution Press, 1979.
Mohanty, Gail Fowler. "Adding Flesh to the Dry Bones of Industrial Research: Rhode Island Handloom Weavers Revealed in Probate Records, 1810-1821." Paper presented at the Dublin Seminar for New England Folklife on Early American Inventories. Deerfield, Massachusetts, July 11-12, 1987. Photocopied.
Montgomery, Charles F. "The Connoisseurship of Artifacts." In *Material Culture Studies in America*, ed. Thomas J. Schlereth, 143-152. Nashville, TN: American Association for State and Local History, 1982.
Morgan, Philip D. "Work and Culture: The Task System and the World of Lowcountry Blacks, 1700-1880." In *Material Life in America, 1600-1860*, ed. Robert Blair St. George, 203-32. Boston: Northeastern University Press, 1987.
Morrison, Toni. "An Interview with Toni Morrison." Interview by Tom LeClair (New York, 1981). *Anything Can Happen: Interviews with Contemporary American Novelists*, ed. Tom LeClair and Larry McCaffery, 252-61. Urbana, IL: University of Illinois Press, 1983.
Nachtigall, Barbara. "Inventory Analysis for the Refurnishing Plan of the Moses Pierce/Nathaniel Hichborn House." Paper presented at the Dublin Seminar for New England Folklife on Early American Inventories. Deerfield, Massachusetts, July 11-12, 1987. Photocopied.
Nash, Gary B. *Forging Freedom: The Formation of Philadelphia's Black Community, 1720-1840.* Cambridge: Harvard University Press, 1988.
Ostroff, Susan. "Life in Pawtucket, Rhode Island before Slater Mill: What Can Be Learned from Probate Records, 1756-1789." N.p., 1982. Photocopied.
Otto, John Solomon. "Race and Class on Antebellum Plantations." In *Archaeological Perspective on Ethnicity in America: Afro-American and Asian American Culture History*, ed. Robert L. Schuyler, 3-13. Farmingdale, NY: Baywood Publishing Co., Inc., 1980.
Owens, Leslie Howard. *This Species of Property: Slave Life and Culture in the Old South.* New York: Oxford University Press, 1976.

Pease, Jane H., and William H. Pease. *They Who Would Be Free: Blacks' Search for Freedom, 1830-1861*. Studies in American Negro Life, ed., August Meier. New York: Athenaeum, 1974.

Pessen, Edward. *Jacksonian America: Society, Personality, and Politics*. rev. ed. The Dorsey Series in American History. Homewood, IL: The Dorsey Press, 1978.

Peterson, Harold L. *American Interiors from Colonial Times to the Late Victorians: A Pictorial Source Book*. New York: Charles Scribner's Sons, 1971.

Pierson, William Dillon. *Black Yankees: The Development of an Afro-American Subculture in Eighteenth-Century New England*. Amherst, MA: University of Massachusetts Press, 1988.

Pleck, Elizabeth H. *Black Migration and Poverty: Boston, 1865-1900*. New York: Academic Press, 1979.

———. "Women's History: Gender as a Category of Historical Analysis." In *Ordinary People and Everyday Life: Perspectives on the New Social History*, ed. James B. Gardner and George Rollie Adams, 51-65. Nashville, TN: American Association for State and Local History, 1983.

Prown, Jules David. "Mind in Matter: An Introduction to Material Culture Theory and Method." In *Material Life in America, 1600-1860*, ed. Robert Blair St. George, 17-37. Boston: Northeastern University Press, 1987.

Quarles, Benjamin. *Black Abolitionists*. New York: Oxford University Press, 1969.

Rabinowitz, Howard N. "Race, Ethnicity, and Cultural Pluralism in American History." In *Ordinary People and Everyday Life: Perspectives on the New Social History*, ed. James B. Gardner and George Rollie Adams, 23-49. Nashville, TN: American Association for State and Local History, 1983.

Rapoport, Amos. *House Form and Culture*. Foundations of Cultural Geography Series. Englewood Cliffs, NJ: Prentice-Hall, Inc., 1969.

The Rhode Island Black Heritage Society. *Creative Survival: The Providence Black Community in the 19th Century*. Catalog of the exhibition at the Rhode Island Black Heritage Society. Providence, RI: The Rhode Island Black Heritage Society, [1984].

Richter, Julie, and Linda Sturtz. "Using Probate Inventories to Study the Slave Population of Colonial York County, Virginia." Paper presented at the Dublin Seminar for New England Folklife on Early American Inventories. Deerfield, Massachusetts, July 11-12, 1987. Photocopied.

Rothstein, Mervyn. "Toni Morrrison, in Her New Novel, Defends Women." *New York Times*, August 26, 1987, p. 17(C).

Salmon, Marylynn. "Women and Property in South Carolina: The Evidence from Marriage Settlements, 1730-1830." In *Material Life in America, 1600-1860*, ed. Robert Blair St. George, 291-309. Boston: Northeastern University Press, 1987.

Schlebecker, John T. "The Use of Objects in Historical Research." In *Material Culture Studies in America*, ed. Thomas J. Schlereth, 106-13. Nashville, TN: American Association for State and Local History, 1982.

Schlereth, Thomas J. "Collecting Ideas and Artifacts: Common Problems of History Museums and History Texts." *Roundtable Reports* (Summer/Fall 1978): 1.

———. "Historic House Museums: Seven Teaching Strategies." Chap. in *Artifacts and the American Past*. Nashville, TN: American Association for State and Local History, 91-119.

———. "Material Culture Studies in America, 1976-1986." In *Material Culture Studies in America*, ed. Thomas J. Schlereth, 1-75. Nashville, TN: American Association for State and Local History, 1982.

Schuyler, Robert L., ed. *Archaeological Perspective on Ethnicity in America: Afro-American and Asian American Culture History*. Farmingdale, NY: Baywood Publishing Company, Inc., 1980.

———. "Sandy Ground: Archaeology of a 19th Century Oystering Village." In *Archaeological Perspective on Ethnicity in America: Afro-American and Asian American Culture History*, ed. Robert L. Schuyler, 48-59. Farmingdale, NY: Baywood Publishing Company, Inc., 1980.

Scott, Patricia Bell. "Debunking Sapphire: Toward a Non-Racist and Non-Sexist Social Science." In *But Some of Us Are Brave: Black Women's Studies*, ed. Gloria T. Hull, Patricia Bell Scott, and Barbara Smith, 85-92. Old Westbury, NY: The Feminist Press, 1982.

Seale, William. *Recreating the Historic House Interior*. Nashville, TN: American Association for State and Local History, 1979.

Shammas, Carole. "The Determinants of Personal Wealth in Seventeenth-Century England and America." *Journal of Economic History* 37 (September 1977): 675-89.

———. "The Domestic Environment in Early Modern England and America." *Journal of Social History* 14 (1980): 3-24.

———. "Mammy and Miss Ellen in Colonial Virginia?" Paper presented at the Conference on Women in Early America, the Colonial Williamsburg Foundation and the Institute of Early American History and Culture. Williamsburg, VA, November 5-7, 1981. Photocopied.

Shapiro, Linn, ed. *Black People and Their Culture: Selected Writings from the African Diaspora*. Washington, DC: Smithsonian Institution, 1976.

Shepherd, Raymond V., Jr. "Stenton Inventory, 1752: An Avenue to Information." Paper presented at the Dublin Seminar for New England Folklife on Early American Inventories. Deerfield, Massachusetts, July 11-12, 1987. Photocopied.

Skramstad, Harold K., Jr. "Interpreting Material Culture: A View from the Other Side of the Glass." In *Material Life in America, 1600-1860*, ed. Ian G. M. Quimby. 175-200. Boston: Northeastern University Press, 1987.

Smith, Billy G. "The Material Lives of Laboring Philadelphians, 1750-1800." In *Material Life in America, 1600-1860*, ed. Robert Blair St. George, 233-60. Boston: Northeastern University Press, 1987.

Smith, Daniel Scott. "Underregistration and Bias in Probate Records: An Analysis of Data from Eighteenth-Century Hingham, Massachusetts." *William and Mary Quarterly*, 3d. ser., 32 (January 1975): 100-10.
Smith, Kathryn S. "Household Inventories as Sources for the Study of Nineteenth-Century Non-Elites." N.p., 1982. Photocopied.
Spear, Allan H. *Black Chicago: The Making of a Negro Ghetto, 1890-1920*. Chicago: University of Chicago Press, 1967.
Sprague, Laura Fecych. "The Cutts Inventory and Mansion House." Paper presented at the Dublin Seminar for New England Folklife on Early American Inventories. Deerfield, Massachusetts, July 11-12, 1987. Photocopied.
Stack, Carol B. *All Our Kin: Strategies for Survival in a Black Community*. New York: Harper and Row Publishers, 1974.
Stearns, Peter N. "The New Social History: An Overview." In *Ordinary People and Everyday Life: Perspectives on the New Social History*, ed. James B. Gardner and George Rollie Adams, 3-21. Nashville, TN: American Association for State and Local History, 1983.
Stetson, Erlene. "Studying Slavery: Some Literary and Pedagogical Considerations on the Black Female Slave." In *But Some of Us Are Brave: Black Women's Studies*, ed. Gloria T. Hull, Patricia Bell Scott, and Barbara Smith, 61-84. Old Westbury, NY: The Feminist Press, 1982.
St. George, Robert Blair, ed. *Material Life in American, 1600-1860*. Boston: Northeastern University Press, 1988.
Stowe, Harriet Beecher. *Uncle Tom's Cabin, or Life among the Lowly*. With an Afterword by John William Ward. A Signet Classic. New York: New American Library, 1966.
Sweeney, Kevin M. "Furniture and the Domestic Environment in Wethersfield, Connecticut, 1639-1800." In *Material Life in America, 1600-1860*, ed. Robert Blair St. George, 261-90. Boston: Northeastern University Press, 1987.
Thernstrom, Stephan. *The Other Bostonians: Poverty and Progress in the American Metropolis, 1880-1970*. Cambridge; Harvard University Press, 1973.
_____. *Poverty and Progress: Social Mobility in a Nineteenth-Century City*. Cambridge; Harvard University Press, 1964.
Trautman, Patricia. "Dress in Seventeenth-Century Cambridge, Massachusetts: A Statistical Reconstruction." Paper presented at the Dublin Seminar for New England Folklife on Early American Inventories. Deerfield, Massachusetts, July 11-12, 1987. Photocopied.
Vlach, John Michael. *The Afro-American Tradition in Decorative Arts*. Cleveland, OH: Cleveland Museum of Art, 1978.
Wade, Melvin. "'Shining In Borrowed Plumage': Affirmation of Community in the Black Coronation Festivals of New England, ca. 1750-1850." In *Material Life in America, 1600-1860*, ed. Robert Blair St. George, 171-82. Boston: Northeastern University Press, 1987.
Walsh, Lorena S. "Urban Amenities and Rural Sufficiency; Living Standards and Consumer Behavior in the Colonial Chesapeake, 1643-1777." *Journal of Economic History* 43, no. 1 (March 1983): 109-117.
Ward, Barbara McLean. "Women's Property and Family Continuity in Eighteenth-Century Connecticut." Paper presented at the Dublin Seminar for New England Folklife on Early American Inventories. Deerfield, Massachusetts, July 11-12, 1987. Photocopied.
Warner, Sam Bass, Jr. *Streetcar Suburbs: The Process of Growth in Boston, 1870-1900*. Cambridge; Harvard University Press, 1962.
Washburn, Wilcomb E. "Manuscripts and Manufacts." In *Material Culture Studies in America*, ed. Thomas J. Schlereth, 101-5. Nashville, TN: American Association for State and Local History, 1982.
Websters Third New International Dictionary of the English Language Unabridged. Springfield, MA: G. & C. Merriam Company, 1981.
Welter, Barbara. "The Cult of True Womanhood: 1820-1860." In *The Underside of American History: Other Readings (Vol 1: to 1877)*, ed. Thomas R. Frazier, 217-40. 3d. ed. New York: Harcourt Brace Jovanovich, Inc., 1978.
Wilson, William Julius. *The Declining Significance of Race: Blacks and Changing American Institutions*. 2d ed. Chicago: University of Chicago Press, 1980.
_____. *The Truly Disadvantaged: The Inner City, the Underclass, and Public Policy*. Chicago: University of Chicago Press, 1987.
Winch, Julie. *Philadelphia's Black Elite: Activism, Accommodation, and the Struggle for Autonomy, 1787-1848*. Philadelphia: Temple University Press, 1988.
Wohl, A. S. "The Housing of the Working Classes in London, 1815-1914." In *The History of Working-Class Housing: A Symposium*, ed. Stanly D. Chapman, 15-54. Totowa, NJ: Rowman and Littlefield, 1971.
Zaretsky, Eli. *Capitalism, the Family and Personal Life*. State and Revolution. New York: Harper & Row, Publishers, Harper Colophon Books, 1976.
Zunz, Olivier. *The Changing Face of Inequality: Urbanization, Industrial Development, and Immigrants in Detroit, 1880-1920*. Chicago: University of Chicago Press, 1982.

INDEX

A-ACP
  see Afro-American Communities Project
Abolition 8, 133
Adelphic Union Library Association 116, 127, 132
Administrator 3, 4, 68-72, 76, 88, 97, 101, 132, 135, 149
  administratrix 3, 4, 120
Afro-American Communities Project (A-ACP) 6, 7
Ambush, Edward 17, 23, 24
Andrews, Gustavius 67
Appraisal 35, 36, 38, 67, 71, 92, 127
  appraising 4, 149
Auction 39, 90, 93, 121, 151
Bedding 38-39, 52-56, 62, 67, 78, 83-86, 109-110, 113, 115, 145, 153, 155
Bible 24, 25, 54, 67, 115, 129, 131, 133
Biner, Charles 99, 104
Black Abolitionist Papers 132, 133, 136, 139, 140, 142, 143, 146, 149, 155
Blair, Phineas 6, 68, 69, 72, 76, 97, 103, 128, 130, 149
Book 19, 68, 88, 89, 99, 116
Brent, John Lewis
  see Lewis, John
Brooks, John 96, 104, 148
Brown, John W. 72-77, 99, 105-107, 109, 114, 118, 124, 125, 147, 150
Business stock 78-81, 89, 91, 93, 98, 99, 103, 154
Businessmen 9, 97-100, 103, 104, 108-117, 120, 124, 125, 142, 145, 152
Capen, Phineas 6, 89, 90, 127, 149
Carr, Lois Green 35-37, 44, 46, 67, 82, 102
Cary, N.C. 89, 149
Cash 4, 30, 38, 71, 73, 76, 78-81, 89, 91, 93, 98-100, 102, 103, 117, 120, 124, 128, 131, 132, 138, 146, 149, 150, 154
China 78, 86-89, 111-113, 115, 145, 152, 155
Civil War 3, 4, 6-8, 14, 19, 25, 31, 33, 51, 66, 67, 71, 94, 108, 154
Clark, Mary 68, 69, 71
Clark, Thomas 68, 69
Class, Charles B. 67
Clock
  see timepiece
Clothier 96
Clothing 20, 38, 39, 52-55, 62, 67, 74, 77, 79, 83, 84, 97, 98, 100, 102, 105, 113-115, 126, 128, 142, 144, 150, 151
Cole, Thomas 72, 74, 75, 77-79, 89, 96, 98-100, 102, 105-107, 109, 110, 112, 113, 116, 117, 120, 121, 124, 125, 127, 131, 132, 134-136, 141-143, 145, 146, 149, 150, 152, 154, 155
Cooking fixtures
  see Heating and Cooking Fixtures
Creditor 3, 38, 96, 118, 134-136
Crisscrossing pattern 72, 74, 77, 79-81, 94, 124

Debt 38, 73, 92, 93, 96
Discrimination 8, 17, 18, 28-30, 147
Domestic labor 9
Dower 3, 39, 89-91, 94, 96, 118, 119, 148, 151
First Independent Baptist Church 127, 136
Funeral 4, 71, 91, 93, 101, 117, 120
Garrison, William Lloyd 136, 137, 142
Geographic mobility 15, 17
Gray, Peter 99, 100, 104, 120
Hairdresser 26, 72, 74, 77-79, 96, 98-100, 113, 116, 127, 139, 144
Hall, Primus 99, 104, 106-110, 112, 114, 116, 118-121, 125, 131, 134, 135, 137, 139, 140, 142, 143, 146, 150, 152, 153
Harris, P.M.G. 35, 44
Heating and Cooking Fixtures
  cooking fixtures 83, 84, 110
Hershberg, Theodore 14, 15, 21, 28, 148, 152
Hilton, John T. 74, 75, 77, 78, 89, 94, 127, 134, 136-143
Homeowner 17, 33, 155
Horton, James O. 6
Household goods 25, 31-33, 39, 47, 53, 56, 67, 78-82, 84, 85, 88, 89, 93, 98-109,
  amenities 32, 34, 47, 55, 56, 58, 62, 67, 81, 82, 84-89, 105-115, 125, 145, 152
  luxuries 19, 32, 34, 46, 57-58, 64, 67, 81, 82, 86-89, 105-115, 125, 145, 152
  necessities 6, 13, 17, 19, 32, 42-43, 55, 58, 67, 81-89, 105-114, 124-125, 128, 133, 145, 152
Howe, James 98, 105, 109, 112, 114, 117, 129, 112-115, 120, 124, 125, 145, 150, 151, 152-154
Hoyte, Calvin 72, 97, 98, 103, 104
Immigrant
  German 28
  Irish 8, 9, 28, 66
Insolvent 4, 70, 72, 89-93, 102, 116-118, 125, 147
  insolvency 3, 4, 73, 76, 91, 118, 120
Inventory 5, 6, 8, 24, 29, 34, 36, 39, 60, 63, 68, 70-78, 83, 84, 88, 89-92, 96, 100, 101, 104, 105, 109, 114, 116-119, 124, 126-130, 134, 135, 149-151, 153
Jackson, Amy 67-72, 89, 93, 94, 96, 98, 108-110, 115, 117, 124, 125, 129-131, 145, 149, 150, 152
Jackson, Thomas 68
Jinnings, William 98, 120
Jones, Alice Hanson 3, 34-36, 71, 81, 100
Jones, Arthur 96, 104
Kinship 19, 27, 29, 32
Kitchenware 83, 84, 110
Labbottiere, Edward 72-75, 77, 100, 101, 124
laborer 20, 26, 34, 77, 96, 98, 100-104, 108, 110-113, 115, 116, 120, 128, 142, 143, 145, 152

Lawson, Edward 100, 105-108, 110, 112, 115, 120, 121, 125, 131, 132, 145, 147, 149, 150, 152, 154
Lawyer 131
Lebsock, Suzanne 31, 42, 43
Lewis, John 72, 98, 100, 102, 104, 128
Lindert, Peter H. 36, 37
Literacy 24, 39, 54, 56, 64, 68, 71, 81, 86-88, 109, 111-116, 126, 129-134, 144, 151-153, 156
Main, Gloria L. 35, 36, 45, 48, 68, 155
Mariner 68, 72, 103
Menard, Russell R. 35, 44
Mirror 26, 55, 67, 115
Morris, Robert 6, 91, 131, 135, 136, 140, 146
Mortgage 71, 90, 91, 94, 101, 102, 117, 119, 151, 154
Mulatto
  see skin color
Native American 28
Occupation 19-21, 25, 26, 31, 37, 38, 41, 42, 46, 48-50, 96, 98, 99, 103, 104, 108, 110-114, 120, 125, 127, 129, 131, 144, 152
Personal estate 3, 5, 38, 42, 67, 70, 78-81, 89-91, 93, 98, 100, 101, 102-105, 117-119, 128, 129, 148, 151
Philadelphia Social History Project (PSHP) 14, 18
Phillips, Willard 67, 69, 72
Property 3, 4, 8, 13, 15-17, 21, 23, 24, 26, 27, 31-34, 36-38, 44, 47, 59-61, 64, 67, 70, 77, 78, 89, 90, 92-94, 96, 97, 100, 102, 103, 109, 117-119, 127-129, 144, 146, 150, 151, 152-156
PSHP
  see Philadelphia Social History Project
Racist 8, 9, 25, 30
  racism 8, 9, 22, 26, 30, 153
Real estate 3, 33, 38, 49, 52, 53, 67, 70-72, 75, 76, 78-81, 89, 90, 91-94, 96-99, 101-103, 117-119, 121, 124, 128, 129, 141, 143, 147, 148, 150, 151, 153-156
Religion 19
  church 19, 21, 22, 42, 58, 127, 136, 139
Riley, William 74, 75, 77-79, 81, 94, 100, 105, 120, 124, 131, 134, 135, 138-140, 146, 150
Robinson, Henry 104-112, 114, 125, 152
Robinson, John 74, 75, 77, 79, 89, 91, 92, 99, 105-109, 113, 116, 117, 120, 121, 124-126, 131, 134, 135, 138-141, 145, 146, 147, 149, 152-154
Rogers, John 74, 75, 77, 79, 117, 119, 131, 135, 138, 139, 146
Russell, Chloe 72-77, 100-102, 104, 124, 131, 150
Senex, Eunice 68-70, 150
Sewall, Samuel E. 6, 69, 90, 149
Sewall, Thomas R. 67
Sexism 22, 30
Scarlett, John E. 72, 74, 75, 77, 79, 89-91, 99, 105, 124, 134, 135, 140, 141, 145, 150
Silver 53, 55, 58, 67, 86-88, 104, 111-113, 115, 137, 145, 152, 155
Skin color 26
  mulatto 9, 15, 23, 26, 27, 131, 145, 146

Slave 4, 8, 16, 17, 19, 21-24, 27, 34, 42, 48, 59, 63, 67, 133, 142
  slavery 8, 9, 14, 16, 17, 19, 22, 26, 27, 29, 32, 33, 132, 136, 143, 153
Smith, Freeman
  see Smith, John
Smith, John 97, 98, 103, 104
Smith, Kathryn S. 35, 41, 46, 63
Smith, Lucinda 105, 154
Sprague, Joseph 100-102, 104, 131, 136, 143, 146, 154
Stratification 15, 16, 19-21, 26, 37, 47-52, 63
Tax 15, 24, 31, 32, 36, 41-43, 92
  taxes 4, 8, 92, 118
Timepiece
  clock 87, 143
  watch 87, 88, 103, 104, 153, 155
Walsh, Lorena S. 34, 36, 37, 46, 57, 67, 82, 102, 152
Watch
  see timepiece
Wealth 3, 5, 15, 16, 19-21, 24, 26, 28, 31, 32, 34-57, 59-61, 63, 64, 67, 68, 70, 71, 78, 80-82, 84, 89, 91-94, 96-100, 102, 104, 105, 107, 108, 116-120, 125-127, 142, 144, 147, 151, 152, 154-156
Widow 3, 38, 39, 48, 67, 72, 75, 89-91, 93, 94, 96, 98, 100, 101, 103, 104, 108-111, 115, 117-120, 128, 129, 145, 148, 149, 151, 152
Williams, Charles
  see Hoyte, Calvin
Williams, Peter 99, 100, 105-110, 114, 125, 145, 154
Wills 3-6, 38, 42-44, 67-69, 71, 79, 102, 129, 131, 156
  testate 4, 5, 67, 88, 101, 129, 131, 132, 155
Working Women
  see Women
Women 9, 15, 20, 22, 26-31, 33, 34, 41-43, 50, 57, 59-61, 63, 82, 98-100, 103, 127, 131, 142, 144, 145, 148-152, 155

For Product Safety Concerns and Information please contact our EU representative GPSR@taylorandfrancis.com
Taylor & Francis Verlag GmbH, Kaufingerstraße 24, 80331 München, Germany

www.ingramcontent.com/pod-product-compliance
Lightning Source LLC
Chambersburg PA
CBHW050430240426
43661CB00055B/2334